I am glad that you have written this book and I cong
in America. I think, therefore, that your book ought to find a market and quite a few readers should profit from its fine presentation with excellent examples illustrating the discussion. This should prove an indispensable textbook for seminaries and colleges teaching NT Greek.

**—Dr. Chrys C. Caragounis**

Professor of New Testament Exegesis, Lund University, Sweden; author of *The Development of Greek and the New Testament: Morphology, Syntax, Phonology, and Textual Transmission*

Dr. Philemon Zachariou has provided us with a much-needed corrective to the pronunciation of New Testament (i.e., Hellenistic Κοινή) Greek. For too many years, Erasmus's artificial system of pronunciation has dominated the study of the New Testament, and has even kept students of the New Testament from recognizing significant phonological nuances and wordplays that impact our interpretation of important texts. Dr. Zachariou's clear explanations, helpful charts, and acoustically pleasing audio files make this book a valuable learning aid both to the beginning Greek student and to the established scholar who would like to switch from Erasmian pronunciation to an accurate Historical Greek Pronunciation.

**—Dr. George Gunn**

Professor of New Testament Greek, Shasta Bible College and Graduate School, Redding, California

Professors of Koine Greek have too quickly assumed either that the Erasmian pronunciation was historically accurate or that reconstructing the pronunciation of the first century is impossible. Zachariou deftly exposes the groundless nature of both suppositions. Through careful historical and linguistic work he makes a compelling case that Hellenistic Greek pronunciation is much closer to that of modern Greek than it is to the artificial construct of Erasmus. Highly recommended for every student and professor of Greek!

**—Daniel R. Streett**

Associate Professor of Biblical Studies, Houston Baptist University

It is high time that the so-called "Erasmian" pronunciation of ancient Greek is recognized for what it is—a diverse range of artificial pronunciations that typically reflect the native language of the speaker—and that the "Modern" Greek pronunciation which, after all, is our only living guide to the sound of Greek, be restored to its rightful place as the universal standard in biblical, and therefore Hellenistic, Greek pronunciation. This point has of course been made before, but the latest manifestation of it may be found in Philemon Zachariou's new book. By building upon the latest research and compiling the pertinent evidence, Zachariou argues cogently for the antiquity of the

"Modern" Greek pronunciation, and convincingly shows what a hazardous travesty it is to replace this historical pronunciation with an "Erasmian" one. Given that the majority of those teaching and learning the Greek of the Bible continue to persist with some kind of "Erasmian" pronunciation, Zachariou's work serves as a necessary corrective, and is an important and timely contribution to the field.

**—Dr. Jody A. Barnard**

Professor of New Testament Greek, UK; author of *The Mysticism of Hebrews*

Dr. Zachariou's work adds to the strong evidence supporting the unity of the Greek language, in this instance as it pertains to phonology. He persuasively argues that the Erasmian pronunciation is not based on sound principles or reasoning, neither is it necessitated by the extant data, which rather validates the Historical Greek Pronunciation as being the way the language was spoken from well before the time of the New Testament. His unveiling of some of the forces at work historically and currently in academia to hold on to Erasmus's theory should lead to self-evaluation, especially for Bible scholars who are slow to recognize the need for and value of change in relation to this topic.

**—Dr. David S. Hasselbrook**

Pastor of Messiah Lutheran Church, Missoula, Montana; author of *Studies in New Testament Lexicography*

"In the 1500s, the chancellor of the University of Cambridge decreed that students who used the Erasmian pronunciation be expelled. How, then, have we gone from such eschewing of Erasmian to the nearly wholesale adoption of it in today's English-speaking colleges and seminaries? Zachariou expertly illumines this history and charts the path toward the recovery of the historical pronunciation of ancient Greek in the modern academy."

**—Mark Dubis**

Professor of Biblical Studies, Union University

"If the use of the artificial Erasmian system for learning Classical Greek is scientifically questionable, its application to the Koine of the Hellenistic era is even less justified. . . . Thanks to Zachariou's work, students and instructors of Greek can now have an analysis of the evolution of the Greek phonological system from Classical Greek to Koine and down to the present. Linguistic comparisons show that the current pronunciation of Greek legitimizes its use not only for learning post-Classical Greek, but also Classical Greek."

**—Santiago Carbonell**

Professor of Greek, Department de Cultura Clàssica, IES Cotes Baixes, Spain

"When your name is Philemon Zachariou, you care about the correct pronunciation of Greek words. But Dr. Zachariou cares a whole lot more about helping people learn the original language of the New Testament and bringing them into greater intimacy with the word of God. He has spent decades teaching Greek successfully, and this book helpfully brings his insights to the aid of students and teachers. As a fellow Greek teacher, I recommend this book to anyone who loves the New Testament."

**—Joseph Castleberry**
President, Northwest University

"For several years now, ancient Greek scholarship has been increasingly critical of the so-called Erasmian pronunciation system that has governed our reading of the language for nearly five centuries. The evidence against Erasmus is overwhelming, but academic institutions and their teachers have been slow to abandon the inaccurate and unhelpful ways handed down to them. As the tide slowly begins to turn, many will want an accessible reference work that demonstrates the weaknesses of Erasmus and the evidence that points to a truly Greek pronunciation of Greek. Dr. Zachariou has produced just such a work. Highly recommended."

**—Constantine R. Campbell**
Senior Vice President of Global Content, Daily Bread Ministries; formerly Professor of New Testament at Trinity Evangelical Divinity School; author of *Advances in the Study of Greek*

# Reading and Pronouncing Biblical Greek

# Reading and Pronouncing Biblical Greek

## Historical Pronunciation *versus* Erasmian

PHILEMON ZACHARIOU

WIPF & STOCK · Eugene, Oregon

READING AND PRONOUNCING BIBLICAL GREEK
Historical Pronunciation versus Erasmian



Wipf & Stock
An Imprint of Wipf and Stock Publishers
199 W. 8th Ave., Suite 3
Eugene, OR 97401

www.wipfandstock.com

PAPERBACK ISBN: 978-1-7252-5448-0
HARDCOVER ISBN: 978-1-7252-5449-7
EBOOK ISBN: 978-1-7252-5450-3

Manufactured in the U.S.A. JUNE 15, 2020

Grateful acknowledgment is here given to the Hellenic Ministry of Culture for its communication regarding my transcription of photographed Attic inscriptions in the publication, *Athenian Democracy Speaking through its Inscriptions* (2009), as exhibited in the appendixes.

Gratitude is also expressed to Wikimedia Commons for releasing into the public domain photographed images of 5th century BC voting ostraka, an image of which is displayed in the appendixes.

To my wife, Margie

πολλαῖ μὲν θνητῶν γλῶτται
μία δ' ἀθάνατος

# Contents

# Acknowledgments

To MY STUDENTS AT Capital Bible College (later Northwest University) I express my gratitude for their enthusiasm about learning Greek and their excitement about seeing this work taking shape before their very eyes as their questions, discoveries, comments, and corrections kept driving me back to the drafting table for adjustments.

I am grateful to Dr. Gus Plessas, professor emeritus at California State University, whose early assessment of the manuscript, combined with his passion for the Greek language, served as a reassuring compass.

Many thanks also, for an invaluable perusal of the manuscript, to Rev. Dr. Joseph Kostelnik, a lover of Greek.

A word of appreciation is due in memory of the late Dr. Clayton K. Harrop, chair of the Greek Department at Golden Gate Baptist Theological Seminary in Mill Valley, California, whose first words in inviting me to teach New Testament Greek for the seminary were, "Here we teach the Modern Greek way," as the pronunciation key in his New Testament Greek manual attests.

I am immensely indebted to Dr. Chrys C. Caragounis, professor of New Testament exegesis at Lund University, Sweden, for examining and critiquing most generously, expeditiously, and unreservedly vital portions of the manuscript. His astounding knowledge of Greek, voluminous works, and profound linguistic and biblical insights can only be matched by his love for his mother tongue.

I am no less indebted to Dr. George Gunn, professor of New Testament Greek at Shasta Bible College and Graduate School, for his insightful comments without which vital areas of this book would be found wanting.

Likewise, many thanks to Dr. Santi Carbonell of Universidad de Alicante, Spain, whose valuable comments in the earlier stages of the manuscript determined the depth and breadth of some areas presented.

Words of deep appreciation go to Dr. Bradley H. McLean, professor of New Testament language and literature at Knox College, University of Toronto, Canada, for an incisive evaluation of the manuscript that helped sharpen the focus of the project.

Words of appreciation go as well to Dr. Nikolaos Adamou of Holy Trinity Seminary, New York, whose diagnostic remarks helped bring this project's goal into clearer view.

I wish to express my gratitude also to Dr. Harvey C. Pittman, professor of Greek and academic dean at International Seminary, Florida, for his intense involvement in examining the manuscript and for his excitement about seeing this book and the workbook in the hands of many students.

I am particularly indebted to Rev. Dr. David S. Hasselbrook, pastor of Messiah Lutheran Church, Missoula, Montana, for graciously devoting time to examining the final version of the book and for affirming the worthiness of its purpose.

Many thanks as well to Dr. Jody A. Barnard, professor of New Testament Greek in the United Kingdom, for his thorough examination of this book, which resulted in a number of vital corrections and in the addition of valuable points of discussion.

Philemon Zachariou

# Abbreviations

| | |
|---|---|
| AD | Anno Domini |
| AG | Ancient Greek |
| aor. | aorist |
| BC | Before Christ |
| BG | Biblical Greek |
| c. | century |
| cf. | compare |
| CG | Classical Greek |
| CIA | Corpus Inscriptionum Atticarum |
| CIG | Corpus Inscriptionum Graecarum |
| dat. | dative |
| e.g. | for example (Lat. *exempli gratia*) |
| EM | Epigraphical Museum |
| f. | feminine |
| fn. | footnote |
| gen. | genitive |
| GNT | Greek New Testament |
| Heb. | Hebrews |
| HG | Hellenistic Greek |
| HGP | Historical Greek Pronunciation |
| i.e. | that is (Lat. *id est*) |
| IE | Indo-European |
| IG | Inscriptiones Graecae |
| KG | Koine Greek |
| KJV | King James Version |
| Lat. | Latin |
| lit. | literally |
| LXX | Septuagint |
| m. | masculine |

| | |
|---|---|
| MS, MSS | Manuscript, Manuscripts |
| Matt | Matthew |
| MG | Modern Greek |
| n. | neuter |
| nom. | nominative |
| NT | New Testament |
| NTG | New Testament Greek |
| orig. | original(ly) |
| OT | Old Testament |
| Rev | Revelation |
| SEG | Supplementum Epigraphicum Graecum |
| Sept. | Septuagint |
| SIG | Sylloge Inscriptionum Graecarum |
| TR | Textus Receptus |
| vs. | versus |

# Why This Book

*Reading and Pronouncing Biblical Greek* addresses the oft-asked questions:

- How was "Koine" Greek pronounced in New Testament times?
- How similar is the pronunciation of Modern Greek to the Koine of the New Testament?
- How similar are the sounds of Koine and Attic Greek?
- Why is Erasmian so prevalent? Is it imitative of Classical Greek?

To that end, it traces the origins of Koine sounds to classical and pre-classical times and follows their development so diachronic comparisons can be made; and it describes the origins and spread of Erasmian and assesses its effects on Greek scholarship and learning.

The last chapter describes the Greek sounds, while the appendixes examine Attic inscriptions at the Epigraphical Museum in Athens as presented in a special publication by the Hellenic Ministry of Culture.

# Pronunciation Matters

New Testament Greek textbooks typically devote a page or two to some pronunciation key. While different authors at times share some of the same examples in their keys, their description of Greek sounds often varies. As a matter of fact, at times one author's description of a given vowel may fit the description of a different vowel in another author's key. Such pronunciation inconsistencies speak of the need for some uniform approach to reading and pronouncing New Testament Greek.

The need for such an approach, however, remains a moot issue in the vast majority of theological institutions and universities in America and abroad where Erasmian is used. Brilliant scholars who are somewhat or even appreciably familiar with the historical development of Greek sounds, yet overshadowed by formative training, typically see no issue with the particular manner in which they teach their students to read and pronounce Greek. Consequently, many deem it unnecessary, if not collegiately inexpedient, to adopt the pronunciation of Neohellenic (Modern Greek). After all, today's Greek spelling and sounds are a modern development, whereas Erasmian is imitative of Attic Greek—or so these scholars have been led to think.

This study describes the historical sounds of Greek and the graphemes that represent them and shows that these sounds are preserved in mainstream Neohellenic. Ample evidence in the light of historical research indicates that these sounds can be traced to the inscriptional record of the Hellenistic period and to their origins in classical or pre-classical times.

To that end, I have incorporated works by native as well as nonnative Greek scholars in order to form an added dimension of understanding of the historical development of the Hellenic language in general and of its phonology in specific. I have also incorporated references to works by Erasmian advocates in order to not only spotlight their treatment of the historical evidence, but also to create an awareness of the main ramifications of that treatment.

A number of questions may have by now been raised in your mind. It is hoped that the essence of your questions is reflected in the *Questions* section that follows, as this work considers such questions legitimate and fair and is devoted to substantiating the answers.

# Questions

## GREEK PRONUNCIATION

- After two millennia since Christ, doesn't Neohellenic sound as different from the Κοινή *Koine* of Biblical Greek as, say, Modern English from Chaucer's Anglo-Saxon?
- If we had evidence that Κοινή sounded much like Neohellenic, what might that evidence be?
- Even if Κοινή sounded much like Neohellenic, isn't today's Greek spelling, syllabification, and reading different from that of Biblical Greek, which complicates matters for English-speaking students and instructors?
- Are there any Bible colleges, seminaries, or other entities that teach Κοινή Greek the way Greek is pronounced today? If so, what is their reasoning?

## ERASMIAN PRONUNCIATION

- If for five centuries now Erasmian has been the predominant pronunciation in universities and theological institutions, is it not because Κοινή, like Attic Greek, is a dead language and therefore unrelated to today's Greek?
- Why change the way Greek has been traditionally taught in our universities, Bible colleges, and seminaries, since professors of Greek are all in unity regarding the Erasmian way Κοινή is pronounced?
- Scholars advocate the use of Erasmian in an attempt to approximate that melodious Attic Greek dialect of classical Athens, the speech of Plato and Aristotle. Isn't that the ideal pronunciation for our Bible and Ancient Greek students today?

Could you elucidate?
Answer: Certainly. Please read on . . .

> The [Greek] pronunciation commonly used in American colleges and seminaries is an attempt to approximate that used by the Athenians during the classical period of Greece (fifth and fourth centuries BC).

This assertion by a New Testament Greek scholar (discussed later) is in reference to the so-called "theoretical," "academic," or "standard" pronunciation of Greek. Invented in the early 1500s, this pronunciation is credited to the Dutch scholar Desiderius Erasmus (1466–1536), so it is commonly known also as Erasmian. The Erasmian pronunciation supposedly approximates the way Plato and Aristotle spoke Greek in classical Athens. As it will be shown in this study, however, Erasmian is artificial and inconsistent and has never been a part of the Greek speech.[1]

In Erasmus' day, while the Greek national voice remained silenced by the Ottoman Turks after the fall of Constantinople in 1453, unprecedented international interest in Classical Greek and in the newly printed Greek New Testament led non-Greek Renaissance intelligentsia to lump together everything Greek from antiquity down to the Christian era under one label: *Ancient Greek*. In other words, Erasmus had no reason to distinguish between the pronunciation of Aristotle's Attic Greek and Paul's Κοινή, for they both spoke "Ancient Greek."

Unlike Erasmus himself, however, Erasmian proponents today view the pronunciation of New Testament Κοινή as being different from that of Classical Greek due to phonological changes they presume Greek underwent before New Testament times as a result of Alexander's spread of Κοινή; yet they indiscriminately apply Erasmian to Classical Greek and New Testament Greek alike. Seen in this light, what the above assertion essentially says is that Aristotle's Erasmian pronunciation of Classical Greek is a more appropriate model for New Testament Greek than Paul's own pronunciation of Κοινή.

This implication raises questions about the pervasive presence of Erasmian—and in recent years, of other quasi-Erasmian varieties of pronunciation—in the study of Biblical and Classical Greek. Close inquiry reveals that Erasmian is more than just a pronunciation issue. Therefore the move being made in this study for the pronunciation warranted by the historical record eventually transcends the very question of pronunciation itself and elicits attention as well to other aspects of the Greek language and learning that are impacted by Erasmian and which as a result are currently at stake.

But let us now bring temporary closure to the above foretaste of the Erasmian issue and resume the topic in chapter 4, that is, after a discussion of the historical background of the Greek language, the formation of Κοινή, and the development of the historical Greek sounds.

1. The term *Erasmian* is used here as a blanket term that encompasses all Erasmian-like pronunciations of Greek, including "restored" and other such varieties.

PART ONE

# Authentic Greek Sounds

# Chapter 1

# The Development of Κοινή

## 1.1 THE FIRST HELLENES (GREEKS)

Several waves of Hellenic-speaking peoples are traditionally known to have migrated southward in the Greek peninsula between 2000 and 1000 BC, the most significant being the Achaeans (οἱ Ἀχαιοί), the Ionians (οἱ Ἴωνες), the Dorians (οἱ Δωριεῖς), and the Aeolians (οἱ Αἰολεῖς).

The Achaeans descended on the mainland of Greece and the islands after 2000 BC. Over time, they subjugated and mingled with the Pelasgians, an indigenous people of uncertain origin—though probably of Hellenic stock. Around 1450 BC the Achaeans invaded also the island of Crete and occupied Knossos, the center of the brilliant Minoan civilization whose origins are traced to the third millennium BC. Subsequently, a fusion of the Achaean and Minoan cultures gave rise to the Mycenaean civilization with its center in Mycenae, a city south of Corinth. The Mycenaeans are as well the Achaeans of the Trojan War (around 1200 BC) as recounted in Homer's the *Iliad* and the *Odyssey*.

Around 1100 BC the Ionians likewise descended and occupied east and central Greece, many Aegean islands, and the central portion of the western coast of Asia Minor, which was named Ionia. Thereafter, the Achaeans and the Ionians became victims of a third and harsher invasion by a Hellenic-speaking people known as the Dorians—e.g., the Spartans were Dorians. The Dorians spread down the mainland of Greece and conquered nearly all of Greece, save Attica and Euboea. This forced many Achaeans to flee to the islands, Attica, Euboea, and to Asia Minor where they became known as Ionians. The Dorian invasion, which presumably submerged the Mycenaean civilization, contributed to the "Dark Age" of Greece that lasted for four hundred years,[1] after which classical Greece began to emerge.

1. The four-hundred-year span begins with the fall of the Mycenaean civilization (1200 BC) and the appearance of the Ionic script around 800 BC. Some authorities allude to a three-hundred-year

## 1.2 PERIODS OF THE HELLENIC LANGUAGE

Hellenic is the oldest recorded living language and has been spoken in the Greek peninsula and surrounding islands for well over four thousand years. Based on the written record, Hellenic, an Indo-European language,[2] may be divided into two broad periods: ancient, 1500 BC–AD 600; and modern, AD 600–2000. Ancient period: Mycenaean, 1500–1200 BC; Dark Age, 1200–800 BC; Archaic or Epic, 800–500 BC; Classical (Attic), 500–300 BC; and post-Classical, 300 BC–AD 600, comprising Hellenistic period Koine, 300 BC–AD 300, and Proto-Byzantine Koine, AD 300–600. Modern period: Early Neohellenic/Byzantine, AD 600–1000; Middle Neohellenic/Late Byzantine (Medieval), AD 1000–1500; and Late Neohellenic, AD 1500–2000.[3]

Today's Hellenic is Κοινή Νεοελληνική [kiní neoelinikí] (*Neohellenic Koine*) "Common New Hellenic" (officially as of 1976). The name for *Greece* is Ἑλλάς *Ellas* (*Hellas*), and *Greek* is Ἑλληνική *Elliniki* (*Hellenic*). The English adaptation of *Greek* is derived from the Latin *Graecus*, which originates from Γραικός *Graikos*, the name of a Boeotian tribe in Greece that emigrated to Italy in the 8th c. BC. It is by that name the Hellenes were known in the West. Hellenic here refers particularly to Classical Greek, and Hellenistic[4] to the six-hundred-year period of Greek following Alexander the Great. Thus, New Testament Greek, widely known simply as *Koine* Κοινή [kiní] "common," is Hellenistic Greek.

Note: Henceforth the name *Greek*, rather than *Hellenic*, is used—except in certain cases. Similarly, the name *Neohellenic Greek*, or simply *Neohellenic*, rather than *Modern Greek*, is used—except in select cases—for (a) Νεοελληνική Κοινή *Neohellenic Koine* is the official name of today's Greek language and the language into which the historical Greek speech evolved; and (b) from a phonological perspective, the sounds of Greek are not modern or new but of an unbroken past (3.6). It is in fact this continuity of the Greek speech that makes it technically impossible to investigate the linguistic nature of one of its historical periods to the exclusion of the others.

With this bird's-eye view of the development of Greek as a historical backdrop, let us now take a look at the roots and formation of Κοινή.

span beginning with the submerging of the Mycenaean culture by the Dorians (1050 BC) and the beginning of some inscriptional records (750 BC).

2. *Indo-European* is a term applied to a group of cognate languages including the majority of European language groups—Albanian, Baltic, Celtic, Germanic, Greek, Italic, and Slavonic—as well as Armenian, Indo-Iranian (Hindi and Persian), and Sanskrit. English, being a Germanic language, is Indo-European.

3. Adapted from the work by Caragounis, *Development of Greek*, 22.

4. *Hellenistic* is from Ἑλληνίζω [elinízo] *I Hellenize* "I make Greek."

## 1.3 ORIGIN OF KOINH

Ancient Greek was diversified into distinct but mutually intelligible dialects—Aeolic, Attic, Doric, and Ionic. It was chiefly in the Ionic dialect and partly in the Aeolic that the epic poems of Homer, the *Iliad* and the *Odyssey*, appeared around 850–800 BC. During the classical period (500–300 BC), and with the rise of Athens to prominence following the defeat of the Persians in Greece (490–479 BC), Attic,[5] the dialect of Athens and an offshoot of Ionic, began to produce masterpieces of literature, a characteristic of the "Golden Age of Athens" (479–404 BC). With its superiority over the other Greek dialects sustained by Athens' undisputed cultural, political, and military prowess, Attic prevailed as the standard language of the Greek world, which led to its eventual adoption under Philip II, or earlier, as the language of Macedonia.

**Κοινή did not come directly from the artistic literary Attic but from the Attic vernacular.**

The unification of Hellas by Alexander the Great shortly after the beginning of his rule (336 BC), which brought nearly all Hellenes together, led to the amalgamation of the Greek dialects under the predominance of Attic into what became known as post-Classical or Κοινή "common (tongue)." This Κοινή did not come directly from the artistic literary Classical Attic used in the writings of Sophocles, Thucydides, Plato, Demosthenes, or Aristotle but from the Demotic Attic, the vernacular spoken in Athens at that time but whose literary level was deeply influenced by the artistic literary Classical Attic (1.10).

## 1.4 SPREAD OF KOINH

During his expeditions of world conquest (334–323 BC), Alexander spread the Κοινή to all his conquered lands, thereby ushering in the Hellenistic Age. The spreading of Greek over most of the known world was perhaps the most significant development of the Hellenistic Age. Greek "became the mother tongue of the new communities in Egypt, Syria, Asia Minor, Mesopotamia and the Iranian world."[6] The conquest of Greece by the Roman Empire (146 BC) could not restrain the spreading of Κοινή, which by then had attained world-speech status. In fact, at the time of Christ, Greek was the language of trade and the cultural language of the Roman Empire, the *lingua franca* familiar to all educated persons and of the majority of the populace from Rome eastward.

The extent to which Κοινή had been established as a world-speech in the beginning of the Christian era may be measured in part by the following notable events: Paul composed his letter Πρὸς Ῥωμαίους *To (the) Romans*, that is, to the church at Rome, in Greek (AD 56–57); the letter Πρὸς Ἑβραίους *To (the) Hebrews*, apparently addressed to the Jewish people, was likewise written in Greek (before AD 70); Cicero

5. *Attic* comes from Ἀττική *Attica*, the name of the region containing the city of Athens.

6. Browning, *Medieval and Modern Greek*, 22.

(1st c. BC) and other educated Romans like him studied in Athens; and the Roman Emperor Marcus Aurelius (AD 121–180) wrote τὰ εἰς Ἑαυτόν, his personal memoirs known as *Meditations*, in Greek. Says Jannaris, "It is this Panhellenic or *new Attic* that marks an already advanced stage in the direction of *Modern Greek*."[7]

## 1.5 THE SEPTUAGINT WRITTEN IN KOINH

When Alexander founded the city of Alexandria in Egypt (331 BC), he assigned a part of it to a colony of Jews. In this way, and through a gradual dispersion of the Jews westward, a large body of Hellenized Jews sprang up who, while they thought and felt as Hebrews, yet spoke Greek. This situation gave rise to the need to have the Old Testament Scriptures translated into Κοινή. The translation, commenced around 285 BC, became better known as the Septuagint (LXX).[8] The LXX was the only Bible known to most Jews in the world in the nascent Christian era and the Bible used by the writers of the NT. It is of significance that the conviction of a Creator God enters the stream of Greek literature through the Septuagint, thereby preparing the Κοινή for the NT.

## 1.6 THE KOINH OF THE NT

The Κοινή of the NT is not the language of the Classical Attic masterpieces of literature nor is it some form of Egyptian, Jewish, or Christian Greek, nor a sacred "Biblical Greek" tongue.[9] The discovery in Egypt during the nineteenth century of well-preserved heaps of papyri from the Hellenistic Age (2.2) revealed that the language of the NT is the language naturally evolved from the Classical Attic vernacular and whose continuation is Neohellenic, today's Greek. Thus, the Κοινή spoken by Hellenized Jews during NT times had evolved from the same Classical Attic vernacular as the Κοινή spoken also by contemporary mainline non-Hellenized Greeks in Athens.

A comparison therefore of the NT writings with Classical Greek must be made with caution because they cannot be compared against the literary works of the "Golden Age" of Greece for two reasons: (a) they were written by Hellenized writers and therefore cannot be viewed as representatives of current mainline Greek among

7. Jannaris, *Historical Greek Grammar*, 6.

8. From Latin *septuaginta* "seventy." The name was applied around the time of Bishop Augustine (AD 354–430) of Hippo, a Roman city in Algeria, and is based on the embellished tradition that seventy-two Jewish emissaries in Alexandria (six from each Jewish tribe—the number being rounded off to seventy and represented by LXX) were commissioned by Ptolemy II Philadelphus, a Greek-born king of Egypt, to translate the Hebrew Scriptures into Κοινή Greek. Commencement of the translation is variously placed between 285 and 282 BC. The translation is said to have been completed in seventy-two days, but it is likely that initially the Pentateuch was translated, and that LXX was extended later to cover the entire Greek translation of the Hebrew manuscripts.

9. While Κοινή refers to the Greek language *per se*, "Biblical Greek" refers to the Κοινή as applied by Hellenized Jews to record their sacred writings in general and the writings of the New Testament in specific.

Greeks, and (b) they were written in Κοινή, with most of Paul's writings, Hebrews, parts of Acts, and much of Peter, James, and Jude being in literary Κοινή; and the gospels, along with parts of the other NT books, being more representative of the colloquial or popular Κοινή. The literary Κοινή of the NT, however lofty, was not the Atticistic Greek used by contemporary Atticists.[10]

## 1.7 BYZANTINE GREEK

Following Emperor Diocletian's most savage persecution of all Christians in the eastern parts of the Roman Empire, a persecution that continued unabated until 311, Emperor Constantine I, by a miraculous reversal of events within two years, made Christianity in 313 a legal religion. In 324 Constantine, the first Christian Roman emperor, moved the capital of the Roman Empire from Rome to "New Rome" in Byzantium, an ancient Greek city renamed in AD 330 *Constantinople* "city of Constantine" (modern Istanbul). Under Emperor Theodosios some years later, Christianity became the state religion of the entire Roman Empire.

Upon Theodosios' death in 395, the Roman Empire became divided into Eastern and Western Roman Empire, and under Emperor Justinian (527–565) Greek was declared the official language of the Byzantine Empire, as the Eastern Roman Empire came to be known. The Byzantine Empire, having survived the Frankish Crusades and Venetian expeditions of the 12th and 13th centuries, endured for over a millennium until the Ottoman Turks ransacked Constantinople in 1453.

Byzantium was a Greek-speaking society. Byzantine schoolboys studied Attic and read Homer and the old Athenian authors. It was during Byzantine times that the Κοινή and scholarly studies in Greek were kept alive, copies of manuscripts multiplied, and the Greek NT was preserved. In fact the Greek Bible did not make its way to the West until after the fall of Constantinople in 1453. At that time Byzantine scholars fled to the West, especially Italy, bringing with them as well invaluable treasures of ancient Greek and Roman manuscripts.[11] It was the Byzantine text of the Eastern Church that became the basis of Desiderius Erasmus' 1516 edition of the Greek NT during the Reformation, including the King James Version in 1611.

10. From the 1st c. BC on, Greek writers composed literary works in *puristic* or Atticistic Greek, i.e., Greek imitative of artistic/literary Classical Attic. The Atticists were zealously followed in practice to various degrees by subsequent generations of literati from Byzantine times down to the present (1.10).

11. "Of the 55,000 Ancient Greek texts in existence today, some 40,000 were transmitted to us by Byzantine scribes." Brownworth, *Lost to the West* (front and back flap of the book's jacket).

## 1.8 BYZANTINE GREEK: KOINH'S LINK TO NEOHELLENIC GREEK

The relation of today's Greek to Byzantine Greek is comparable to the relation of the latter to the Κοινή of the Christian era. Up to AD 600, particularly in its earlier stages, Byzantine Greek was identical with the Κοινή of the early Christians. (See illustration below.) Additionally, once Greek became Christianized, there developed a heavy dependence on Classical Attic which, concurrent with the Byzantine vernacular, found a mighty shelter as the sacred language of the Greek Church. Jannaris describes this situation as follows:

> Just as classical Attic had served as a model for all pre-Christian antiquity, so ecclesiastical Attic succeeded and continued as a fixed and sacred standard for all post-Christian literature. . . . Ecclesiastical Attic was the language of the ritual daily read and heard in the Greek Church; . . . the diction of all schoolbooks, the entire course of education being religious in spirit and bearing. Likewise the official language of the Emperor and his court, that of the vast administration, of the law courts and the numberless clergy, was essentially ecclesiastical or modernized Attic. . . . Now there was but one grammar: the Attic.[12]

Thus, practically from the NT era on, especially from AD 330, Greek remained homogeneous within the Byzantine Empire. Robertson concurs by saying that "the vernacular Κοινή lived through the Roman and Byzantine periods and survives today as the modern Greek," and that "the modern Greek popular speech does not differ materially from the vernacular Byzantine, and thus connects directly with the vernacular κοινή."[13]

The following chart depicts the continuation of Κοινή from the end of the classical period to the present.

**Continuation of Κοινή**

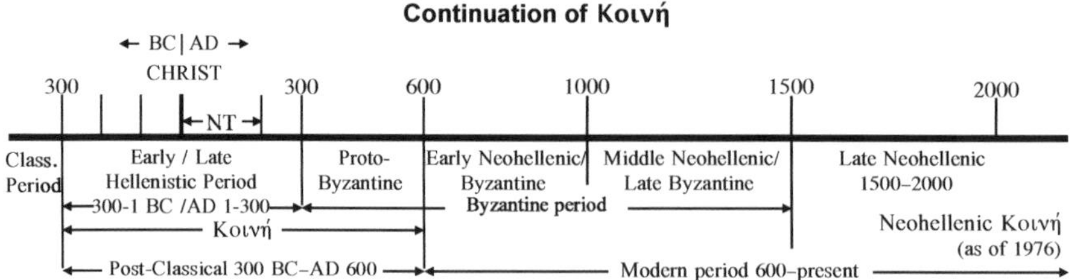


12. Jannaris, *Historical Greek Grammar*, 11.

13. Robertson, *Grammar of the Greek New Testament*, 22, 44.

## 1.9 NEOHELLENIC: A CONTINUATION OF KOINH

Because of the pioneer work of philhellenes during the Turkish oppression such as Adamantios Koraës (1748–1833), Διδάσκαλος τοῦ Ἔθνους *Teacher of the Nation*; world-renowned native Greek linguists George Hatzidakis (1848–1941) and Antonios Jannaris (1852–1909); and others, it is clear among professionals today that Neohellenic is part of the living stream of the NT Κοινή. Blackwelder acknowledges, "Modern Greek scholars like Hatzidakis and Professor [Evangelinos Apostolides] Sophocles have done a great deal to show the connection between the Koine, the Byzantine, and the Modern Greek," and assures the student of NT Greek that various points of grammar and syntax are made clearer in the light of today's Greek vernacular.[14]

**"Few even among professional scholars are aware how small the difference is between the Greek of the N.T. and a contemporary Athenian newspaper."**

A comparison of Κοινή and Neohellenic grammar is beyond our scope. Suffice it to say that Neohellenic is simpler at the vernacular, though less so at the Katharevousa, level. As Robertson observes, "Few even among professional scholars are aware how small the difference is between the Greek of the N.T. and a contemporary Athenian newspaper."[15]

On the flip side of Robertson's observation, non-Greek scholars at times cannot differentiate between NT Greek and Modern Greek. On the wall inside an evangelical church in Athens, for example, is an inscription of the Lord's Prayer from Matthew 6:9–13 (see frame below). A prominent modern-day scholar opines that the prayer is in Modern Greek—or, is it?

"This is the Lord's Prayer," says Mounce, "inscribed on the inside of an evangelical church in Greece. It is modern Greek. Here it is in Koine, without the textually uncertain ending."[16]

ΠΑΤΕΡ ΗΜΩΝ Ο ΕΝ ΤΟΙϹ ΟΥΡΑΝΟΙϹ
ΑΓΙΑϹΘΗΤΩ Τ'ΟΝΟΜΑ ϹΟΥ
ΕΛΘΕΤΩ Η ΒΑϹΙΛΕΙΑ ϹΟΥ ΓΕΝΗΘΗΤΩ
ΤΟ ΘΕΛΗΜΑ ϹΟΥ ΩϹ ΕΝ ΟΥΡΑΝΩ ΚΑΙ
ΕΠΙ ΤΗϹ ΓΗϹ ΤΟΝ ΑΡΤΟΝ ΗΜΩΝ ΤΟΝ
ΕΠΙΟΥϹΙΟΝ ΔΟϹ ΗΜΙΝ ϹΗΜΕΡΟΝ ΚΑΙ
ΑΦΕϹ ΗΜΙΝ ΤΑ ΟΦΕΙΛΗΜΑΤΑ ΗΜΩΝ
ΩϹ ΚΑΙ ΗΜΕΙϹ ΑΦΙΕΜΕΝ ΤΟΙϹ ΟΦΕΙΛΕΤΑΙΞ
ΗΜΩΝ ΚΑΙ ΜΗ ΕΙϹΕΝΕΓΚΗϹ ΗΜΑϹ ΕΙϹ
ΠΕΙΡΑϹΜΟΝ ΑΛΛΑ ΡΥϹΑΙ ΗΜΑϹ ΑΠΟ ΤΟΥ
ΠΟΝΗΡΟΥ ΟΤΙ ΞΟΥ ΕϹΤΙΝ Η ΒΑϹΙΛΕΙΑ ΚΑΙ
Η ΔΥΝΑΜΙϹ ΚΑΙ Η ΔΟΞΑ ΕΙϹ ΤΟΥϹ ΑΙΩΝΑϹ
ΑΜΗΝ

Πάτερ ἡμῶν ὁ ἐν τοῖς οὐρανοῖς·
ἁγιασθήτω τὸ ὄνομά σου·
ἐλθέτω ἡ βασιλεία σου· γενηθήτω
τὸ θέλημά σου, ὡς ἐν οὐρανῷ καὶ
ἐπὶ τῆς γῆς· τὸν ἄρτον ἡμῶν τὸν
ἐπιούσιον δὸς ἡμῖν σήμερον· καὶ
ἄφες ἡμῖν τὰ ὀφειλήματα ἡμῶν,
ὡς καὶ ἡμεῖς ἀφήκαμεν τοῖς ὀφειλέτες

14. Blackwelder, *Light from the Greek New Testament*, 27–28.
15. Robertson, *Grammar of the Greek New Testament*, 24.
16. Mounce, *Biblical Greek Grammar Workbook*, 40.

ἡμῶν· καὶ μὴ εἰσενέγκῃς ἡμᾶς εἰς

πειρασμόν, ἀλλὰ ῥῦσαι ἡμᾶς ἀπὸ τοῦ

πονηροῦ. [shorter ending]

Contrary to Mounce's claim, the upper (framed) rendition of the Lord's Prayer, written in Byzantine uncials (capitals), is not in "modern" Greek; it is actually from the *Textus Receptus* (TR).[17] The lowercase rendition is in modern type. Both renditions are in the Κοινή "Koine" of the New Testament and are identical in wording and spelling. The only difference, besides the letter type, is that the uncial rendition—here accurately reproduced—has ἀφίεμεν "we forgive" (TR), while the lowercase rendition has ἀφήκαμεν "we forgave" and a shorter ending (Nestle-Aland).[18] Modern-day Greeks can read and understand the uncial rendition—as well as the lowercase one—though not because it is Modern Greek.

Other scholars espouse the notion that today's Greek differs from that of the NT as does Modern English from Anglo-Saxon or the English of fourteenth-century Chaucer. Such an assumption cannot stem from a close acquaintance with Neohellenic nor with the tenacious nature the Greek language and its phonology and orthography have displayed for nearly two and a half millennia. As Browning comments:

> Since then [Homer's time] Greek has enjoyed a continuous tradition down to the present day. Change has there certainly been. But there has been no break like that between Latin and the Romance languages. Ancient Greek is not a foreign language to the Greek of today as Anglo-Saxon is to the modern Englishman. . . . Perhaps connected with this continuous identity over some three and a half millennia is the slowness of change in Greek. . . . Earlier stages of the language are thus accessible to speakers of later stages, . . . [a] peculiar situation created by a long and continuous literary tradition which makes all elements of Greek from antiquity to the present day in a sense accessible and "present" to any literate Greek.[19]

Largely as a result of Alexander's conquests, the Hellenic dialects, under the predominance of Attic, were fused into a common tongue. So radical was the unification of these dialects that, in direct contrast to the fate of other Indo-European dialects, particularly the Germanic and Romance groups—which grew farther and farther apart—they have survived merged into one language whose continuity over the centuries down to Neohellenic has curbed change to glacial slowness.[20] The following diagram illustrates this:

17. "Received Text" formed the translation base for the King James Version in 1611.

18. Nestle et al., *Novum Testamentum*.

19. Browning, *Medieval and Modern Greek*, vii, 2–3, 13.

20. Hellenic encompasses not different languages but mutually intelligible dialects, the main ones being Aeolic, Attic, Doric, Ionic. Κοινή, developed from Attic, became *Neohellenic Κοινή*.

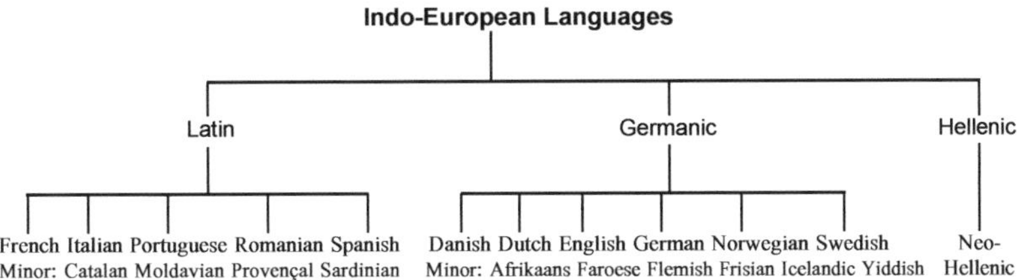


## 1.10 GREEK DIMORPHIA

By "Ancient" or "Classical" Greek, one typically means the Classical Greek of Athens, the extolled language of the masterpieces of classical literature of the 5th and 4th c. BC, and whose earlier literature (until 600 BC) was recounted in verse. But did the average Athenian of antiquity converse with his fellow citizens in metrical poetry or rhymed song? Hardly.

Classical Greek consisted of two contemporaneous forms: the artistic literary Attic, and the Demotic or vernacular. The artistic form was artificially lofty and highly refined in grammar and expression, while the vernacular, deeply influenced by the artistic at the literary level, was the informal speech of everyday Athens (p. 150). It is mainly this Attic vernacular, as we have seen, that became the Κοινή of Hellenistic times and was applied to the Septuagint and the NT. Though distinct in expression, the artistic literary Attic and the Attic vernacular shared one and the same alphabet and phonological system. This phenomenon of *dimorphia* ("two forms" [of the same language]), improperly referred to as *diglossia* ("two tongue-ness"), was revived in Hellenistic times when artistic Classical Attic, waning under Roman rule, was resuscitated by the Atticists—mainline Greek writers using Atticistic Greek, that is, Greek imitative of artistic Classical Attic. This practice continued through Byzantine and Neohellenic times.

Today's literary Greek is *Katharevousa*[21] "puristic" (officially "ended" in 1976) and has its roots in the artistic literary Classical Attic, while *Dimotiki* "Demotic" has its roots in the Demotic or Classical Attic vernacular, which became Hellenistic Κοινή. In 1976 Greece adopted *Neoelliniki* "Neohellenic" *Koine* or "Common New Greek" as the official name of her language, a "middle ground" for the two forms that, in actuality, reflects a rich vernacular ever drawing upon the vast resources of Katharevousa.

As was the case with the artistic Classical Attic and the Classical Attic vernacular, Katharevousa and Dimotiki share the same historical alphabet, virtually the same spelling rules and grammatical features, and the same phonological system, all such features being traceable to Classical Attic. As Caragounis puts it, "Neohellenic . . . is

21. Katharevousa is used primarily by the Athenian polytonic newspaper ΕΣΤΙΑ, in written works by the Greek Orthodox Church, and in speech by church representatives. Special interest groups in Greece advocate the return to the polytonic writing, an accentuation system that was abolished in 1982 and which is associated more with Katharevousa.

the latest phase of the Attic dialect, the outcome of a continuous linguistic evolution through the Koine, Byzantine, and Mediaeval Greek, preserving all the basic grammatical categories intact."[22]

## 1.11 HISTORICITY OF THE GREEK ALPHABET

In considering the question of Greek pronunciation, an understanding of the historicity of the Greek alphabet is necessary. As seen earlier, the Achaeans were the first Greek-speaking people who descended on the mainland of Greece sometime after 2000 BC. The Achaeans conquered the Minoans in Crete, and a fusion of the Achaean and Minoan cultures gave rise to the Mycenaean civilization, named after Mycenae. Mycenaean is the oldest attested form of the Hellenic language. The Mycenaeans produced the oldest written record of Greek called *Linear B*, a writing system used between 1500 and 1200 BC. The *Linear B* syllabary consisted of about ninety pictographs, each representing a syllable, including signs for the five vowels /i, e, a, o, u/ (2.5; 6.5).

It is commonly believed among authorities that around 1000 BC the Greeks began to abandon their pictographic writing system and progressively adopted the Phoenician alphabet, a Semitic form of writing that represented only consonant sounds (like Hebrew), and to which they ingeniously added symbols for their five phonemic vowel sounds.[23] Scant primitive inscriptions show that in its beginning stages the alphabet was incomplete and deficient, with various similar symbols having different phonetic values in different regions. This suggests that the alphabet found its way into the various Greek communities not simultaneously but at various intervals and by various channels.

Eventually the Ionians, the kinsmen of the Athenians, perfected their alphabet, a regional alphabet the Athenians began to adopt from the mid-5th c. BC. In 403 BC Athens, under Archon Eucleides' rule, ratified the Ionic alphabet as the official Attic alphabet.[24] All previous Attic Greek literature now had to be transcribed into the new scholastic orthography, ἡ μετ᾽ Εὐκλείδην γραμματική *the post-Eucleidean grammar*.[25] It must be noted that although the ratification of the Ionic alphabet involved

22. Caragounis, *Development of Greek*, 59.

23. In Plato's time these five phonemes are represented by the letters α, η, ι, which are named ἄλφα, ἦτα, ἰῶτα, respectively; and nameless ε, ο, υ, ω (*Kratylos*, 393d), which are identified as εἶ, οὖ, ὗ, ὦ (Jannaris, *Historical Greek Grammar*, 26). The name ψιλόν *psilon* "simple" in ἔψιλον *epsilon* (ε) and ὕψιλον *ypsilon* (υ), used by the Byzantines, denotes that ε and υ are monoliteral in contradistinction to their biliteral homophones αι and ει, οι, υι, respectively. Similarly, the homophones ο and ω were named ὄμικρον *omicron* "small o" and ὠμέγα *omega* "great/large o" (not μακρόν *macron* "long"!) to facilitate orthography during dictation to Byzantine school children and MS copyists (2.3, fn.). In NT times Ω is still nameless: ᾽Εγὼ τὸ Ἄλφα καὶ τὸ Ὦ, *I (am) the Alpha and the O(mega)* (Rev 22:12).

24. The Attic alphabet is exactly the same twenty-four-letter alphabet used in Greece today and which, since about the 8th c. AD, features also lowercase letters.

25. Significantly, Neohellenic, particularly Katharevousa, still follows the Attic orthography. As of

orthographical changes such as would effectuate grammatical distinctions in writing hitherto not possible (2.21), it was executed not under the banner of a spelling reform *per se* but of a new script. For had it been termed a "spelling reform," it would not have passed off without being met by public opposition and outcry, not without vehement criticism from contemporary satirists and other artists. Instead, it was ratified "quietly and without a public stir."[26]

At the same time it must be borne in mind that when Athens began to adopt the Ionic alphabet in the mid-5th c. BC there was much confusion in orthography because of two contemporaneous writing systems: the Chalcidic,[27] or old Attic type, and the Ionic, or new Attic type. For instance, old Attic E was later in the century represented by E(ε), EI(ει), H(η), or HI(ῃ); O by O(ο), Ω(ω), or OY(ου); EI by EI(ει) or HI(ῃ); and OI by OI(οι) or ΩI(ῳ). Accordingly, the old Attic spelling ΦΕΡΕ could be read later in the century as φέρε, φέρει, or φέρῃ, and ΛΟΓΟΙ could be read as λόγοι or λόγῳ.

Thus, whereas prior to the mid-5th c. BC we see E and O dominating the older Attic script, from the second half of the 5th c. BC we begin to notice the encroachment of Ionic H, Ω, OY, the replacement by Λ Γ Π Ζ Σ of their older counterparts, the appearance of ΧΣ(ΚΣ) as Ξ and of ΦΣ(ΠΣ) as Ψ, and the new role of defunct "aspirate" H[h] as the vowel H(η).

But the newly adopted Ionic alphabet did not instantaneously supplant the older Attic; the latter in fact persisted until late Hellenistic times. And although the newer script represented grammatical distinctions more efficiently, orthographical errors of an acoustic nature, particularly in private Hellenistic inscriptions and papyrical records by the less educated, abounded. Significantly, such errors bequeathed to the historical linguist a well-marked map to the origins and formation of the historical Greek sounds.

It is thus from around the mid-5th c. BC, when Attic incorporated Ionic H, Ω (officially in 403 BC), that we can more confidently rely on the *written* evidence to track the historical sounds of Attic Greek, discussed in chapter 2.

## 1.12 PHONOLOGICAL DEFINITIONS

As we proceed to examine the phonological development of Κοινή, a streamlined definition of certain phonological terms may prove helpful.

about 1976, Dimotiki uses -ει, -εις, -ομε/-ουμε in the present indicative and subjunctive alike, while literary Katharevousa still uses the traditional subjunctive endings -ῃ, -ῃς, -ωμεν.

26. Jannaris, *Historical Greek Grammar*, 532.

27. Before the 5th c. BC the Greek alphabet was divided into two main branches, Chalcidic (western) and Ionic (eastern). Chalcidic or Chalcidian is from Χαλκίς (-ίδος), a city on the island of Εὔβοια near Athens.

| | |
|---|---|
| a. *phonology* | The study of the sound system of a language. |
| b. *pronunciation* | The manner in which sounds are articulated during normal speech. |
| c. *orthophonic* | *Correct-sounding.* The isolated pronunciation of a single sound segment, syllable, or word. |
| d. *isochronous* | *Equally-timed.* Describes the quantity or length of vowels and syllables during their orthophonic pronunciation. |
| e. *phonetic* | The physical, acoustic qualities of a speech sound. IPA[28] *phonetic* symbols are enclosed in square brackets: [b], [s], [v]. |
| f. *phoneme* | The smallest meaningful sound in a language that can convey a distinction in meaning, as that between *b* in *bat* and *p* in *pat*. IPA *phonemic* symbols are enclosed in forward slashes: /b/, /s/, /v/. |
| g. *allophone* | An alternative pronunciation of a phoneme. The 't' in *top, stop, little, better* represents *variant sounds* (allophones) of the phoneme / t /. |
| h. *grapheme* | A letter of an alphabet. |
| i. *graph* | Any of the possible forms of a grapheme. Also, a *monograph*. |
| j. *allograph* | An alternative spelling of a grapheme (letter) or combination of graphemes that represents the same speech sound. The variant spellings of the [s] sound in *sir, class, city, science*, are *variant graphs* (allographs) of the speech sound [s] or phoneme / s /. |
| k. *sound* | Phonetic value assigned to a letter or cluster of letters; the letter itself. |

## 1.13 ORTHOPHONIC PRONUNCIATION AND ITS SIGNIFICANCE

Pronunciation in a *narrow* sense may be understood as the orthophonic utterance of an isolated speech sound, syllable, or word. In a *broad* sense, pronunciation may be viewed as part of intonation, which entails additional features that fall within the acoustic properties of regular speech: stress, pitch-accent, juncture, rhythm, length, and voice quality. The broad sense presupposes a living language or voice recordings of native speakers. Thus, the further back in time we go prior to the end of the nineteenth century, that is, before the recording of human voice was possible, the more dependent we are on the written aspect of the Greek language regarding the identification and description of speech sounds. In determining therefore how to read and pronounce Biblical Greek (as the title of this work goes),[29] we will adhere primarily to the narrow (orthophonic) approach.

Upon attempting however to compare the pronunciation of the Κοινή of the NT with that of Neohellenic, we are at once faced with a linguistic paradox: Κοινή and Neohellenic, in addition to being direct descendants of Attic, share the same twenty-four-letter Classical Attic alphabet and orthography. The question then arises: What

28. *International Phonetic Alp*habet. For the value of IPA symbols, see p. 90

29. *Reading* in the title of this book signifies the association of a letter (or letters) with a sound; *Pronouncing*, the actual articulation of the sound associated with that letter (or letters).

sound should a given Κοινή letter be compared against? What, in other words, should be the reference point for the Κοινή pronunciation? Attic? If Attic, what should be the reference point for Attic itself? Latin? Persian? Sanskrit? That would have been a likely approach had Attic been dead. But looking at the evolutionary spectrum of Greek, with Attic at one end and Neohellenic at the other, we are reminded that the continuity of Greek speech makes it technically impossible to investigate the linguistic nature of one of its historical periods to the exclusion of the others (1.2). Thus Neohellenic cannot be left out of the loop in terms of possible clues; for without the living sounds of Neohellenic we would have no reliable basis for assuming even the sound of ἰῶτα (ι) in Byzantine times, let alone Hellenistic or classical times, not to mention the more controversial sounds.

At the same time it becomes clear that once the value of a Κοινή letter or digraph is established and subsequently traced to Neohellenic, it may be said that that Κοινή sound is preserved in Neohellenic. It follows that the degree of similarity in pronunciation between Neohellenic and Κοινή is commensurate with the number of orthophonically similar sounds.[30]

With this significant point in mind, the aim in the ensuing discussion will be to ascertain the extent to which the Κοινή and Neohellenic sound systems are similar (or different), with Attic serving as a gauge for sound development from classical times to the present. It is thus of paramount importance that we establish the sounds Attic letters represented around the time of Plato and Aristotle. The sounds most disputed (chiefly by Erasmians) are the following:[31]

Monoliterals or monographs (single letters): β, γ, δ, ζ, θ, φ, χ, υ, ο, ω, η, h[32]

Biliterals or digraphs (pairs of letters): αι, ει, οι, υι, ευ, αυ, ηυ

The remaining sounds are normally not disputed: α, ε, ι, ου, κ, λ, μ, ν, ξ, π, ρ, σ, τ, ψ. Digraphs γγ, γκ, γξ, each beginning with "nasal γ," are normally of no concern. For digraph γχ, see the individual letters γ, χ above. "Spurious diphthongs" ᾳ, ῃ, ῳ are normally treated the same way as α, η, ω.

In chapter 2 each disputed sound is discussed and compared with its Neohellenic equivalent, though not in the above order. Certain sounds are further discussed in subsequent chapters. Included in the discussion are phonological aspects that come into focus and which are also held in dispute, such as vowel length (quantity) and pitch-accent (tone).

30. Questions about Greek pronunciation usually entail the idea of how Modern Greek compares to the Greek of other periods. A casual response may provoke a volatile reaction such as, "You mean to say that after two thousand years Modern Greek sounds like Koine?" When asked about pronunciation, I steer my response to individual sounds. After all, individual sounds are the building blocks of pronunciation.

31. A letter (grapheme) is not a sound; it is a symbol that represents a sound. In this study a letter referred to as a sound must be understood as the phonetic value assigned to it (cf. 1.12.k).

32. h stands for "aspirate" [h] as in *have*.

Finally, and as already mentioned, the discussion in this work incorporates references to works by two sides of scholars: native-born and nonnative Greek scholars, and Erasmian scholars. Thus portions of the discussion in the following chapters are devoted to critiquing various views by Erasmian advocates regarding Attic, Κοινή, and Neohellenic sounds. The aim is to bring to bear the basis for those views in order to show how that basis measures up to the historical evidence.

# Chapter 2

# The Phonology of Κοινή and Its Similarities to Neohellenic

## 2.1 A SPECIFIC LINGUISTIC PERIOD

Attic Greek did not die nor did it give birth to a new language;[1] rather, it continued to develop through Hellenistic and Byzantine times down to the present. From Alexander the Great until technically AD 600, Greek is known as Κοινή *Koine* [kiní]. Thereafter it may be referred to as Early/Middle/Late Neohellenic (cf. 1.2), and presently as Neohellenic Κοινή or simply Neohellenic. This chapter examines the development of the phonology of Κοινή and compares it with that of Neohellenic. Because certain features of Κοινή had been established by or were initiated within classical times, reference will be made as well to their period of origin or initiation. Of immediate concern then becomes the time period from classical through NT times, as the diagram below shows:

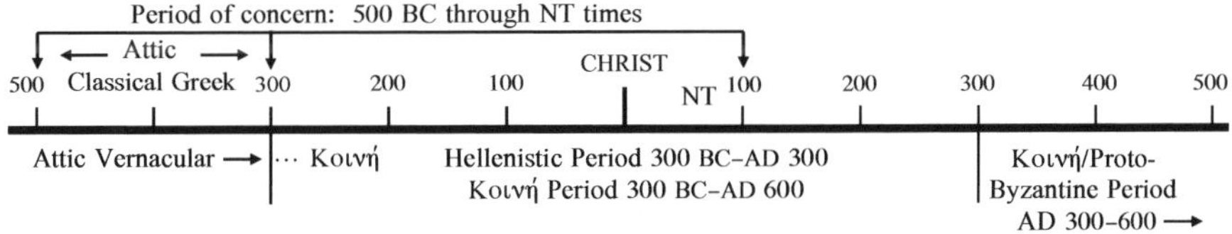


1. Wallace's analogy of a physical but not linguistic birth of Κοινή in 330 BC can be misleading: "Just as a newborn baby does not immediately speak, it took some time before Koine took shape." (Wallace, *Beyond Basics*, 18.) Such descriptions, regardless of intent, can lead to the erroneous notion that Κοινή was an "infant" tongue, not the continuation of Attic.

## 2.2 IOTACISM

English-speaking students of NT and Classical Greek are typically told that in Neohellenic the [i] sound is represented six different ways: ι, η, υ, ει, οι, υι; and that this "modern" Greek method of pronouncing these letters and digraphs began to develop around medieval times. This method, students are further told, could not have been true of Classical Greek as there was no reason for the Athenians, a people of the subtlest intellect, to have assigned the same phonetic value to such a variety of symbols.[2] As it will be shown, however, this variety of spellings for the same sound—that of ἰῶτα *iota* (ι)—is not a modern invention but rather the result of a centuries-old linguistic progression that reached classical Athens.

Numerous mounds of thousands of well-preserved Greek papyri and *ostraka* (potsherds) from the Hellenistic period were discovered in Egypt toward the end of the nineteenth century—personal letters and records, shopping lists, business contracts, wills, etc.—which date between the beginning of the 3rd c. BC and 7th c. AD, i.e., from Alexander's conquest of Egypt onward,[3] and which would have been understood by the NT authors. While the finds included fragments of ancient literary works, the nonliterary papyri formed an overwhelming proportion, the majority having been written by scribes and ordinary individuals with poor orthography skills and who haphazardly interchanged alphabet letters that stood for the same sound. This interchange of letters means that a writer would misspell a word using, for instance, ι for ει, η, υ, or οι simply because he spelled not according to prescribed grammatical rules but acoustically. This practice tells us which letters stood for the same sound for Κοινή speakers and which sounds were phonemically distinct. Below are but a few samples of the innumerable Hellenistic-period spelling errors found in papyri dated between the 2nd c. BC and the 1st c. AD.

### 2.2.1 Interchange of ι-Sound Letters in Hellenistic Papyri

| | **Misspelled word** | **Corrected** | **Interchange shown** | | |
|---|---|---|---|---|---|
| 2nd c. BC[4] | πλ**ι**στα | πλ**ει**στα | ι | for | ει |
| | αναβαιν**ι**ς | αναβαιν**ει**ς | ι | for | ει |
| | υγ**ει**αινειν | υγ**ι**αινειν | ει | for | ι |
| | γ**ει**νωσκειν | γ**ι**νωσκειν | ει | for | ι |

2. Notably, English i-sounds are spelled thirty different ways (5.7).

3. Until the Persian invasion of Egypt around AD 618–19, Egypt had been a part of the Byzantine Empire. Egypt was subsequently conquered by the Muslims in AD 639. There were sporadic finds of Greek papyri in Egypt in the early 1800s, but more substantial amounts were found from 1877 on.

4. Deissmann, *Ancient East*, 187.

| | | | | | |
|---|---|---|---|---|---|
| 1st c. BC[5] | μισθωμ**ε** | μισθωμ**αι** | ε | for | αι |
| | **ει**ερεος | **ι**ερεως | ει / ο | for | ι / ω |
| | σ **υ** | σ **οι** | υ | for | οι |
| | εχ**ι**ς | εχ**ει**ς | ι | for | ει |
| | μισθωσ**ι** | μισθωσ**ει** | ι | for | ει |
| | τελεσ**ι**ν | τελεσ**ει**ν | ι | for | ει |
| 1st c. AD[6] | δαν**η**ων | δαν**ει**ων | η | for | ει |
| | π**υ**ουμενων | π**οι**ουμενων | υ | for | οι |
| | ετ**ι** | ετ**η** | ι | for | η |
| | οφ**ι**λομεν | οφ**ει**λομεν | ι | for | ει |
| | χ**ο**ρ**ει**ς | χ**ω**ρ**ι**ς | ο / ει | for | ω / ι |
| | ημ**υ**σον | ημ**ι**σον | υ | for | ι |

Each misspelled word (above) is pronounced as its corrected counterpart, with the phonetically interchangeable letters betraying their common sound. Clearly, spelling [i] a half-dozen different ways in the 1st and 2nd c. BC could by no means be viewed as a "modern" Greek invention. As shown, this applies to the equations ω = ο and αι = ε as well.

Blass says that the interchange of ει and ι is "rather frequent in the early Hellenistic period."[7] While that may be true, it does not mean that this interchange was nonexistent or even infrequent prior to that time, i.e., in the classical period. In fact, pre-Hellenistic inscriptions show not only the interchange of ι for ει, but also of all ι-sound letters.

Compare, for instance, the above Hellenistic misspellings with the following samples of misspellings from the classical or pre-classical period (6th to 4th c. BC) in the neighboring regions of Attica, Boeotia, and Euboia. Bear in mind that misspelled words and names recur at times even right alongside their correct spelling.[8]

## 2.2.2 Interchange of ι-Sound Letters in the Pre-Classical and Classical Period

| **Interchange** | **Misspelling / c. BC** | **Correct spelling** | **Misspelling / c. BC** | **Correct spelling** |
|---|---|---|---|---|
| ι for ει | Αριστοκλιδης 6–5 | Αριστοκλειδης | Κλιταρχος 6 | Κλειταρχος |
| | Νεοκλιδης 6–5 | Νεοκλειδης | Αριστογιτον 5 | Αριστογειτων |
| | Θαλια 6 | Θαλεια | ευτελια 5 | ευτελεια |
| | Χιρων 6 | Χειρων | Σταγιριται 5 | Σταγειριται |
| | Καλλιγιτον 5 | Καλλιγειτων | Χαροκλια 5 | Χαροκλεια |
| | Χαλκιαται 5 | Χαλκειαται | Αριστιδου 4 | Αριστειδου |
| | εχις 4 | εχεις | οριχαλκος 4 | ορειχαλκος |

5. Jenkins, *American Society of Papyrologists*, 32, 34.

6. Brown, *Bulletin of Papyrologists*, 6.

7. Blass, *Greek Grammar*, 13.

8. Samples from Caragounis, *Development of Greek*, 365–70; Jannaris, *Historical Grammar*, 47–52.

| | | | | |
|---|---|---|---|---|
| ι for υ | δακριον 6–5 | δακρυον | Λισικλες 6 | Λυσικλης |
| | Ηιποτελε 6–5 | Ηυποτελε | Ηιποκιμενος 6–5 | Ηυποκειμενος |
| | Τιρινθι 6–5 | Τιρυνθι | Διονισια 5 | Διονυσια |
| | Αριστονιμο 5 | Αριστονυμῳ | Διονισιγενες 5 | Διονυσιγενης |
| | Διονισος 5 | Διονυσος | Λισιστρατος 5 | Λυσιστρατος |
| | Κρισευς 5 | Κρυσευς | Κρισηις 5 | Κρυσηις |
| | Πιθις 5 | Πυθις | ημυσυν 4 | ημισυ |
| ι for η | Αθινα 5 | Αθηνα | Αρις 5 | Αρης |
| | Διμοσθενις 5 | Δημοσθενης | Ευφιβος 5 | Ευφηβος |
| | Ηιπποκρατης 5 | Ιπποκρατης | σιμα 4 | σημα |
| | Πιδασης 5 | Πηδασης | τινδε 4 | τηνδε |
| οι for υ | μοιχον 5 | μυχον | Ποιθικου 4 | Πυθικου |
| | Κοιβων 4 | Κυβων | Ποιτιος 4 | Πυτιος |
| υ for υι | Ηιλεθυα 6 | ιλεθυια | απαληλυθυας 5 | απαληλυθυιας |
| | κωδυας 4 | κωδυιας | οργυας 4 | οργυιας |
| ει for οι | δυειν 4 | δυοιν | τειχωι 4 | τοιχωι |
| | Περιθειδης | Περιθοιδης | Φαληρει 4 | Φαληροι |
| ι for οι | περιαλιφην 4 | περιαλοιφην | Μιραι 6 | Μοιραι |

**ι, ει, η.** The interchange in classical times of ι, ει, and η in particular is further corroborated by Plato's Socratic dialogues according to which the Athenians substituted ει or η for ι (*Kratylos* 418c):

νῦν δὲ ἀντὶ μὲν τοῦ ἰῶτα, ἢ εἶ [ἢ] ἦτα μεταστρέφουσιν
"and so now instead of ι they change to ει or η"
οἱ μὲν ἀρχαιότατοι ἱμέραν τὴν ἡμέραν ἐκάλουν,
οἱ δὲ [ὕστερον] εἱμέραν,[9] οἱ δὲ νῦν ἡμέραν
"the most ancients called ἡμέραν [*day*] ἱμέραν,
and others [later] εἱμέραν, and now they call it ἡμέραν"[10]

**Plato lived in the midst of the transition to the new Attic alphabet.**

Plato's testimony regarding ει = η = ι must be understood within the context of the orthographic issues Plato himself faced during Athens' transition to a new writing system (1.11). The alternative—and absurd—explanation of Plato's remarks would be that in his time the Athenians pronounced ἡμέρα and other variably spelled words three different ways!

**οι, ι.** Thucydides (460–395 BC) informs us that the Athenians were uncertain whether an oracle had warned of λοιμός *plague* or λιμός *famine* (cf. Luke 21:11). The oracle said, ἥξει Δωριακὸς πόλεμος καὶ λοιμὸς ἅμ᾽ αὐτῷ, *There will come a Dorian war and a plague with it.* Sturtevant however attempts to explain away the Athenians' confusion through Thucydides' remarks surrounding the historical background of

9. Other sources use ἑμέραν. This is in line with the fact that older Attic ε stood also for ει (1.11). So in Plato's time ε(ι)μέραν [imeran] was now read also as ἡμέραν. Clearly, Plato's point is with respect to the interchangeability of ι and ει, and now also η (see first quote above) with no hint at any difference in quality or quantity between these three vowels.

10. Plato also says that the name of Ποσειδών, *Poseidon*, who walks in the water as if he were ποσιδεσμος "with his feet bound," is spelled with ι (Ποσιδών), but that ε is added (Ποσειδών) merely "for the sake of propriety" (*Kratylos* 402e), in essence reiterating the equation ει = ι.

the oracle: "If the two words had been pronounced alike," remarks Sturtevant, "there could have been no disagreement as to what had been 'said.'"[11] But that is exactly the point: there was confusion among the Athenians, and the confusion could not have come about if λοιμός sounded different from λιμός (e.g., like Allen's "mixed diphthong" [oi] in *toy* or *coin*).[12] That οι at any rate is confused with ι in classical times is supported also by the fact that οι interchanges as well with ει and which, since earlier times, sounded like ι (cf. above table).

**υ, ι.** Evidence of υ = ι in the late archaic period (from 600 BC) is cited by Threatte, e.g., Ἀριστονίμο for Ἀριστονύμο, Διονισιγένες for Διονυσιγένες, Τύρινθι for Τίρυνθι, etc., with words such as ἥμυσυ for ἥμισυ, Εὐτιχίς for Εὐτυχίς, Σύρυλα for Σύριλλα being attributed to assimilation.[13] The confusion of υ and ι is further corroborated by the fact that υ interchanges with η and οι, both of which had also begun to acquire the sound of ι already by the 4th c. BC; and that υ interchanges also with ει by the 5th c. BC.[14] Timayenis says that in the 6th c. BC "the pronunciation of υ as an ι was not unknown to the ancients" and cites:

> δρίος for δρύον, μόλιβος and μολύβδαινα, τρυφάλεια for τριφάλεια, μυστίλλω for μιστύλλω, μίτυλος for μύτιλος, βύβλος for βίβλος, ῥύπτω for ῥίπτω, ψιμύθιον for ψιμίθιον, πύστις for πίστις, ἴψος for ὕψος, ἰψηλός for ὑψηλός, ἰπέρ for ὑπέρ, ἰπαρ for ὑπαρ, all of which "show how easily υ was exchanged with ι."[15]

The foregoing samples of spelling errors speak of a phonological process known as *iotacism* (or *itacism*). The term originally described the pronunciation of η as *iota* ι [i] but is now used to include other letters used for this sound. Clearly, the effects of iotacism are traceable to classical times; its origins, to pre-classical. Iotacism may be illustrated thus:

**Iotacism**

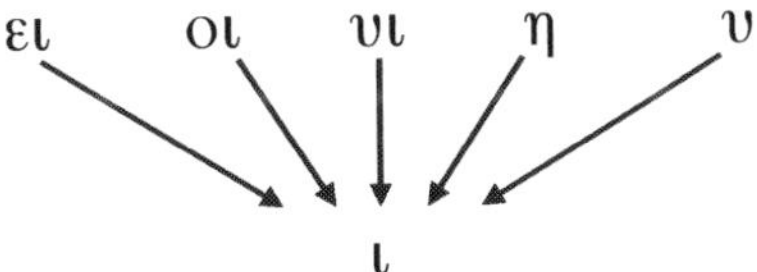


11. Sturtevant, *Greek and Latin*, 145.
12. Allen, *Vox Graeca*, 80–81.
13. Threatte, *Attic Inscriptions*, 261–62.
14. See examples on preceding page.
15. Timayenis, *Modern Greek*, 151–52

Robertson refers to the evidence of iotacism in the 1st c. BC in Attica, saying that αι = æ, ει = ι, η = ι, υ = ι, υι = υ, οι = ι,[16] and that "in Attica in the first century B.C., in spite of Archinos' law, the inscriptions use sometimes αι and αε, ει and ι, η and ι, υ and ι, υ and υι, ι and ει interchangeably."[17] Like Blass, however, Robertson makes no allusion to the classical or pre-classical origins of iotacism.

**αι, ε** and **ω, ο**. Concurrent with iotacism was the leveling of αι = ε and ω = ο. Blass holds that "the confusion of αι and ε began in ii BC according to the testimony of the papyri," and that of ω = ο "appeared the earliest iii/ii BC."[18] However, the testimony that predates the papyri traces αι = ε and ω = ο to 4th–5th c. BC. The interchange of αι (æ) and ε in classical times can be seen in words such as Ἀρισταίου for Ἀριστέου, 450 BC; πεδίαρχος for παιδίαρχος, 4th c. BC; Ἐλέρα for Ἐλαίρα, 5th c. BC. The addition of ι after αι in Ἐλαιῖται 452 BC, ἐλαίινος 378 BC, Ἀθηναιικόν 300 BC further confirms that αι was pronounced as ε. That αι was pronounced monophthongally in classical times is supported also by the fact that in Boeotia borrowed monoliteral Ionic η before 400 BC was used in place of αι, as in χηρε for χαῖρε, Θειβηος for Θειβαῖος, κη for καί, θεράπηνα for θεράπαινα, etc.[19]

The interchange of ω and ο is seen from the mid-5th c. BC when Attic borrowed Ionic ω. Allen curiously places the equation ω = ο six hundred to seven hundred years later, saying that the distinction between "long" ω and "short" ο in pronunciation began to disappear "in the 2–3 c. AD . . . and consequently ο and ω began to be confused in spelling."[20] But the inscriptional evidence does not support Allen's claim. See, for instance, p. 140, where Ω interchanges with Ο in 5th/4th c. BC. Likewise, we see Σάμων for Σάμον (433/2 BC), λιπόν for λιπών (326 BC), Διώνυσος for Διόνυσος, and Δίφιλως for Δίφιλος (5th–4th c. BC).[21]

## 2.3 IOTACISM IN THE NT MSS

The interchange between letters that stand for the ι-sound is seen also in copies of the New Testament manuscripts (MSS). Since the vast majority of NT MSS are Byzantine, this type of orthographical error is seen in every MS copied prior to the fall of Constantinople in 1453. From a historical linguistics standpoint, however, these errors are not altogether disheartening:

> From around the middle of the II[nd] century A.D. on we are able to add to the evidence of the inscriptions and the papyri of Greek texts also the evidence of

16. Robertson, *Grammar of the Greek New Testament*, 238.
17. Robertson, *Grammar of the Greek New Testament*, 182.
18. Blass, *Greek Grammar*, 14–15.
19. Jannaris, *Historical Greek Grammar*, 53–54.
20. Allen, *Vox Graeca*, 173.
21. Caragounis, *Development of Greek*, 373.

> the New Testament manuscripts. And this evidence does not disappoint! All of the NT MSS contain orthographical mistakes. This is only natural, given the situation so clearly demonstrated . . . [earlier], that the values that were being given to various vowels and diphthongs since classical times were making it difficult to spell correctly, if the scribe was ignorant of etymological orthography and was guided, instead, acoustically.[22]

There are thus no spelling errors of the type seen in the Hellenistic papyri that are not seen in copies of the NT MSS. To show the frequency of orthographical errors in the NT MSS, Caragounis lists 492 errors found in one MS alone, P. Bodmer II (Papyrus 66),[23] which dates to AD 200.[24] Below are but a few samples:

### 2.3.1 Interchange of Letters in the NT MSS

| Interchange | Error | Corrected | Interchange | Error | Corrected |
|---|---|---|---|---|---|
| ι for ει | λεγι | λεγει | ει for η | Ιωαννεις | Ιωαννης |
| ι for υ | ιοι | υιοι | ει for ι | εδειδαξεν | εδιδαξεν |
| ι for οι | πιει | ποιει | ε for αι | ετεις | αιτεις |
| υ for ι | υμυν | υμιν | αι for ε | ποιηται | ποιητε |
| η for υ | ηπερ | υπερ | ο for ω | ανοθεν | ανωθεν |
| η for ει | ηργασμενα | ειργασμενα | ω for ο | εκπορευσωνται | εκπορευσονται |
| οι for ει | ευρισκοι | ευρισκει | (Compare this table with 2.2.1 and 2.2.2.) | | |

## 2.4 IOTACISM TODAY

One may wonder why Greek still allows these same allographs (variations in spelling) of the ι-sound today. There are grammatical reasons for it, though suffice it to say that the difference in meaning between two *homophones* (words that are spelled differently but sound alike) is determined by spelling; and spelling, by orthographical rules. For example, μέλλει [méli] means "(s/he) intends," μέλει [méli] means "(it) concerns," μέλη [méli] means "members," and μέλι [méli] means "honey." All four words are pronounced alike: *méli*. A semiliterate Greek person may misspell these words, yet he pronounces each of them correctly because to him the allographs ει, η, ι represent

22. Caragounis, *Development of Greek*, 497.

23. Caragounis, *Development of Greek*, 502–14.

24. After the Christian era, scribes copied NT MSS privately or publicly. Early in the Middle Ages copying increased as the practice took place in *scriptoria*, "places of writing," where many scribes were simultaneously engaged in dictation (replication) by following a lector's reading. The likelihood for error depended on the scribe's linguistic competence, academic training, physical disposition, and so on. A scribe less familiar with grammatical and orthographical rules was more likely to be guided by his ear and thus use one letter for another that stood for the same sound, as in ὑμῦν for ὑμῖν, or εὑρίσκοι for εὑρίσκει, as the above table shows.

the same sound. As for the meaning of each word, it becomes clear to him by the context. For instance, if his wife hands him a shopping list that includes the word μέλη, he knows that she wants him to buy "honey"—not "members"! That is exactly what happened in classical times—Plato bearing witness (2.2.2)—as well as in Hellenistic, Byzantine, and Neohellenic times.

It may be argued that inscriptions tell us more about orthography than pronunciation. However, it must be underscored that the unbroken tradition of faulty readings, emerging at the beginning of the inscriptional period and continuing through the classical, Hellenistic, Byzantine, and Neohellenic periods, and judged throughout by the same standard—the same historical writing and spelling system—is the best proof of the diachronic presence of the historical sounds and pronunciation of Greek; for the same interchanges found in the Hellenistic papyri and Byzantine MSS are traced to classical times, all of which are mirrored in Neohellenic, as will be further shown below.

## 2.5 A FIVE-VOWEL SYSTEM

The original sound of Υ(υ) [i] was [u], but it is difficult to trace the process that brought about the change from [u] to [i]. Descriptions, however, of υ sounding like the German ü or French u and eventually becoming ι as late as medieval times vary and are hypothetical at best. Browning uses the Slavonic name Curila from Greek Κύριλλος in an attempt to support the hypothesis that as late as the 9th c. AD υ was still ü and had not become ι. But in the same breath Browning rectifies his reasoning, conceding that "loan-words throw light on the development of the borrowing languages rather than that of Greek."[25] Rightly so, for the name Lord Byron, for instance, in Greek is Λόρδος Βύρων [lórðos víron], in which υ (= [i]) can hardly be relied upon for tracing the English diphthong [aˈ] in Byron [baˈrən].

Transliteration of loanwords is not always a reliable substitution for phonetic transcription. Besides, the equalization υ = ι originated before NT times, and older inscriptions from 6th–5th c. BC down to Byzantine times give multiple instances of υ = ι, as already shown (2.2.1; 2.2.2). The fanciful theory that the Greek vowel system "i e a o u ü" became "i e a o u" during the late Roman Empire after ü became i is hardly convincing in light of the historical record—though telling of the Erasmian position. Thus, iotacism and the inclusion of attested α /a/ and Ionic ου /u/ yield a five-phoneme vocalic system in Attic and Κοινή, the same as in Neohellenic:

Pre-/Hellenistic vocalic phonemes: /i, e, a, o, u/

Neohellenic vocalic phonemes: /i, e, a, o, u/[26]

25. Browning, *Medieval and Modern Greek*, 56.

26. Throughout antiquity until mid-/late 5th c. BC, the Attic alphabet shows five vowel symbols, ι, ε, α, ο, υ, corresponding to the Latin and Neohellenic vowels /i, e, a, o, u/, the same as the Mycenaean vowels (1.11; 6.5).

## 2.6 FRICATIVIZATION OF POSTPOSITIVE -Υ

Another significant phonological change that took place in pre-Hellenistic times was the *fricativization* of the vowel υ of the "diphthongs" (digraphs) αυ, ευ, ηυ. *Fricative* is a term that describes a consonant produced with continuous friction of air passing through the mouth. Thus fricativization is the change of a vowel, semivowel, or plosive (stop) into a fricative consonant. For example: [u] > [w] > [v], or [t] > [th] > [θ].

The fricativization concept may be illustrated by the situation in which a German speaker, in trying to produce the English semivowel [w] as in *wary*, places the lower lip against the upper teeth thereby producing the sound [v]. Here the German speaker is said to have *fricativized* the nonfricative English sound [w] as the fricative [v].

A fricative, or *spirant*, is a single sound segment produced with simultaneous aspiration induced by turbulence in the airflow mechanism. During the fricativization process the vowel ὕψιλον υ of the digraphs αυ ευ ηυ became a *labiodental fricative consonant* (*[au, eu, iu] > [aw, ew, iw] > [av, ev, iv] / [af, ef, if]). Hence, υ is now β as in *vat* when voiced, and φ as in *fat* when voiceless, as follows:

**Fricativization of υ in αυ, ευ, ηυ**

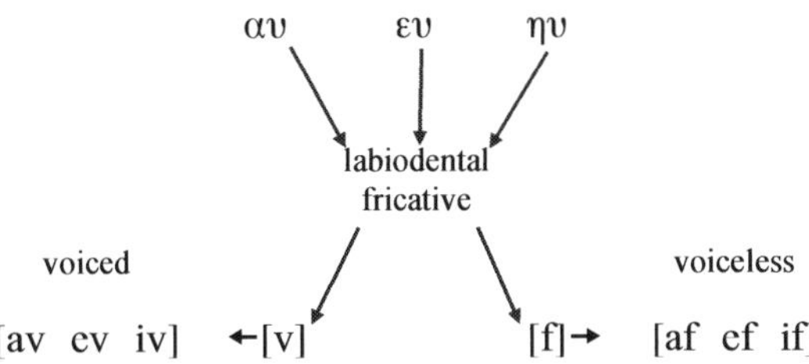


"In the labial series," Browning says, "we have ample evidence in the form of such errors of spelling as κατεσκέβασαν for κατεσκεύασαν 'installed', ῥαῦδος for ῥάβδος 'staff' etc. from the first century B.C."[27] Changes of this type, however, are traced further back than the 1st c. BC. For example, Ναϝπακτίων for Ναυπακτίων, 6th–5th c. BC, in which *digamma* ϝ, an archaic Phoenician symbol that sounded like the *v* in *vine*, was since the 5th c. BC substituted by β or fricativized υ. Examples: ἀμοίϝαν for ἀμοιβάν, 6th c. BC; Εὔανδρος side by side with Εὔβανδρος, 4th c. BC; ἕυδομον for ἕβδομον, 3rd c. BC.[28] The effects of fricativization, in place well before Hellenistic times, are reflected on the table below.

27. Browning, *Medieval and Modern Greek*, 27.

28. Caragounis, *Development of Greek*, 375.

## 2.7 EFFECTS OF FRICATIVIZATION BEFORE HELLENISTIC TIMES

| Before vowels and voiced consonants the υ of αυ, ευ, ηυ becomes voiced β [v]: | | | | |
|---|---|---|---|---|
| αυ | sounds like αβ as in *bravo* | αυλη | [avli] | *courtyard* |
| ευ | sounds like εβ as in *ever* | ευαγγελιζω | [evaŋgelizo] | *I evangelize* |
| ηυ | sounds like υβ as in *evil* | ηυλογησε | [ivlojise] | *(he) blessed* |
| Before voiceless consonants and at end of words it becomes voiceless φ [f]: | | | | |
| αυ | sounds like αφ as in pilaf | αυτος<br>Ησαυ[29] | [aftos]<br>[isaf] | *he*<br>*Esau* |
| ευ | sounds like εφ as in effort | ευχαριστω<br>ιερευ | [efharisto]<br>[ieref] | *I thank*<br>*priest!* (voc.) |
| ηυ | sounds like ηφ as in reef | ηυξανε | [ifksane] | *was increasing* |

## 2.8 FRICATIVIZATION MIRRORED IN NEOHELLENIC

The imprint of the fricativization effects is clearly seen in Greek today. Compare the pre-Hellenistic examples given above with the following Neohellenic examples:

| Before vowels and voiced consonants the υ of αυ, ευ, ηυ becomes voiced β [v]: | | | | |
|---|---|---|---|---|
| αυ | sounds like αβ as in *bravo* | αυλη | [avli] | *courtyard* |
| ευ | sounds like εβ as in *ever* | ευαγγελιζω | [evaŋgelizo] | *I evangelize* |
| ηυ | (ηυ- formal, ευ- informal) | ηυλογησε | [ivlojise] | *(he) blessed* |
| Before voiceless consonants and at end of words it becomes voiceless φ [f]: | | | | |
| αυ | sounds like αφ as in pilaf | αυτος<br>Ησαυ | [aftos]<br>[isaf] | *he*<br>*Esau* |
| ευ | sounds like εφ as in effort | ευχαριστω<br>ιερευ/ιερεα | [efharisto]<br>[ieref, ierea] | *I thank*<br>*priest!* (voc.) |
| ηυ | (ηυ- formal, αυ- informal) | ηυξανε | [ifksane] | *was increasing* |

29. The pronunciation of Ἡσαῦ [isáf] comports with Hebrew *Esau*. Final [f] (fricativized υ) is in conformity with Greek phonology, hence [isáf]—compare "T" ταυ [taf], ἱερεῦ [ieréf] *priest* (voc.), βασιλεῦ [vasiléf] *king* (voc.). Intervocalically, Hebrew [v] as in *Levi* is transliterated υ in the LXX, thus Λευί [leví] *Levi*, Λευιτικόν [levitikón] *Leviticus*, Εὕα [éva] *Eve*, Δαυίδ [ðavíð] *David*, Νινευή [nineví] Ninevah, showing that the fricativization of υ as [v] predates the LXX, that is, it was in place well before the Hellenistic period.

## 2.9 FURTHER FRICATIVIZATION EFFECTS

**There is no linguistic justification for the pronunciation of Κοινή ευ as "you."**

The following list shows that in Κοινή regular verbs whose stem ends in π, β, or φ form their future and aorist active by adding the fricative tense formative -σ- to their stem. The combination, whether π + σ, φ + σ, or β + σ, results into ψ [ps]:

| Stem Ending: π φ β | Fut./Aor. Affix: σ | | | | | | Future | Aorist |
|---|---|---|---|---|---|---|---|---|
| βλέπ-ω | + σ | = | βλέπσ-ω | > | ψ | > | βλέψ-ω | ἔβλεψ-α |
| ἀλείφ-ω | + σ | = | ἀλείφσ-ω | > | ψ | > | ἀλείψ-ω | ἤλειψ-α |
| διατρίβ-ω | + σ | = | διατρίβσ-ω | > | ψ | > | διατρίψ-ω | διέτριψ-α |

Consider now the verb πιστεύω *I believe* whose stem ends in ευ (= εβ), thus [pis-tévo]. In Κοινή, πιστεύσω [pistéfso] (fut.) and ἐπίστευσα [epístefsa] (aor.) ευ becomes [ef] due to the voiceless σ that follows, so ευ + σ = [efs]. In literary (formal) Neohellenic πιστεύσω and ἐπίστευσα are used as in Κοινή. Alternatively, in the vernacular (informal) ευ + σ = [eps], hence πιστέψω and ἐπίστεψα. So it is with a good number of other such verbs: ψαρεύω *I fish* ψαρέψω, ἐψάρεψα; φυτεύω *I plant* φυτέψω, ἐφύτεψα; χορεύω *I dance* χορέψω, ἐχόρεψα. Doubtless, the Neohellenic rendering of πιστεύσω / επίστευσα alternatively as πιστέψω / ἐπίστεψα is rooted in the fricativization process whereby informal –υ + σ > ψ [ps], just as –β + σ = ψ [ps]. For instance:

| | | | | | | Present | | Future | Aorist |
|---|---|---|---|---|---|---|---|---|---|
| Κοινή / Neohellenic: | ιβ | + | σ | = | [ips] | διατρίβ-ω | > | διατρίψω | διέτριψα |
| Neohellenic (informal): | εβ | + | σ | = | [eps] | πιστεύ-ω | > | πιστέψω | ἐπίστεψα |
| Κοινή / Neohellenic (formal): | εβ | + | σ | = | [efs] | πιστεύ-ω | > | πιστεύσω | ἐπίστευσα |

The point. Pronouncing πιστεύω [pistévo] (pres.) as Erasmian [pɪstjúoᵘ], πιστεύσω [pistéfso] (fut.) as Erasmian [pɪstjúsoᵘ], and ἐπίστευσα [epístefsa] (aor.) as Erasmian [èpɪstjúsa] is as if to say that Neohellenic [eps]/[efs] in πιστέψω/-εύσω, ἐπίστεψα/-ευσα resulted from [jus] (i.e., what was Κοινή [jus] as in *use*, in Neohellenic became [eps]/[efs])—a far cry from a probable linguistic development. There is thus no linguistic justification for the Erasmian pronunciation of Κοινή ευ as [ju].

## 2.10 THE CONSONANTS Φ, Θ, Χ

In pre-Homeric times the Greeks used the digraphs ΠΗ, ΤΗ, ΚΗ to represent the monographs Φ, Θ, Χ respectively. The symbol Η (or 𐌇) had originally been used for aspiration, but there is no indication that ΠΗ, ΤΗ, ΚΗ consisted of two sound segments each, i.e., voiceless stop + aspirate *ph, th, kh* as in *uphold, hothouse, sinkhole.* This is supported by the fact that in pre-classical times the Greek-invented Chalcidic monographs Φ Θ Χ gradually replaced these digraphs. This replacement indicates that ΠΗ, ΤΗ, ΚΗ were not aspirated plosives but *aspirated continuants*, that is, single sound segments that naturally require *continuous friction* of air (aspiration) in order for them to be *fricative*, H signifying their fricativeness. For if ΠΗ, ΤΗ, ΚΗ denoted their exact phonetic value as [ph, th, kh], why should they have been abandoned for Φ Θ Χ which do not visually indicate aspiration? It follows that the replacement of digraphs ΠΗ, ΤΗ, ΚΗ by the monographs Φ Θ Χ reflected not a phonetic change but simplified spelling—e.g., as in replacing the digraph PH in PHone by the single F as in Fone, since F is a simpler allograph of PH (cf. Span. teléFono, or PHilippines vs. Filipino where PH = F).

The Romans at first transcribed ΠΗ as PH, but when ΠΗ was replaced by Φ they transcribed it as F. Since Latin, however, had no equivalents for the two fricative sounds Θ and Χ, the Romans continued to transcribe Θ as TH and Χ as CH, "H" indicating fricativeness. But under Erasmian influence, the use of PH for Φ returned.

Further evidence of the status of φ θ χ is borne out by the fact that the κ of the preposition ἐκ remains unaffected before the stops π τ κ (ἐκ πόλεως, ἐκ τούτου, ἐκ Κορίνθου), whereas before the continuants φ θ χ it often changes into its continuant associate χ as in ἐχ Χαλκίδος, ἐχ Θετταλίας, ἐχφέρω (ἐκ+φέρω).

### 2.10.1 Sidney Allen's Treatment of φ, θ, χ and π, τ, κ

This section critiques Sidney Allen's argument regarding φ, θ, χ and π, τ, κ as laid out in his *Vox Graeca* (1987).

In his description of Attic Greek consonants, Allen, a leading Erasmian authority, classifies φ, θ, χ as voiceless aspirated plosives [ph, th, kh], with their unaspirated variety being π, τ, κ [p, t, k]. "Their distinctiveness," says Allen, "is demonstrated by minimally different pairs such as πόρος/φόρος, πάτος/πάθος, λέκος/λέχος."[30] Knowing that Modern Greek φ, θ, χ are voiceless fricatives (i.e., not plosives), Allen says that his main task is to prove that their development into fricatives did not happen until a later date, at any rate outside the classical period.[31]

In critiquing Allen, an attempt to summarize the meandrous and multilayered thought pattern in this section of his work might prove futile, hence the need for extra detail here. Thus, Allen prefaces the discussion of his "proof" by pointing out the distinction between aspirated and unaspirated plosives in Sanskrit and in a modern language that developed from Sanskrit, Hindi, saying that that distinction, being allophonic, can also be found in English. He then alludes to Hellenistic grammarians who categorized the two varieties of plosives as smooth letters (γράμμα) ψιλόν and aspirated letters (γράμμα) δασύ, in Latin rendered *lenis* and *aspera* respectively, though the Latin terms in Priscian are *tenuis* and *aspirate*.[32]

30. Allen, *Vox Graeca*, 14.

31. Allen, *Vox Graeca*, 18.

32. Allen, *Vox Graeca*, 15.

Allen then introduces the unaspirated plosives π, τ, κ by saying, "*The fact* [italics mine] that aspirated and unaspirated plosives were distinguished in Greek means that aspiration must be suppressed in the latter if confusion is to be avoided; such a pronunciation comes more readily to native speakers of e.g. French than to those of English or German."[33] Notably, with his introductory remark Allen shows that he already treats as fact the very distinction he is trying to prove; and in describing that distinction, he has so far brought into the discussion Sanskrit, Hindi, Latin, Priscian, French, English, and German.

Next, Allen ties the pronunciation of "a very early period" to Grassmann's Law, "whereby the first of two originally aspirated syllable-initials in a word loses its aspiration."[34] The examples Allen gives are ἔχω and ἕξω, which he renders [ekho] and [hekso] respectively; and τριχός and θριξί, the initials of which he renders [t] and [th] respectively.[35] Later in his discussion Allen uses Grassmann's Law as well in connection with reduplication: πέφευγα, τίθημι, κέχυμαι.[36] What Grassmann's Law theoretically asserts regarding Greek, however, pertains to "a very early period," as Allen puts it, thus it cannot serve as evidence that in Classical Greek, a comparatively much later period, φ, θ, χ were aspirated plosives, rather than aspirated continuants (fricatives). Nor does by the same token [h] in ἕξω (Allen's [hekso]) prove that "aspirate" H [h] was pronounced at all in the 5th c. BC, particularly when H started being used as the vowel ἦτα (η). (See discussion on *aspiration*, 2.18.)

For the discussion of Attic consonants Allen leans on Hellenistic grammarians. "The grammatical tradition," he goes on, "divides the consonants into two primary categories, ἡμίφωνα ['half-voiced'] and ἄφωνα ['voiceless']."[37] This distinction is given by Dionysios Thrax (170–90 BC), who says ζ ξ ψ λ μ ν ρ σ are ἡμίφωνα and β γ δ κ π τ θ φ χ ἄφωνα. Thrax's distinction, however, is given from a poetically euphonic and aesthetic rather than a phonological standpoint (see below). Today no phonetician would classify these two groups of consonants as half-voiced and voiceless, respectively, since the "half-voiced" group includes voiced ζ λ μ ν ρ, and the "voiceless" group includes voiced β γ δ (if we go by the literal meaning of Thrax's terms). Allen, however, says that the two groups correspond to continuants and plosives, respectively; hence he justifies the classification of θ φ χ as plosives.

But further on Allen admits that grammarians from the same era as Thrax, e.g., Stoic Diogenes Babylonios (2nd c. BC), classify φ, θ, χ with the ἡμίφωνα ζ ξ ψ λ μ ν ρ σ—which would make φ, θ, χ not plosives but fricatives(!). Allen, however, brushes Babylonios' classification aside "simply [as] a Stoic aberration."[38] With aberration

33. Allen, *Vox Graeca*, 15.
34. Allen, *Vox Graeca*, 15.
35. Allen, *Vox Graeca*, 15–16.
36. Allen, *Vox Graeca*, 20.
37. Allen, *Vox Graeca*, 19.
38. Allen, *Vox Graeca*, 23.

as his reasoning for dismissing Babylonios, in the same breath Allen also dismisses Plato's classification of φ with ψ, σ, ζ as a fricative (*Kratylos* 427a), asserting, "The classification provides no grounds for assuming a fricative pronunciation of φ."[39] It is not surprising that Allen so casually dismisses Babylonios and Plato, for he has already reached his conclusion—a page earlier—where he declaims:

> The evidence thus seems conclusive that the 5 c. B.C. Attic φ, θ, χ represented *plosives* (as π, τ, κ) and NOT *fricatives* (as σ, or as φ, θ, χ in modern Greek)[40]

—with a capitalized "NOT" apparently strengthening the evidence.

But if Allen's description of φ, θ, χ were to be applied, then ἐχ Χαλκίδος would be ἐkhkhαλκίδος, ἐχ Θετταλίας ἐkhthεετταλίας, and ἐχφέρω ἐkhphέρω, all too cumbersome to pronounce and against the natural flow of the language. Allen therefore advises that [ph, th, kh] should be pronounced each as part of the same syllable, not like "*saphead, fathead, blockhead,* where the plosive and the [h] are divided between separate syllables."[41] Allen's opinion, however, clashes with Smyth's, for the examples Smyth gives for the pronunciation of [ph, th, kh] are *upheaval, hothouse, backhand.*[42]

Allen goes a step further to say that the doubling of these consonants results in an unaspirated stop followed by an aspirated stop, hence πφ, τθ, κχ = [pph, tth, kkh], and offers the vague explanation that "the proof only refers to the time at which the doubling took place, and in many cases this must have been long before the 5 c. B.C."[43] However, Greek phonology does not support [pph, tth, kkh], such pronunciation in fact being unnatural. Clearly, Allen's "proof" so far has no basis.

Having thus far struggled to justify the difference between π, τ, κ and φ, θ, χ, Allen alerts speakers of English to the difficulty they would experience in not only pronouncing but also in hearing the difference between π τ κ and φ θ χ, hence his caveat:

> There is a difficulty which most English speakers are likely to experience—namely, of clearly distinguishing the voiceless *un*aspirated plosives from the aspirated, both in speaking and hearing; and the result of an attempt of the correct pronunciation may thus only bring confusion.[44]

Allen is mindful, though, to offer a pedagogical solution: he advises against trying to produce that distinction and recommends pronouncing φ θ χ as fricatives "in the Byzantine manner"[45]—subtly steering away from saying "Modern Greek"!

39. Allen, *Vox Graeca*, 23.
40. Allen, *Vox Graeca*, 22.
41. Allen, *Vox Graeca*, 28–29.
42. Smyth, *Greek Grammar for Colleges*, 13.
43. Allen, *Vox Graeca*, 21.
44. Allen, *Vox Graeca*, 29.
45. Allen, *Vox Graeca*, 29.

Greek phonology supports [pf] as in σάπφειρος [sápfiros] *sapphire*, [tθ] as in Ἀτθίς [atθís] *Attic (dialect)*, and [kx] ([kç]) as in ἐκχέω [ekxéo] *I pour out*. Jannaris says that if φ θ χ were like p+h t+h k+h, then names such as Σαπφώ, Ἀτθίς, Βάκχος [sapfo, atθis, vakxos], which were simplified to Σαφφώ, Ἀθθίς, Βάχχος [safo, aθis, vaxos] (but never converted to the naturally easier forms Σαππώ, Ἀττίς, Βάκκος [sapo, atis, vakos]), would have been unnaturally pronounced [saphpho, aththis, vakhkhos].[46]

Allen challenges Jannaris by quoting him as saying, "Combinations like φθόνος . . . χθών . . . constitute a physiological impossibility in any actual language."[47] Rightly understood, Jannaris is cogently saying that φθ and χθ are normal in Greek as fricatives, but not as (Allen's) aspirated plosives *p-h + t-h* and *k-h + t-h*, which are not supported by Greek phonology or by that of any language.[48] Allen's argument that this feature is actually normal among modern languages sounds hardly convincing judging by his tendentiously exaggerated (aspirated) transcription of Armenian for *prayer* as [aɣothkh],[49] rather than as [aɣotk].[50]

Allen further alludes to an account by Quintilian, a Roman rhetorician from Spain (1st c. AD), in which Cicero (1st c. BC) laughs at a Greek person who, while standing as a witness in court, is unable to pronounce the F in *Fundanio*.[51] Allen's point is that even in Cicero's time Greek Φ is the aspirated bilabial plosive [ph], not the "modern" Greek fricative [f], also a sound of English. But first let us look at what Cicero's F in *Fundanio* was like.

Scholars have variously attempted to describe Latin F in Quintilian's and Cicero's time. This is shown by the following translation of the same excerpt from Quintilian XII. 10.29:

> For the (F) which is the sixth letter of our alphabet, . . . is no more than a whistle through the teeth; if it goes before a vowel it is no more than a quiver of the lips, and it makes a fracture of all harmony when it precedes, first a consonant, and then a vowel, in the same syllable, or falls in with other consonants.[52]
>
> F, the sixth letter of our alphabet, makes a sound, scarce human, or rather one not proceeding from the voice, because [it is] formed intirely [*sic*] by the air puffed out between the teeth. Followed by a vowel it loses its force, and by a consonant, it breaks the sound, and becomes more harsh and disagreeable.[53]

46. Jannaris, *Historical Greek Grammar*, 58.

47. Allen, *Vox Graeca*, 27.

48. Jannaris, *Historical Greek Grammar*, 58.

49. Allen, *Vox Graeca*, 27.

50. In interviews with native-born Armenian college students, I was assured that my pronunciation of unaspirated [aɣotk] sounded clearly native, whereas Allen's aspirated ending [-thkh] sounded decidedly foreign.

51. Allen, *Vox Graeca*, 23 (regarding Allen's reference to *Quintilian*, I. 4.14).

52. Guthrie, *Quintilian's Institute*, 437.

53. Patsall, *Quintilian's Institutes*, 415.

> For the sixth letter of our alphabet is represented by a sound which can scarcely be called human or even articulate, being produced by forcing the air through the interstices of the teeth. Such a sound, even when followed by a vowel, is harsh enough and, often as it clashes (*frangit*) with a consonant, as it does in this very word *frangit*, becomes harsher still.[54]

Based on the above three (dissimilar) renditions of the same passage, Cicero's F must have been a sound other than [f], for a modern phonetician could hardly associate such bizarre descriptions of a speech sound with the distinctive phonological features of a not-unpleasant sound such as [f]. The closest candidate to Cicero's F, then, would have been *bilabial* fricative [ɸ], a sound which, on the one hand, approximates that of [f] and, on the other, does not restrict the flow of air through the mouth (aspiration) as [f] does. If so, the closest the Greek witness could have come to simulating the effects of [ɸ] would have been voiceless velar fricative [x], e.g., [xuntanio], in which case his lips would have been rounded because of [u], with simultaneous aspiration being produced by [x]. This would have enabled the man to produce aspiration not at the aperture formed by the rounded lips, but between the back of the tongue and the velum—a distinction which, however effective in simulating [ɸ], could escape neither the eye nor the ear of observant Cicero. This comports with Quintilian's account of Cicero's reaction to the witness who, unable to release a rush of airstream through bilabial [ɸu], relied on the aspiration produced by velar [xu].

> nam contra Graeci aspirare F ut φ solent, ut pro Fundanio Cicero testem, qui primam eius litteram dicere non possit, irridet.[55]

> *for the Greeks, on the other hand, are accustomed to aspirate [= aspirated F or φ], whence Cicero, in his oration for Fundanius, laughs at a witness who could not sound the first letter of that name.*[56]

But that Cicero's F could have been *bilabial fricative* [ɸ], i.e., not *labiodental fricative* [f], should not be surprising, since the same sound, though apparently milder in phonation than described above, is enjoyed by many millions of Romance-language speakers today. As Lindsay observes, "It is highly probable that Latin F was at some time bilabial, as it is to this day in Spanish."[57]

The point. My analysis of Quintilian's allusion to Cicero, though plausible, is somewhat conjectural and proves nothing novel about the pronunciation of the sixth letter of the Latin alphabet. It simply shows a possible interpretation other than Allen's. It also shows that drawing attention to an isolated and ambiguous account by some NT-era rhetorician from Spain cannot be equated with evidence. Allen's masterful litanies of cherry-picked multilingual elements, nevertheless, at times culminate with

54. Butler, *Institutio*, 465, 467.

55. Butler, *Institutio*, 68.

56. Watson, *Quintilian's Institutes*, 33.

57. Lindsay, *Latin Language*, 99.

a reference to some historical figure, work, or event, a tactic he uses to boost his ethos. But has Allen, by simply referencing an isolated incident regarding the pronunciation of Latin F, shown that Greek speakers of the day pronounced Φ as [ph] and not as the "modern" Greek sound [f]?

I think not.

Allen has virtually relied on Hellenistic grammarians for a phonological description of the Attic Greek sounds φ θ χ and π τ κ, notwithstanding the peculiar way in which those grammarians classify sounds. But as Roberts soundly remarks, "the terminology of Dionysius' [of Halikarnassos] phonetics is full of difficulties,"[58] and goes on to explain that "[Dionysius' *Composition*] is not a treatise on Greek Pronunciation, or even on Greek Phonetics. . . . There was, in fact, no independent study of phonetics in Greek antiquity; the subject was simply the handmaid in the service of music and rhetoric. . . . [So] in describing the way in which the different letters are produced is not scientific but aesthetic and euphonic."[59]

Dionysios Thrax discusses the relation between φ~π, χ~κ, θ~τ in Classical Attic.[60] If in classical times φ θ χ had been Allen's aspirated stops [ph, kh, th] but by pre-NT or NT times they were beginning to turn (or had already turned) into fricatives, then Dionysios Thrax, as well as Diogenes Babylonios, Dionysios of Halikarnassos, and even Quintilian, whose lives collectively ranged between 230 BC and AD 100, would have most assuredly—and perhaps lamentfully—drawn attention to the Κοινή pronunciation of classical φ θ χ as fricatives, i.e., not as aspirated stops. It is no wonder that none of them even hints at a pronunciation change of these sounds, for apparently they all see classical φ θ χ as fricatives.

Allen has failed to show that Attic Φ, Θ, Χ are the aspirated voiceless plosives [ph, kh, th] and not the monophthongal voiceless fricatives φ, θ, χ [f, θ, x], which continue to be used today.[61]

## 2.11 ROBERT BROWNING'S TREATMENT OF Β Δ Γ AND Φ Θ Χ

Not unlike Allen, Browning says, "In the Hellenistic period . . . voiced plosives [= stops] and aspirated plosives become spirants [= fricatives], voiced and unvoiced respectively. Thus instead of p b ph we get p v f, instead of t d th, t ð θ, instead of k g kh, k ğ x."[62]

It is not clear whether Browning's ph, th, kh are Allen's [ph, th, kh], i.e., pronounced each as part of the same syllable as in "*saphead, fathead, blockhead*," or

58. Roberts, *Dionysius of Halicarnassus*, 294.

59. Roberts, *Dionysius of Halicarnassus*, 43.

60. Davidson, *Dionysios Thrax*, 6.

61. The Anglicized names of Φ, Θ, Χ, popular among modern fraternities and sororities, are Phi, Theta, Chi, commonly pronounced [p$^{h}$a$^{I}$], [θe$^{I}$t$^{hə}$], [k$^{h}$a$^{I}$], respectively.

62. Browning, *Medieval and Modern Greek*, 26.

Smyth's [p+h, t+h, k+h], i.e., each sound pronounced more distinctly as in "*upheaval, hothouse, backhand.*" In either case, Browning, like other Erasmians, follows the general assumption—without any hard evidence—that Attic β δ γ sounded like b d g, and φ θ χ sounded like ph th kh before turning into the fricatives /v ð ɣ/ and /f θ x/ in Hellenistic times. Browning's description of these presumed changes may be represented as follows:

### 2.11.1 Browning's Description of Consonant Changes

| Greek letter | A: Erasmian description of certain Classical Greek consonants | | | B: Presumed changes around NT Hellenistic times generally conceded by Erasmians | |
|---|---|---|---|---|---|
| π | [p] | voiceless bilabial stop | | [p] | (no change) |
| τ | [t] | voiceless alveolar stop | | [t] | (no change) |
| κ | [k] | voiceless velar stop | | [k] | (no change) |
| β | [b] | voiced bilabial stop | > | [v] | voiced labiodental continuant fricative |
| δ | [d] | voiced alveolar stop | > | [ð] | voiced apicodental continuant fricative |
| γ | [g] | voiced velar stop | > | [ɣ] | voiced velar continuant fricative |
| φ | [ph] | voiceless aspirated bilabial stop | > | [f] | voiceless labiodental continuant fricative |
| θ | [th] | voiceless aspirated alveolar stop | > | [θ] | voiceless apicodental continuant fricative |
| χ | [kh] | voiceless aspirated velar stop | > | [x] | voiceless velar continuant fricative |

If, according to Browning, classical [b d g] and [ph th kh] (column *A*) evolved into Hellenistic [v ð ɣ] and [f θ x] respectively (column *B*), the change would have had to blanket the immense Hellenized world at the inception of the Hellenistic period in a very short time and uniformly so; for in pre-NT Hellenistic times there is no evidence of words with [v ð ɣ] having an alternative [b d g] pronunciation, or words with [f θ x] having an alternative [ph th kh] pronunciation. Browning, however, would have us assume that Neohellenic fricatives [f θ x] (e.g., ἑφτά [efta] *seven*, θρέφω [θrefo] *I nourish*, ὀχτώ [oxto] *eight*) typically evolved from Attic [ephta], [threfo], [okhto], respectively, an attempt reminiscent of Allen's treatment of φ, θ, χ and π, τ, κ (2.10.1).

This theory however leaves unexplained the alternative Neohellenic pronunciation of these same words as ἑπτά [epta] *seven*, τρέφω [trefo] *I nourish*, ὀκτώ [okto] *eight*. The question then arises: How does one account for the alternative unaspirated Neohellenic [p t k] in these and other such examples? For either in pre-NT Hellenistic times [ph th kh] evolved both into [f θ x] and [p t k] (in which case many words at some point in their evolutionary process would have been contemporaneously pronounced three different ways each, e.g., [ephta, efta, epta], [threfo, θrefo, trefo], [okhto, oxto, okto]), or [f θ x] in post-NT (Byzantine) times further evolved into [p t k].

Such conjectural absurdities can be laid aside when the cause behind this alternative Neohellenic pronunciation is properly understood: that is, the use of formal stops [p, t, k] or informal fricatives [f, θ, x] *for the same words* is a phenomenon of Greek *dimorphia* (1.10). Dimorphia accounts partly for the alternative (formal/informal) use of sounds in many words. For instance, Katharevousa's use of [p t k] in the words ἑπτά [epta], τρέφω [trefo], ὀκτώ [okto] is considered formal, while Dimotiki's use of [f θ x] for the same words as ἑφτά [efta], θρέφω [θrefo], ὀχτώ [oxto] is considered informal. The sounds π τ κ are not always formal, nor are φ θ χ always informal; in some cases the reverse is true, e.g., ἐλεύτερος [elefteros] is informal, but ἐλεύθερος [elefθeros] is formal.

This dimorphic phenomenon is traced to Classical Attic. For instance, 5th c. BC ostraka show ΘΕΜΙΣΤΟΚΛΕΣ spelled with T (formal) and ΘΕΜΙΣΘΟΚΛΕΣ spelled with Θ (informal). (See p. 152.) This T-Θ interchangeability is indicative of the diachronic formal/informal, i.e., literary vs. vernacular dimorphic nature of Greek (p. 150).

Formal vs. informal applies to other sounds as well: medial μπ, ντ, γγ/γκ, which may be pronounced [mb, nd, ŋg] (formal) or [b, d, g] (informal); and in certain words νδ [nð] is formal, but ντ instead of νδ in the same words is informal (2.13).

The description of consonants (column *B* above) correctly reflects their status in Hellenistic and Neohellenic Greek. However the evidence (2.10) does not support the theoretical correlation in column *A* between β δ γ and [b d g] or φ θ χ and [ph th kh] in the classical period, since the presumed changes in *B* were already in place in the classical period. Browning's premise reflected in *A* is therefore irreconcilable with the evidence.

## 2.12 EUPHONIC B, D, G

*Neohellenic.* The sounds b, d, g are not phonemic: they are formed euphonically through assimilation and are represented in writing by combinatory variants. For example, in ἔμπροσθεν, μ + π = [mb]; in ἀντίχριστος, ν + τ = [nd]; in ἀγκάλη, ν + κ = [ŋg], where "nasal γ" becomes [ŋ]; and in ὄγγος, γ + γ = [ŋg].[63] Medial μπ, ντ, γγ/γκ are pronounced [mb, nd, ŋg], respectively, though informally often as plain b, d, g; and at word juncture in conversational speed optionally by the sound of the letter. No Greek word begins or ends with μπ, ντ, or γκ except in informal and simplified forms, loanwords, and transliterated foreign words—evidence of the nonphonemic status of b, d, g.[64]

63. Nasals ν [n] and μ[m] undergo anticipatory assimilation to a contiguous sound: εν+π = [emp] ἐμπίπτω, εν+ψ = [emps]/[embz] ἔμψυχος; εν+β/φ = [eɱv/f] (allophonic labiodental nasal [ɱ] before labiodentals β, φ) ἐμβαίνω, ἐμφαίνω (cf. *comfort*); εν+μ = [em] ἐμμένω; συν+λ = [sil] συλλέγω; συν+ρ = [sir] συρρέω.

64. Neohellenic words beginning with μπ, ντ are alternative informal forms, the result of phonopathy: μπορῶ [boro] from δέν/ἄν+πορῶ > (ν+π = μπ [mb]) orig. πορῶ; ντροπή [dropi] from ἐντροπή > (ν+τ = ντ [nd]) orig. ἐντρέπω < ἐν+τρέπω. Only a couple of Neohellenic words begin with γκ, as γκρεμνός from τὸν κρεμνόν (ν+κ = γκ [ŋg]), orig. κρημνός (epenthetic ν causing amplification). Initial/final μπ, ντ, γκ are applied to foreign words: μπόμπ *bomb*, Ντόρις *Doris*, Φορντ *Ford*, γκάνγκ *gang*.

*NT MSS*. The use of combinatory variants is seen in the Byzantine MSS. Blass cites occurrences in NT MSS in which the ν of the preposition ἐν is used as γ or μ. Thus ἐγ γαστρί (Luke 21:23), ἐγ Κανᾷ (John 2:11), ἐμ πραΰτητι (Jas 1:21), ἐμ πολέμῳ (Heb 11:34), σὺμ πάσιν (Luke 24:21).[65] The scribe's intent was, it would seem, to provide the phonetic transcription closest to one's pronunciation. It sounded more natural, for instance, to write ἐγ γαστρί [eŋ ɣastri]/[eŋ gastri], which reflected a euphonic pronunciation at the juncture ν + γ as [ŋɣ]/[ŋg], than ἐν γαστρί [en ɣastri]/[en gastri]. Likewise, because ν + κ = [ŋg], ἐν Κανᾷ sounded more natural as ἐγ Κανᾷ [eŋ gana] than [en kana]. (Cf. Engl. *ink* pronounced [ɪŋk] rather than [ɪnk].)

Robertson says, "The most common assimilation between separate words is in words ending in ν"[66] and lists τὴν πόλιν > τὴμ πόλιν (ν + π = [mb]);[67] τὸν λόγον > τὸλ λόγον (ν + λ = λλ), etc. (cf. *in* + *legal* > *illegal*). Likewise, ἐν πραΰτητι becomes ἐμ πραΰτητι [em braítiti], in which ν + π > μ+π = [mb] or even [mp] sounded closer to one's pronunciation than ἐν πραΰτητι [en praítiti]. The same applies to ἐμ πολέμῳ [em bolémo] and σὺμ πάσιν [sim básin]. Likewise, ν + τ = [nd] at word juncture: ἐν τούτοις [en dutis], ἐν τοῖς οὐρανοῖς [en dis uranis]. This assimilation occurs frequently in medial position: ἐμπειρία [embiria], πάντοτε [pandote], ἀγκάλη [aŋgali], ἀγγαρεύω [aŋgarevo]. Thus, like Neohellenic, Κοινή had no need to assign the value of b, d, g to any dedicated alphabet letters and so do away with the use of combinatory variants.

*Attic inscriptions*. Such euphonic spelling at word juncture is seen as well in classical inscriptions: τὸμ πίνακα (for τὸν πίνακα), 449/8 BC; τὸμ φόρον (for τὸν φόρον), 448/7 BC; ἐμ πόλει (for ἐν πόλει); τὸλ λόγον (for τὸν λόγον), 434/30 BC;[68] τὲμ βολέν (for τὴν βουλήν, 435–30 BC; τὸγ γραμματέα (for τὸν γραμματέα), 440–30 BC; ἐμ πινακίῳ (for ἐν πινακίῳ), 341–29 BC; τὴμ μάχην (for τὴν μάχην), 400 BC.[69] (Cf. p. 134, lines 36, 41; p. 135, line 22; p. 139, line 3.) All such occurrences show the same spelling practices as those seen in the Hellenistic and Byzantine periods. Euphonic changes in classical times of stop κ to *continuant* γ (ἐκ > ἐγ) before words beginning with *continuants* β, γ, δ, λ, μ, ν are an indication that γ was a *continuant* (i.e., not the stop [g]): ἐγ Βυζαντίου 444 BC; ἐγ Διός 418 BC; ἐγ λέξοντες 432 BC; ἐγ Μεγάρων 329 BC; ἐγ νήσων 357 BC; etc.[70] (For medial μπ, ντ, γκ/γγ (< νκ/νγ) in Attic, see examples

65. Blass, *Greek Grammar*, 12.

66. Robertson, *Grammar of the Greek New Testament*, 216.

67. When Emperor Constantine renamed Byzantium after himself (1.7), the name of the city became Κωνσταντινούπολις *Constantinoupolis* "City of Constantine" (Κωνσταντίνου *Constantine's* + πόλις *city*). Frequent use of the phrase εἰς τὴν πόλιν *(in)to the city* supplanted the need for identifying one's destination or reference to *the City* by name. The Turkish rendition of Κωνσταντινούπολις as Istanbul (also Stambul) is from εἰς + τὴν + πόλιν > [is + tin + pólin] > [istinbólin] > [istimbóli] > [istamból] > [(i)stambúl]. Here is a living historical example of ν + π > μ + π = [mb].

68. Caragounis, *Development of Greek*, 364.

69. "Searchable Greek Inscriptions/Packard Humanities Institute," *IG I–II*, http://epigraphy.packhum.org.

70. Caragounis, *Development of Greek*, 378–80.

in the preceding paragraph.) But let us now look specifically at the sound δ(Δ) before returning to our discussion of b, d, g.

## 2.13 GREEK δ NOT [d]

The Greek letter δ invariably stands for [ð] as in *the*. In informal speech—and writing—the letter δ of medial -νδ- yields to the letter τ [t], hence -ντ-, in which case voiced ν [n] assimilates voiceless [t] and turns it into its voiced counterpart [d]. When that happens, the combinatory variant ντ is pronounced [nd] or simply [d]. This is illustrated by the following *formal* and *informal* Neohellenic examples:

### 2.13.1 Formal and Informal Spelling and Pronunciation of Medial νδ vs. ντ in Neohellenic

| ***Formal* spelling with νδ = [nð]** | | **Alternative informal spelling of νδ as ντ = [nd]/[d]** | | | |
|---|---|---|---|---|---|
| ἄνδρας | [anðras] | άντρας | [andras] | or [adras] | *man* |
| Ἀνδρέας | [anðreas] | Αντρέας | [andreas] | or [adreas] | *Andrew* |
| δένδρο | [ðenðro] | δέντρο | [ðendro] | or [ðedro] | *tree* |
| ἕνδεκα | [enðeka] | έντεκα | [endeka] | or [edeka] | *eleven* |
| κανδῆλι | [kanðili] | καντήλι | [kandili] | or [kadili] | *oil lamp* |
| μανδολῖνον | [manðolinon] | μαντολίνο | [mandolino] | or [madolino] | *mandolin* |
| μάνδρα | [manðra] | μάντρα | [mandra] | or [madra] | *pen, fold* |
| μανδύλιον | [manðilion] | μαντύλι | [mandili] | or [madili] | *handkerchief* |
| σκανδαλίζω | [skanðaliζo] | σκανταλίζω | [skandaliζo] | or [skadaliζo] | *I scandalize* |
| ὑπανδρεύω | [ipanðrevo] | παντρεύω | [pandrevo] | or [padrevo] | *I marry (trans.)* |
| χονδρικῶς | [xonðrikos] | χοντρικώς | [xondrikos] | or [xodrikos] | *wholesale (adv.)* |

In contrast, in many archaic words preserved in Neohellenic medial νδ is not alternatively spelled ντ; that is, νδ is retained and pronounced [nð] but not alternatively [nd]/[d]: ἐνδεής *poor*, ἐνδέκατος *eleventh*, ἔνδοξος *glorious*, ἔνδυμα *clothing*, κίνδυνος *danger*, μανδύας *cloak*, πανδοχεῖον *inn*, Πίνδαρος *Pindar*, σπονδή *libation*, συνδέω *I join*, σύνδουλος *fellow-servant*, etc. Thus, if Attic /d/ turned into Hellenistic /ð/, why would Greek resort to the use of ντ for both [d] *and* [ð], rather than the old, familiar δ(Δ)? The obvious persistence of unassimilated δ in such archaic words further suggests that the pronunciation of δ as [ð] predates the Hellenistic period; and that for the pronunciation of nonphonemic [nd]/[d] Greek has diachronically relied on the combinatory variant ντ.

**The coevality of β δ γ and b d g is traced to Attic.**

Browning remarks, "The question of the phonemic status of b, d, g is still not settled in regard to modern Greek, so we can scarcely be expected to answer it for late Koine."[71] Actually, the status of b, d, g is not unsettled. As the foregoing two sections indicate, from Attic to the present, Greek has had no need to assign the value

71. Browing, *Medieval and Modern Greek*, 27.

of [b d g] to alphabet letters or otherwise elevate them to phonemic status. These are fluid sounds formed intervocalically or at word juncture and are thus largely optional and idiosyncratic. This is probably a major reason that centuries of influence through loanwords from Latin and other languages containing b, d, g have failed to coax b, d, g into the realm of Greek phonemes.

But if Attic β [v] was plosive [b], then both μ+π and μ+β would have been euphonically indistinguishable as [mb]. And if Attic φ was aspirated plosive [ph], there would have hardly been a distinction between τὸν πόνον and τὸν φόνον, where both ν+π and ν+φ would have likewise been rendered euphonically as [mb]. It follows that the Athenians did not confuse β, δ, γ and b, d, g, for no Attic inscriptionist was ever misled by his ear and so substituted the letter β for π in euphonic cases. In other words, we never see, e.g., ἐμ βόλει (for ἐν πόλει), ἐμ βινακίῳ (for ἐν πινακίῳ), τὸμ βόνον (for τὸν πόνον), which could have very well been the case if Attic β was bilabial stop [b] rather than labiodental fricative [v]. What we do see instead is τὴμ βουλήν [tiɱ vulin] for τὴν βουλήν, where bilabial nasal [m] turns into its labiodental allophone [ɱ] before labiodental fricative β [v] (cf. p. 134, line 36). Besides, β was already confused with ϝ (= [v]) and fricativized υ (= [v/f]) by the 5th c. BC (2.6). The answer to Browning's question may thus be found in the observable diachronic coevality of β, δ, γ with the nonphonemic euphonic b, d, g. Attic β, δ, γ are therefore not duplicate sounds of the stops b, d, g, but phonemes with phonological properties that set them apart as the fricatives /v ð ɣ/, the same as in Κοινή and in Neohellenic. (See *Phonopathy*, p. 147.)

## 2.14 MONOPHTHONGIZATION OF DIPHTHONGS

*Diphthong* means *two phthongs* or *sounds*.[72] This term is nowhere used in Classical Greek literature for it is not older than the Alexandrine grammarians who coined it to refer to *pairs of letters*, not speech sounds.[73] As Jannaris remarks,

> Strictly speaking, Greek, since historical times, knows nothing of real (phonetic or acoustic), but merely graphic diphthongs, the only exception being afforded by the vowel pairs αυ and ευ (ηυ, ωυ), and that only previous to the consonantization of their postpositive υ.[74]

72. An English diphthong may be defined as *a complex speech sound or glide that begins with one vowel and gradually changes to another vowel within the same syllable*—as [eᶦ] in *they* or [aᶦ] in *fine* (not [e-ɪ] or [a-ɪ]). In contrast, no Greek vowel glides into another vowel within the same syllable, for each vowel is a distinct sound segment, which is, or belongs in, one syllable (8.6). Greek has five vowel digraphs or pairs of vowel letters (αι, ει, οι, υι, ου), each pair representing a single vowel sound. Thus, there is no phonological correlation between a Greek *vowel digraph* and an English *diphthong*. As for the digraphs αυ, ευ, ηυ, each consists of one vowel, α, ε, or η, and one consonant, [v] or [f] (see 2.6).

73. Hatzidakis, Ἀκαδημεικὰ Ἀναγνώσματα, 394.

74. Jannaris, *Historical Greek Grammar*, 47.

Thus, no one ever *heard* a Greek diphthong as two vowels (ε-ι, ο-ι, α-ι) occupying one and the same syllable, for in Greek a syllable can have only a single vocalic phthong (8.6).

The digraphs point to a primordial concurrence of alternative vowels, that is, two contiguous vowels each belonging in a different syllable. The result was two alternative accentuation environments: ÁI and AÍ, ÉI and EÍ, ÓI and OÍ, ÓY and OÝ, ÝI and YÍ. This contributed, on the one hand, to the formation of the monophthongized *spurious* or *improper diphthongs* AI(αι), EI(ηι), OI(ωι), with αι, ηι, ωι from the 12th c. AD appearing as Αι, Ηι, Ωι or ᾳ, ῃ, ῳ; and, on the other, to the rise of monophthongized AI(αι), EI(ει), OI(οι), OY(ου), YI(υι),[75] commonly referred to as *genuine* or *proper diphthongs*.

AI was originally written AE [e] (cf. Latin Æ), but by conformity to the spelling of the other proper diphthongs, its second letter E was changed to I(ι), hence AE > AI(αι) = [e].

The monophthongization of diphthongs may be illustrated as follows:

**Monophthongization of "Diphthongs"**

AE EI OI OY YI

| Genuine | | | | | Spurious | | |
|---|---|---|---|---|---|---|---|
| AÉ | EÍ | OÍ | OÝ | YÍ | ÁI | ÉI | ÓI |
| AI | EI | OI | OY | YI | AI | HI | ΩI |
| αι | ει | οι | ου | υι | ᾳ | ῃ | ῳ |

An apparent cause behind monophthongization is the basic rule of *trisyllabotony* "three-syllable-accentuation," a dynamic intrinsic feature of Greek phonology that allows alternative accentuation but restricts it to one of the last three syllables of a word. For example, adding one or more syllables to a word accented on its antepenult causes the accent to shift from its *seat* syllable but remains on the antepenult: ἔρ-χο-μαι > ἐρ-χό-με-θα, κω-μό-πο-λις > κω-μο-πό-λε-ως, εὔ-θυ-μος > εὐ-θυ-μό-τε-ρος. A natural consequence of the alternative accentuation's operation within this restricted field of trisyllabotony was that over time one accentuation, aided by rapidity in normal

75. Some authorities classify υι as a spurious diphthong. Here the focus is the three subscripted ᾳ, ῃ, ῳ.

speech, prevailed over the other and obliterated it.[76] In the case of genuine diphthongs AÉ(αἐ), EÍ(εί), OÍ(οί), OÝ(ού), YÍ(υί), the accent moved to the postpositive sound, with the prepositive sound becoming mute; and in the case of spurious diphthongs ÁI(άι) ÉI(ήι), ÓI(ώι), the accent moved to the prepositive sound, with I becoming a mute subscript (ᾳ, ῃ, ῳ).

The monophthongization of diphthongs, particularly spurious AI(αι), EI(ηι), OI(ωι), is not what Blass embraces as a case in which one "long" vowel by preponderance caused its associate I to become "short" and thereby produced English-like "long-short" sounds in the diphthongs ᾱι, ηι, ωι.[77] On the contrary, I, by virtue of its muteness, acted on its preceding associate as a compensatory lengthening (ἀντέκτασις), its graphic retention as an adscript (later a subscript) signaling the occurrence of phonopathy—in this case, a missing sound (2.15.1).

The monophthongization of diphthongs lies in other causes as well (2.15.1.B), all rooted in the highly inflectional nature of the Greek language and its flexible, though otherwise restrictive accentuation system. Monophthongization probably passed through intermediary stages, with the gradual process affecting each diphthong at different times, though certainly in pre-classical antiquity. However, due to the virtual paucity of the written record from the beginning of the Dark Age (1200 BC) to the beginning of the inscriptional period (600 BC), it is impossible to trace those stages. For instance, the sound [u], originally represented by Greek-invented Y, was gradually represented chiefly by O (for Ionic OY), which persisted till the 3rd c. BC, while the Y of YI, through a preponderance of alternative accentuation (e.g., YÍ), became associated with its postpositive I. In any event, O as [u] can be the result of a contraction (πληροομεν > πληρομεν = πληρουμεν), whereas OY can be (a) the result of compensatory lengthening due to the loss of a sound (λυοτσιν > λυο ' σιν > λυουσιν—with the υ of ου being compensatory), or (b) an original diphthong (φρουδος). Though pre-Eucleidean OY and O can be seen side by side (e.g., TOYTOΣ = τουτους, p. 137), post-Eucleidean OY for [u] is seen standardized (p. 143).[78]

## 2.15 VOWEL QUANTITY (LENGTH)

Scholars commonly theorize that in Classical Greek certain vowels and syllables required longer time to pronounce than other vowels but that this distinction, known as *quantity*, was lost in Κοινή. Might such an assumption, though, stem from technical concepts of post-classical Greek grammarians and Atticists in connection with

76. Jannaris, *Historical Greek Grammar*, 46.

77. Blass, *Pronunciation of Ancient Greek*, 43.

78. On a somewhat related note, Brian Joseph thinks that the sporadic dialectal change [i]>[u] in Ancient Greek and again in Medieval to Modern Greek follows the same pattern (Joseph, "Irregular [u] in Greek"). This, however, speaks more of the tenacious diachronic behavior of Greek even among peripheral dialects, rather than—for lack of written record—of any disrupted ancient dialectal pattern that was supposedly resumed in medieval times.

artificial prosodic features applied to metrical verse where quantity mattered? This section takes up the discussion on quantity and continues through the next section (2.16).

"There is not a word in the whole classical literature about quantity, as understood by us," says Jannaris, "nothing about short, long, or common syllables or vowels, . . . all these technical terms having made their first appearance in late grammatical treatises, that is in Greco-Roman times."[79] If, based on this position, vowel length is not a distinctive phonemic feature of Classical Greek, then all vowels and syllables orthophonically pronounced must be *isochronous* "equally timed" (1.12.d). Granted, accented syllables in regular speech may be imperceptibly to noticeably longer and louder depending on the speaker's intonational patterns, background, mood, or occasion. But that is not what quantity with respect to Classical Greek is all about, so some historical background may prove helpful.

Following the Dark Age of Greece (1.1), from the 7th c. BC to the beginning of the inscriptional period (600 BC), the Greeks became aware of the need for a national education system. As the basis for learning, they adopted their ancestral literature, which was chiefly in Homeric verse. As Durant remarks, until 600 BC "nearly all Greek literature had taken a poetic form; education had transmitted in verse the lore and morals of the race; even early philosophers . . . gave their systems poetic dress."[80] "It is of utmost importance," concurs Davidson, "to realize that the intellectual and moral part of [Greek education] has music and poetry for its starting-point."[81]

Right from the outset the Greeks realized that in their own dialect, more notably in Attic, the current pronunciation of their ancestral Homeric literature reflected changes that entailed the loss of consonants and of vowel sequences that caused versification to be phonetically and metrically anomalous. Attic contractions, which would have been foreign to Homer, now necessitated artificial lengthening to satisfy meter. Noted below is but an indication of the various types of phonological changes and what schoolmasters early in post-Homeric times did to compensate for sound loss in metrically affected syllables.

79. Jannaris, *Historical Greek Grammar*, 526.

80. Durant, *Life of Greece*, 139–40.

81. Davidson, *Aristotle*, 73.

### 2.15.1 Some Methods of Compensating for Homeric Sound Loss

A. The consonant next to (before or after) the missing sound was doubled:

| Older form | Consonant loss | | Missing consonant (') to be doubled | | New Attic form | |
|---|---|---|---|---|---|---|
| ΑΡΣΗΝ | Σ | > | ΑΡ'ΗΝ | > | ΑΡΡΗΝ | *male* |
| ΘΑΡΣΟΣ | Σ | > | ΘΑΡ'ΟΣ | > | ΘΑΡΡΟΣ | *courage* |
| ΜΕΛΙΤΣΑ | Τ | > | ΜΕΛΙ'ΣΑ | > | ΜΕΛΙΣΣΑ | *bee* |
| ΟΛΝΥΜΙ | Ν | > | ΟΛ'ΥΜΙ | > | ΟΛΛΥΜΙ | *I destroy* |
| ΠΑΝΡΗΣΙΑ | Ν | > | ΠΑ'ΡΗΣΙΑ | > | ΠΑΡΡΗΣΙΑ | *boldness* |
| ΣΥΝΛΕΓΩ | Ν | > | ΣΥΛ'ΕΓΩ | > | ΣΥΛΛΕΓΩ | *I collect* |
| ΑΛΙΟΣ | Λ | > | ΑΛ'ΟΣ | > | ΑΛΛΟΣ | *other* |

The double consonant spelling of these and other such Attic words is retained in Neohellenic.

B. A vertical stroke | was inserted by the vowel of the metrically affected syllable:

| Older form | Reduced form | Compensatory mark (stroke) | | New Attic form | |
|---|---|---|---|---|---|
| ΔΕΕΤΕ | ΔΕ'ΤΕ | ΔΕ \| ΤΕ | > | ΔΕΙΤΕ | *you bind* (pl.) |
| ΦΕΡΕΕΝ | ΦΕΡΕ'Ν | ΦΕΡΕ \| Ν | > | ΦΕΡΕΙΝ | *to bring* |
| ΒΑΣΙΛΕϜΕΣ | ΒΑΣΙΛ'ΕΣ | ΒΑΣΙΛΕ \| Σ | > | ΒΑΣΙΛΕΙΣ | *kings* |
| ΕΝΣ | Ε'Σ | Ε \| Σ | > | ΕΙΣ | *into* |
| ΑΡΧΑΝΣ | ΑΡΧΑ'Σ | ΑΡΧΑ \| Σ | > | ΑΡΧΑΙΣ | *authorities* |
| ΤΟΝΣ | ΤΟ'Σ | ΤΟ \| Σ | > | ΤΟΥΣ | *the* (acc. m. pl.) |
| ΕΣΝΑΙ | Ε'ΝΑΙ | Ε \| ΝΑΙ | > | ΕΙΝΑΙ | *to be* |

Thus, when the vowels A, E, O (list B) occurred before a lost sound (which was not always traceable), schoolmasters wrote A|, E|, O|, the added | being a silent vertical stroke.[82] The stroke | originally served as a silent guide, a compensatory mark analogous to the apostrophe ( ' ) in *o'er the fields we go*, where the silent apostrophe compensates for the "loss" of *v* while maintaining the rhythm by the positional lengthening of accented *o*.

Over time, however, the compensatory symbol | as a mere conventional mark ended up giving monophthongized *spurious diphthongs* A|, E|, O| the appearance of the monophthongized *genuine diphthongs* AI, EI, OI. As a result, the two sets became confused. Adding to the confusion was the fact that archaic E stood both for [e] and [i] sounds and which, from around the end of the 5th c. BC on, was represented by E(ε), EI(ει), H(η), or HI(ηι); and archaic O stood both for [o] and [u] sounds and which, from around the end of the 5th c. BC on, was represented by O(ο), Ω(ω), or OY(ου). OY[u] was from the 6th c. to the 3rd c. BC frequently written O.

But how did such sound changes eventually affect subsequent periods of Greek specifically with respect to vowel quantity? The following encapsulates the way those changes gave rise to the artificial application of vowel quantity in Classical Attic:

82. This vertical stroke | was initially not confounded with *iota* I since the latter's archaic Attic form (prior to 6th c. BC) resembled Ϟ or something similar, until it appeared as I(ι). (See p. 153.)

> In Homer we witness a very frequent succession of vowels. In Attic we observe a regular vowel contraction. . . . The old inscriptions . . . show regularly E and O . . . where our texts of Homer and the Attic poets now show ε η ει and ο ω ου respectively. . . . η ω ει ου—the principal exponents of quantity—are absent, or almost absent, from early Attic and previous Greek. . . . The (Attic) inscriptions previous to the Peloponnesian war, know no "natural" quantity. What we find indicated in those . . . which are metrical, is "length by position," and this "position" virtually constitutes the principal indicator of quantity.[83]

It must thus be understood that Attic verse was predicated not upon any inherent quantity within the Attic sound system but upon artificial metrical principles handed down to the Athenians by pre-classical originators. Unlike modern poetry, which is essentially for reading, classical verse had reference to music, whether vocal, instrumental, or both, with meter—not rhyme—at its core.

Now length in verse entailed the accenting, and therefore lengthening, of a syllable to compensate for the loss of a consonant (*antectasis*), a feature known as *ictus* (2.19.3) For classical versifiers, a simplistic and practical way of measuring length was the actual raising of the foot (ἄρσις βραχεῖα *short raising*), which indicated an unaccented, and therefore shorter, syllable; and the actual putting down of the foot (θέσις μακρά *long down position*), which indicated an accented, and therefore longer, syllable—all according to a particular genre of verse (epic, iambic, lyric, tragic, trochaic, etc.) and its metrical foot (dimeter, trimeter, tetrameter, pentameter, etc.), hence iambic pentameter, dactylic hexameter, etc.

Accordingly, Attic teachers and Homerists further dealt with *phonopathy* (phonological anomalies that interfered with rhythmical verse) by developing additional artificial methods and principles: κρᾶσις *mingling*, συναίρεσις *contraction*, ὑφαίρεσις *deletion*, συνίζησις *co-settling*, ἀφαίρεσις *subtraction*, ἔκθληψις *elision*, and the like, "conventional signs such . . . as would not interfere with the sense, form, sound or aesthetic appearance of the text, and yet serve as visible indicators of the underlying phonetic changes."[84]

This point takes us to the adoption of H and Ω initially not as alphabet letters but as compensatory marks respecting quantity in versification.

## 2.16 METRICAL USE OF "LONG" H, Ω

Around the mid-5th c. BC the Athenians adopted Ionic H[85] and Ω. Certain scholars espouse the notion that the Athenians adopted H and Ω either because they lacked symbols for two existing vowel sounds, or because they had just added two new vowel

83. Jannaris, *Historical Greek Grammar*, 525–26.

84. Jannaris, *Historical Greek Grammar*, 528–29.

85. By classical times, H as a sign of aspiration had long been a relic of antiquity (see 2.18).

sounds to their language but had not yet decided what alphabet signs should represent them. Such unfounded assumptions are challenged by the simple question:

> If a phonetic distinction . . . necessitated the retention of η and ω as marks for a long *e*-sound and long *o*-sound respectively . . . is it probable that ignorant scribes and stone-cutters should have never been misled by their ear and so substituted εε for "long" η, and οο for "long" ω?[86]

At the time of their adoption into Attic as compensatory marks, H and Ω had no phonetic value of their own. Thus, if in adopting H and Ω the Athenians had in mind not a phonological feature related to speech, it follows that what they had in mind was a technical, quantitative prosodic feature related to metrical verse, the lifeblood of Greek drama. Let us then look at "length" in this light.

From the mid-5th c. BC, H and Ω were used in Attic verse as compensatory symbols to mark the position of accented and therefore metrically lengthened syllables where E and O respectively had hitherto been placed and viewed as "long by position." As time went by, however, the repeated use of positionally long H and Ω caused them to be regarded as "long" vowels, while vowels not long in the same sense were by default considered "short." H and Ω were thus considered long not by virtue of any intrinsic phonological qualities but technically, that is, metrically or grammatically;[87] for in Classical Greek speech vowels were relatively neither long nor short but isochronous (equally timed).[88]

For example, an honorific Attic decree inscribed in 399 BC—shortly after the adoption of the Ionic alphabet—shows an interchange of letters (spelling error) involving Ω and O, e.g., ΛΕΩΝΤΙΣ for ΛΕΟΝΤΙΣ (p. 140). Such an error shows that Ω and O in Classical Attic speech—not verse—were neither quantitatively nor qualitatively distinguishable. This is in line with Plato's testimony regarding the use of Ω in place of O (*Kratylos* 420b). Plato does not even hint at length as a distinctive feature of Ω.

Thus, prior to the adoption of H and Ω the Greeks knew nothing of "long" or "short" vowels in their speech. Such concepts were in fact invented later by Hellenistic grammarians (e.g., Dionysios Thrax) who developed rules governing metrical verse as follows:[89]

86. Jannaris, *Historical Greek Grammar*, 38–39. That is, no inscriptionist or scribe has ever substituted "long" η for εε, e.g., θη for θεε (voc. of θεος), or "long" ω for οο, e.g., πρωριζω for προοριζω. On the other hand, εε can only turn into ει (not η) as in φερεεν > φερειν, and οο can only turn into ου (not ω) as in πληροομεν > πληρουμεν.

87. O is called μικρόν *omicron* "small" (not "short"), and Ω μέγα *omega* "large/great" (not "long"). These Byzantine names hint at the comparative size of the two letters, not their phonetic/acoustic length.

88. It cannot be contended, for instance, that in normal speech the ancient Greeks made any perceptible distinction in vowel quantity between ἀνώτερος and πότερος, κλήματα and κρίματα, λύωμεν and λύομεν, or that the ου in σπουδάζουσιν was longer than the α in βαπτίζουσιν.

89. Adapted from Τζαρτζάνου (Tzartzanos), Γραμματικὴ τῆς Ἀρχαίας Ἑλληνικῆς Γλώσσης, 7.

**Vowel quantity in Attic Greek is a technicality of the art of metrical verse, not of ordinary speech.**

1. A syllable is *short* (βραχεῖα)—
   if it has a "short" vowel ε or ο
   followed by another short vowel, a
   single consonant, or nothing, as
   νέ-ος, λό-γος, λύ-ε-τε
2. A syllable is *long* (μακρά)—
   a) *by position* (θέσει μακρά)
      if it has a "short" vowel ε or ο
      followed by two or more consonants
      or one double consonant, as
      ἐ-κτός, ἐ-χθρός, ὄ-ντος, δό-ξα
      or ends in a double consonant, as ἅλς
   b) *by nature* (φύσει μακρά)
      if it has a "naturally long"
      vowel η or ω, as κῆ-πος, ᾠ-δή,
      a diphthong, as κρού-ω, χαί-ρειν,
      or a doubtful element is assumed
      long, as Ἄρης

Obviously "short" ε and ο may be considered "long" as well (#2.a), though not by any distinctive phonological designation but by their very *position* (i.e., arbitrary imposition) in the foot of rhythmical verse. Thus it cannot be argued that a syllable with a "short" ε or ο followed by two or more consonants, e.g., the ε in ἔστω or the ο in ὄντος, becomes acoustically shorter when followed by a syllable with a single consonant, e.g., ἔσω, ὄνος.

As a final point respecting quantity it must be noted that, according to Dionysios Thrax, "a long syllable may come about in eight ways, three by nature and five by position."[90] This in itself shows that "quantity is not fixed phonetically or physiologically but merely rests on tradition . . . κατὰ τὴν παράδοσιν καὶ χρῆσιν τῶν παλαιῶν *according to the tradition and usage of the ancients*."[91] Such comments are an allusion to the artificiality of quantity applied to versification in ancient times and passed down to the Attic poets—artificialities that were in turn passed on to post-classical and Byzantine versifiers.

Clearly, vowel quantity in Attic Greek is a technicality of the art of metrical verse, not of ordinary speech; for no one arranges words metrically before uttering them, just as no poet today converses naturally in rhymed verse.

## 2.17 PRONUNCIATION OF H(η) AND Ω(ω)

The adoption of H and Ω in the mid-5th c. BC brought much confusion to the Athenians, as they began to interchange EI, H, and I, as well as O and Ω (2.2.2). In place of I(ι) they used EI(ει) or H(η) (*Kratylos* 418c), and they substituted Ω for O (*Kratylos* 420b). H was initially intended for use in Attic verse as a compensatory "lengthening" symbol to replace the metrically and positionally "long" E.[92] Contrary to that inten-

90. Davidson, *Dionysios Thrax*, 7.

91. Davidson, *Dionysios Thrax*, 7.

92. Older Attic E was nameless and identified as EI εἶ (1.11)—named ἔψιλον by the Byzantines—and

tion, however, H became increasingly interchanged with I. At the same time spurious EI(ηι) was thought to be a combination of E + silent compensatory stroke | to form EI or H, so it became confused with the original (proper or genuine) diphthong EI(ει), which had long been monophthongized and pronounced as I(ι).[93]

Meanwhile, H began to creep into ordinary composition as well. So H(η), its original intent of replacing rhythmically and positionally long E now obscured, was actually thought to be a replacement for monophthongized EI(ει), thus becoming popularly read in ordinary composition as I(ι).[94] Additionally, H was used (a) where older E later stood for H(η), e.g., Ἀριστοκλες 525–500 BC > Ἀριστοκλης, δΕμόσιον 510–500 BC > δΗμόσιον, Ἀθενόν 447/6 BC > Ἀθηνῶν, ΔΕμΕτρα 447/6 BC > ΔΗμΗτρα;[95] and (b) where older EI stood for "long" ηι and read likewise as I(ι), e.g., τΕΙ βολΕΙ > τΗΙ βουλΗΙ (τῇ βουλῇ), τΕΙ στελΕΙ > τΗΙ στελΗΙ (τῇ στήλῃ), adscript (subscript) I being silent (2.15.1).

It was thus in the latter part of the 5th c. BC that Ionic H and Ω made their way into composition, and only in the year 403 BC that they were officially received into the Attic alphabet. This means that pre-Eucleidean works, i.e., works composed prior to 403 BC, made use of E where in post-Eucleidean works we see E, H, EI, HI; and of O where in post-Eucleidean works we see O, Ω, OY (1.11).

This transition is shown in a two-sided pre-Eucleidean Attic decree for the Temple of Athens Nike (427/3 BC) in which Side I uses "old" O in ΠΟΛΗΤΑΣ for ΠΩΛΗΤΑΣ (p. 137), whereas Side II uses "new" Ω in ΚΩΛΑΚΡΕΤΩΣΙ (p. 138). Also, "old" dative ΤΕΙ ΒΟΛΕΙ τῇ βουλῇ on side II is followed by "new" dative ΤΗΙ ΣΤΗΛΗΙ τῇ στήλῃ (p. 138). Meanwhile, versifiers and theorists, accustomed to using ancestral E and O, attached to H and Ω the old E and O values (i.e., old E was /e/ or /i/, and old O was /o/ or /u/), all the more adding to the confused use of E, O, H, Ω, OY.

As for H(η) in particular, it became popularly associated with EI(ει), the latter having been iotacized, hence one ought not to confuse H(η) with E(ε). At the same time, one must distinguish between acoustically interchangeable letters (e.g., EI and I), and alternative formal versus informal usage—a diachronic feature of the dimorphic nature of Greek. For example, the alternative spelling η/ε in the temporal augment of

**Alternative spelling of η/ε in some NT verb forms shows no confusion but formal vs. informal usage.**

stood for [e] and [i] sounds. Example: in ΘΕΟΙ θεοι E is E [e], but in ΕΣ ες (= εις) E is EI [i]. According to Plato's testimony, when older E later stands for EI (ει), it is [i]; and when it stands for H (η), it is again [i] (2.2.2).

93. Examples: Χιρων for Χειρων 580–70 BC, Κλιτίας for Κλειτίας 570 BC, Τιμαρχος for Τειμαρχος 580–70 BC, etc. (see "ι for ει," 2.2.2). The mixing of EI and HI is clearly sampled in the Phanokritos decree (early 4th c. BC) which has "[Τ]ΗΙ ΒΟΥΛΕΙ . . . ΛΙΘΙΝΕΙ" for ΤΗΙ ΒΟΥΛΗΙ . . . ΛΙΘΙΝΗΙ. Hicks and Hill, *Historical Inscriptions*, 188.

94. Examples from the 5th c. BC: Αθινα for Αθηνα, Διμοσθενις for Δημοσθενης, Αρις for Αρης, Ευφιβος for Ευφηβος, Πιδασης for Πηδασης, σιμα for σημα, Καμιρης for Καμηρης (see "ι for η," 2.2.2).

95. Pre-Eucleidean ostraka show ΠΕΡΙΚΛΕΣ, which in post-Eucleidean became ΠΕΡΙΚΛΗΣ. See also p. 146 regarding pre-Eucleidean E = /e/ or /i/, but post-Eucleidean E = /e/, and H = /i/.

some NT verbs indicates not a confusion of η and ε, but formal (η) versus informal (ε) usage: ἤμελλεν (Heb 11:8), ἔμελλεν (John 11:51); ηὕρισκον (Acts 7:11), εὕρισκον (Luke 19:48); ηὐχαρίστησαν (Rom 1:21), εὐχαρίστησεν (Ac 27:35)—Nestle-Aland.[96] The same holds true in Neohellenic: the H in Ηνωμένες Πολιτείες της Αμερικής *United States of America* becomes E (Ενωμένες) in informal Dimotiki. This formal/informal distinction involves other sounds as well (cf. 2.11.1; 2.13).

Some scholars apparently equate a surge in spelling frequency seen early in Hellenistic times with the development—even the origin—of that occurrence. Threatte, for instance, views the identity of ε and η early in Roman (Hellenistic) times as a vowel isochrony, saying that "η and ε must have become very similar at this time . . . but no complete identity of η and ε like that of ο and ω was reached, for η was already becoming closer and eventually became identical with ι."[97] But whereas Threatte treats earlier inscriptions mainly orthographically, he now treats them phonetically by applying vowel *isochrony* "equal-timeness" to speech, i.e., outside metrical verse; for by "isochrony" he means that "long" vowels η and ω in Hellenistic times started to become equally-timed with ε and ο respectively. Though the frequency of interchange between η and ι increases early in Hellenistic times, the fact remains that their interchange in pre-Hellenistic times reflects a change already initiated and in effect. Threatte apparently fails to equate the evidence of isochrony in Hellenistic times with the interchange of η and ι in classical times.

It must also be pointed out at this juncture that although we see the older Attic E used in place of Ionic H down to Byzantine times (partly due to alternative formal vs. informal usage, error, regional preferences, or even the effects of spelling on speech), it is of no consequence; for we are speaking not of peculiarities or relics of pronunciation in isolated places, but of the mainstream historical pronunciation that has the future. Once the significance of this is realized, it is frivolous to cite any example of the confusion of H and E.[98]

## 2.18 ASPIRATION

**In Plato's time H had no acoustic value other than that of the vowel H.**

One century ago, James Moulton wrote regarding the presumed phonological changes in Greek during the Κοινή period, "de-aspiration was the prevailing tendency . . . as

96. Nestle et al., *Novum Testamentum*. Worth noting is that in the 13 different types of interchanges totaling 492 orthographical errors in P. Bodmer II (Papyrus 66) not a single case of η for ε or the converse is shown (see 2.3). And in the Oxyrhynchus, Tebtunis, Amherst and other Hellenistic and Byzantine papyri the distinction between ε and η appears standardized.

97. Threatte, *Attic Inscriptions*, 160.

98. Dietrich lists ξερασία *drought* (for ξηρασία), ὑπερεσίαν *service* (for ὑπηρεσίαν), including words in which ε is used for other [i] sounds: Ἀρεστείδης (for Ἀριστείδης), Μελτιάδης (for Μιλτιάδης), ἐρήνη *peace* (for εἰρήνη), Τένδερα (for Τέντυρα) in *Byzantinisches Archiv*, 11–13. Such cases reflect alternative usage or regional preferences and prove nothing.

Modern Greek shows."[99] "Aspiration . . . was lost during the period of the Koine," echoes Gignac.[100] Moulton and Gignac hold that the loss of aspiration in Greek occurred in Hellenistic times. Such assertions lead to the assumption that aspiration in Classical Attic, indicated by the symbol H [h], was a phonological feature with distinctive acoustic properties. But was aspiration really even a part of the Classical Attic speech?

We know that Aeolic and Doric had no aspiration; and that in Ionia by the 7th c. BC aspiration had ceased to exist. In pre-classical Attic, however, the use of H is uncertain. This uncertainty, says Caragounis, reflected in "the frequent occurrence of H with ρ, λ, γ, etc. and ϝ (digamma)—where aspiration is impossible—indicates that the sense of aspiration had been lost.[[101]] This together with the evidence . . . respecting the extremely erratic use of H shows conclusively that aspiration had ceased in Athens already before the end of the classical period. When observed in script, it was as an old relic, not as a living item of language . . . —just as it has been till our own day!"[102]

In a similar vein of thought, Threatte says that after 450 BC "the comparative frequency of H = η . . . may be due to its previous existence in the Attic alphabet with the value of [h]. . . . occasionally there are special instances . . . where H = η in almost all places, and there is no H = [h] . . . but the phenomenon begins essentially ca. 460–450 B.C."[103] This all the more indicates that in the mid-/late-5th c. BC Attic H as a sign of aspiration was a legacy of the past.

As Jannaris remarks, "with the close of the 5th c. B.C., the aspiration was altogether done away with . . . or . . . lingered as a mere Phoenician antiquity."[104] This probably explains why Plato never described aspiration in his etymologies of names in *Kratylos;* and Aristotle, who explains that the distinction between οὗ *whose* and οὐ *no* consists in stress, does not even hint at aspiration as part of their difference. Thus, the official designation of H(η) in 403 BC as the vowel "Hta" met no aspiring rivals, which explains why the Athenians had no problem deciding to continue using it as such.

Some scholars espouse the notion that H was the aspirate *h* with acoustic consonantal properties (such as described below) until 403 BC but the vowel H (η) afterward. If so, Socrates must have had to hurriedly adjust his Attic pronunciation at age sixty-six and Plato in his mid-twenties! Could it be, then, that H in classical Athens

99. Moulton, *Prolegomena*, 44.

100. Gignac, *Grammar of the Greek Papyri*, 137.

101. Some examples Caragounis gives are: ληέων for λέων (7th–6th c. BC); κηόρη for κόρη (7th–6th c. BC); μηεγάλου for μεγάλου (6th c. BC) (*Development of Greek*, 390).

102. Caragounis, *Development of Greek*, 390–91.

103. Threatte, *Attic Inscriptions*, 42–43.

104. Jannaris, *Historical Greek Grammar*, 64. Jannaris adds that the breath marks, allegedly invented in the 3rd c. BC, had no bearing on the pronunciation of Κοινή but only served as artificial links to antiquity; and that the smooth breathing mark ( ' ) in particular is never found in the inscriptions and papyri or in the oldest MSS, and makes its first appearance in the MSS of the 7th c. AD, the practice having met with favor among the Byzantine successors.

had no acoustic value any more than the mute H in French, Italian, Portuguese, and Spanish, or ( ᾿ ) and ( ῾ ) (up until 1982) in Neohellenic? An examination of Allen's views regarding Attic H may help provide clear answers.

### 2.18.1 Sidney Allen's Treatment of Attic "Aspirate" H[h]

This section examines Sidney Allen's key arguments (italicized) regarding "aspirate" H as laid out in his *Vox Graeca* (1987), pp. 52–55.

Claim #1. "*The existence of this phoneme in classical Attic is clearly established*," declares Allen as he begins his description of "aspirate" H. He then proceeds to classify H as a consonantal phoneme with acoustic properties like those of the *h* in English, describing it as "*a pure voiceless aspirate* or '*glottal fricative*.'" Allen's designation of H /h/ as an Attic phoneme necessarily means that the presence or absence of H makes a difference in meaning. This distinction, Allen assures us, is all the more significant in that in Classical Attic the "*false writing of H is rare*."

Upon examining a number of Attic inscriptions it can be determined whether the presence or absence of H makes a difference in meaning (as in *herring* and *erring*); and if not, whether the difference might be some rare false writing (as in writing *hour* for *our* or *our* for *hour*), in which case the meaning would be determined by the context.

A decree for the Temple of Athens Nike, inscribed in 424/3 BC,[105] shows that H is used both as h and as η practically side by side, where the spelling TEI HIEPEAI τει hιερεαι (= τῃ hιερεᾳ) near the top of the inscription appears again a few lines below as THI IEPEAI τηι ιερεαι (= τῃ ιερεᾳ), where H[h] is missing. This means either that the two spellings form a minimal pair where the presence or absence of H makes a difference in pronunciation *and* meaning, in which case "glottal fricative" H /h/ would be a phoneme;[106] or, that the two variant spellings are read and pronounced alike and without a difference in meaning, in which case H would have to be mute in order for the two spellings to be read and pronounced alike. Since the context clearly indicates that in either case the word is one and the same—therefore the two are pronounced alike—H could only be a grapheme (letter), not a phoneme.

Might this inaccuracy in spelling be just what Allen calls a "rare false writing" of H? In other pre-Eucleidean Attic decrees from the same period (448 to 409 BC)[107] several occurrences of words that would normally be aspirated are shown without aspiration:

105. See p. 138.

106. As Allen points out by quoting R. Jakobson, "As a rule, languages possessing the pairs voiced/voiceless, aspirate/nonaspirate, have also a phoneme /h/" (*Vox Graeca*, 53).

107. Based on Attic decrees in the Epigraphical Museum of Athens as presented in the publication, *Athenian Democracy*.

ΕΚΑΣΤΟΝ for ΗΕΚΑΣΤΟΝ;[108] ΕΚΑΣΤΟ for ΗΕΚΑΣΤΟ, ΥΙΕΣΙΝ for ΗΥΙΕΣΙΝ;[109] ΟΣΠΕΡ for ΗΟΣΠΕΡ, ΟΜΟΛΟΓΟΣΙΝ for ΗΟΜΟΛΟΓΟΣΙΝ, ΕΚΑΤΕΡΟΙ for ΗΕΚΑΤΕΡΟΙ, ΕΚΑΣΤΟ for ΗΕΚΑΣΤΟ, ΕΚΑΣΤΟΣ for ΗΕΚΑΣΤΟΣ, ΕΛΛΕΣΠΟΝΤΟΦΥΛΑΚΑΣ for ΗΕΛΛΕΣΠΟΝΤΟΦΥΛΑΚΑΣ, ΕΔΡΑΣ for ΗΕΔΡΑΣ, ΕΟΣ for ΗΕΟΣ, ΟΙ ΣΤΡΑΤΗΓΟΙ for ΗΟΙ ΣΤΡΑΤΗΓΟΙ;[110] ΕΜΕΡΟΝ for ΗΕΜΕΡΟΝ;[111] ΑΝΤΙ ΟΝ for ΑΝΤΙ ΗΟΝ, and Ο for ΗΟ.[112]

These multiple occurrences of "de-aspirated" words from six different decrees (including the one discussed above) prove beyond any doubt that (a) the "false writing of H," particularly when one takes into account the multiple occurrences of "aspirated" spellings of some of the same words in the same inscriptions, is hardly rare; and that (b) mute H does not qualify as an Attic phoneme.

Claim #2. "*The symbol H in its consonantal value dropped out of general use after the introduction of the Ionic alphabet.*"

An audience would have to be too passive, if not also too naïve, to receive words uttered in such a nonchalant fashion for a linguistic event of tectonic magnitudes. One should only try to imagine waking up one morning and, upon turning on the TV news, being appalled at hearing that according to recent legislative action, and effective immediately, the initial letter "h" of every English word would now be permanently deleted from speech (except in certain "stereotyped phrases") as well as from all printed materials, whether governmental, academic, or private.

The implications of such a linguistically debilitating situation for speakers of English would be nonetheless no match for the gargantuan task that must have befallen Socrates, Plato, and all speakers of Attic in 403 BC. For in addition to instantly having to change H from a consonant to a vowel—besides having to adapt to a technically whole new alphabet—they must have had to hurriedly adjust their pronunciation of every Attic Greek word hitherto pronounced with the initial "glottal fricative" phoneme /h/.

One too quick to relegate such notions to sheer fantasy should first ascertain whether Allen's perfunctory portrayal of the demise of the "phoneme" /h/ is not an attempt to piggyback a potentially earth-shattering happening atop a government-sanctioned momentous event that went seemingly unnoticed and with relative ease. To claim that as a consequence of the introduction of the Ionic alphabet /h/ simply dropped out of general use, not only as a symbol but also as a phoneme, is to pass off the function of a phoneme as a superficial stylistic option. Any linguist would avow that the role of phonemes transcends pronunciation, for phonemes are the arteries of oral communication, the primary conveyors of the life of meaning. How could then

108. See p. 134.

109. See p. 136.

110. See p. 141.

111. See p. 135.

112. See pp. 142, 147.

this highly artistic classical tongue, so elevated to phantasmagoric echelons—without public stir, without signs of civil strife and remonstrance by a society teeming with educators, philosophers, playwrights, satirists, demagogues, politicians, historians, orators, versifiers, poets, musicians, artisans, sculptors, painters, and the hosts of the proud citizens of Athens—possibly become so quietly, so arbitrarily, and so abruptly subject to phonological mayhem?

Claim #3. "*That [h] had been lost, as in modern Greek, by the 4 c. A.D. is indicated by its frequent omission or misplacement of Gothic transcriptions.*"

Allen's reliance on Gothic transcriptions in support of his claim regarding the fate of Attic H[h] by the 4th c. AD is uncanny given the fact that Allen could have made the same observation with respect to 5th c. BC Attic inscriptions. Had Allen looked at the historical record more closely, he might have figured out that the legislative action behind dropping H[h] from Attic in 403 BC was actually repeated for the same major reason "in modern Greek" in 1982 when Neohellenic dropped the symbols of aspiration ( ᾿ ) and ( ῾ ). For, whether in 5th c. BC, in 4th c. AD, or in modern times, aspiration was as burdensome in Greek writing as it was unrelated to Greek speech. Allen's unsubstantiated claims related to Attic H[h] conclusively lack merit.

## 2.19 SUPRASEGMENTAL (PROSODIC) FEATURES

The Κοινή sound system is not that of an isolated or dead language but of one with an unbroken oral and literary record, the language naturally evolved from Attic Greek and whose continuation is Neohellenic. The evidence of the phonological features of Κοινή may thus be searched beyond the written records, which limit search to the analysis of single sound segments. There are other features that may be considered such as *suprasegmental* or *prosodic*, which fall within the acoustic properties of speech: stress, pitch-accent, rhythm, length, word juncture, and voice quality. These are all part of *intonation*, the voice contours or tone variations expressed in speech. Prosodic features of this type are *qualitative prosody* and are the characteristics of one's intonational patterns and speech style.

Granted, no audible record of Κοινή exists, thus no one can reconstruct its prosodic features; but at least one can look to the Neohellenic sound system for plausible clues. To that end, this next section purports to briefly clarify the usage of some terms in connection with prosody so as to lead specifically to *two points* (see below).

To begin with, it must be pointed out that there are two types of prosody, *qualitative* and *quantitative*. These two terms overlap in nomenclature and concepts yet are different in application, so we must distinguish between them.

A couple of qualitative prosody features have already been touched on in connection with speech: *juncture* (2.12), and *length* (2.15). Another such feature is *accent*. Because *accent* is part of quantitative and qualitative terminology and concepts, we must further distinguish between (a) the conventional accent marks (tones) used in writing, (b) the phonological pitch-accent related to the tonal (intonational) aspects of regular speech, and (c) the rhythmical or prosodic accent (ictus) in metrical verse.

## 2.19.1 Accent Marks (Tones)

Ἡ ὀξεῖα ( ´ ) *the acute* and ἡ βαρεῖα ( ` ) *the grave* were the only accentuation terms and marks known to classical antiquity (*Kratylos*, 399b). These reading marks are normally absent from Attic inscriptions and earlier papyri and are applied to poetical works to symbolize the rhythm produced by the regular recurrence of ´ and `, that is, by ἄρσις βραχεῖα *short raising (of the foot)*, and θέσις μακρά *long down position (of the foot)*. Such diacritic symbols "were employed to begin with . . . almost exclusively in poetical works,"[113] says Jensen, his remark being in harmony with "length" in relation to rhythm in versification, not in actual speech.

Accentual marks and other such diacritics are otherwise credited to Aristophanes of Byzantium (257–180 BC), a grammarian and librarian at the Library of Alexandria. Aristophanes devised the breathing marks, the comma, the period, the apostrophe, the hyphen, and other marks, a system of complementary symbols that over time encompassed ten signs, αἱ δέκα προσῳδίαι *the ten prosodies*. These signs were perceived as prosodic marks—prosody (προσῳδία) now denoting accentuation—and were devised primarily in an attempt to guide one's reading and interpretation of the old classical works.

After scanty use for centuries, and following a reform of accentuation undertaken by grammarian Theodosios of Alexandria around AD 400, accent marks and diacritics reappeared and further evolved. The systematic application of accent marks to MS texts dates since the seventh century, and from the thirteenth century onward accentuation became obligatory and used on every word. It may thus very well be that the evolution and actual use of accent (or stress) marks in Byzantine times—marks originally meant for metrical verse—may have contributed to the traditional notion that in Hellenistic times Greek changed from a tonal to a stress language (see below).[114]

## 2.19.2 Phonological Accent (Intonation)

**Historical question-forming tonal patterns are preserved in Neohellenic.**

Whether in ancient or modern times, each Greek word has one, and only one, pitch-accent (stress-accent). As is the case with the use of accentual marks, the phonological pitch-accent

113. Jensen, *Sign, Symbol and Script*, 470.

114. In 1982 the Greek Parliament abandoned the use of breath marks in Dimotiki to simplify spelling since Neohellenic has no aspiration. It also introduced a simplified accentuation system whereby the traditional accents marks ( ´ ` ˜ ) were replaced with a *single accent mark* ( ´ )—hence, *monotonic*—which is placed over the vowel of the accented syllable. All such diacritic symbols find use in Katharevousa (1.10).

is restricted to one of the last three syllables of a word and cannot recede beyond the third syllable from the end. Pitch-accent has always been an intrinsic feature of Greek speech. Caragounis explains:

> This stress-accent . . . has ever since held its iron grip upon the language; its rules and principles are still unchanged in Modern Greek. . . . This tenacity of the Greek accent finds satisfactory explanation only in its having been an integral part of the language; from the beginning (not merely from the 1st c. A.D.) it has held the language together, it has given it meaning and rhythm.[115]

Stress in Neohellenic is hardly perceptible. In practical terms, Neohellenic stress may be better understood as tonal accent or pitch, though pitch is hardly totally free of stress or even length. Compared to English, today's Greek is more of a tonal than a stress language (8.4). By implication Κοινή, too, is characterized as a tonal language.

This leads to the first of two points: Looking to Neohellenic for further clues regarding tonal features in Κοινή and in fact Classical Attic, one can identify the prosodic features related to the way interrogative statements are formed. Thus, in forming questions, Neohellenic, unlike English (which relies on periphrastic constructions or the reordering of words to turn sentences into questions), depends on qualitative rising-falling intonational patterns. This feature serves as added evidence that the historical question-forming pitch-accent tonal patterns of Greek (irrespective of idiosyncratic variations) are preserved in Neohellenic.

## 2.19.3 Rhythmical Accent (Ictus)

As already seen, *ictus* is the accenting of a syllable due to *antectasis* (the lengthening of a vowel sound in order to compensate for the loss of a Homeric sound) and thereby sustain rhythm in metrical verse.

**Rhythm in metrical verse has led many a scholar to characterize Classical Greek as a flawless tonal tongue.**

Now both pitch-accent *in speech* and rhythmical accent (ictus) *in verse* are subject to the intrinsic feature of Greek trisyllabotony, but they can be different in application. Phonological pitch-accent, for example, is used in speech according to grammatically-prescribed trisyllabotony patterns used by the general consensus of native Greek speakers. In this case, speakers naturally accent or stress a word while pronouncing all syllables isochronously (i.e., with equal length), hence without distinguishing between "long" and "short" vowels. Rhythmical accent, on the other hand, is used in verse to artificially lengthen an accented syllable (ictus) with emphasis on maintaining metrical rhythm. This method of lengthening a syllable is not natural nor is it defined by any intrinsic phonological properties of its vowel.

115. Caragounis, *Development of Greek*, 388–89.

The foregoing three cursory descriptions and distinctions of *accent* were necessitated in order to place particular emphasis on the manner in which accent is used in connection with the tonal rhythm in Greek verse; hence, the second point:

It is generally thought that Attic Greek was a tone language and that during Hellenistic times its musical pitch-accent gave way to stress. Thus the characterization of Neohellenic by the traditional philologist as a stress language seems to give him reason for keeping Classical Greek elevated to phantasmagoric Olympian echelons as a stress-free melodious tonal dialect of an idolized golden epoch, a tongue admirably filled with musical contours of metered long and short sounds, as though Attic Greek had been all poetry in song (and without a vernacular?), with the Greek of today being drastically different or even unrelated to it.

A more accurate view of Classical Attic would be to see it not only in the light of its artistic expression but also of its pragmatics. While the artistic side of Classical Attic, of which we do have a record, is artificial in expression, its vernacular side, of which we have virtually no record, is the natural, everyday language spoken in Athens. The Athenians' intense interest in perfecting especially the art of rhythm in metrical verse—the heartbeat of education in classical times—has apparently (mis)led many a Greek scholar to characterize Attic Greek as a flawless tonal tongue.

It is no wonder that in sheer contradistinction to artistic Attic, the Attic vernacular, particularly at the colloquial level, was referred to as κοινή "common (tongue)."[116] Regardless, it must always be borne in mind that both the artistic and the common expression of Attic Greek are of one and the same tongue and that the two share one and the same set of phonemic sounds.

## 2.20 ORTHOGRAPHY AND THE SOUND Z

Some orthographic peculiarities have already been noted (2.12, fn.). In closing, one more peculiarity must be pointed out, that of Z(ζ) [z] in place of Σ(σ) [s]. In Neohellenic the spelling of σ belies its pronunciation as ζ before voiced consonants. Χάρισμα *charisma*, for instance, is pronounced [hárizma], hence σ+μ > ζ+μ = [zm]. That this applies to Classical Greek as well is supported by the fact that Z is sometimes seen in place of Σ: πρεζβευτοῦ for πρεσβευτοῦ, Πελαζγικόν for Πελασγικόν, Ζμύρνα for Σμύρνα (4th c. BC).[117] The euphonic spelling of Z for Σ before voiced consonants is seen as well in NT MSS. This practice did not disappear until the 5th c. AD, its disappearance being an adjustment in orthography, not in speech; for, as in the days of old, in Greek speech today the letter σ [s] before a voiced consonant turns euphonically into a ζ [z] sound.[118]

116. The term κοινή, used prior to Hellenistic times by the various Greek dialects, carried a pejorative sense. (Cf. Latin *vulgate*, the common speech of the people, especially the uneducated.)

117. Caragounis, *Development of Greek*, 381.

118. A person may opt to pronounce χάρισμα [harisma] and Σμύνα [smirna], but as a rule the

As already seen, Erasmians base many of their assumptions regarding Attic Greek sounds on descriptions by Dionysios Thrax (170–90 BC) and later Alexandrine grammarians. These grammarians, however, were not phoneticians, thus their description of certain sounds may be misconstrued. One such sound is ζ, with regard to which Dionysios says that it is composed of σ and δ,[119] hence ζ = σδ [zð], or Erasmian [zd]. On the same plea, Apollonios Dyskolos (2nd c. AD), an Alexandrine grammarian, says, ὅταν δὲ ἤθελον συγγράψαι λέξιν ἔχουσαν τὴν τοῦ ζ ἐκφώνησιν, ἔγραφον τὸ σ καὶ τὸ δ ἀντὶ τοῦ ζ *when [the Athenians] wanted to write a word having the sound ζ, they wrote σ and δ in place of ζ*."[120] This however is a reference to the actual occurrence of σδ in composition, e.g., εἰσδέχομαι, where σ before voiced δ euphonically becomes ζ, hence [zð]. By itself ζ is [z], not [zð], let alone [ðs], which is foreign to Greek.

Specifically with regard to the pronunciation of Z as [dz], it is probable that Erasmians are misled by the supposed resemblance of the Greek Z to the Latin "Z" sound. As Quintilian remarks, "The ζ of the Greeks sounds melodious and sweet, but that of the Romans, rough and unmusical."[121] Compare, for instance, the English *z* in *zebra*, which sounds like the Greek Z [z], with the Italian *z* in *zebra*, which sounds like [dz].

Jannaris observes, "That ζ [z] from the outset represented a *simple* sound appears plainly from the fact that it figures, even in the oldest inscriptions, as a *simple* or monoliteral symbol (in the shape of I)."[122] See, for instance, p. 135, where pre-Eucleidean Ξ and Ψ are represented by the letters ΦΣ (line 24) and ΧΣ (line 33), while the sound "Z" is represented not by ΣΔ but by the monoliteral I (lines 15, 24). It is obviously for the same reason that Z, unlike Ξ and Ψ, has nowhere in inscriptions appeared (mistakenly) as the digraph ΣΔ. As Geldart remarks, "Etymologically it is extremely doubtful whether ζ ever stands for δς, and certain that it never stands for σδ, the fact being that σδ and δς are ways of approximating the sound of ζ."[123]

Plato dispels doubt about Z when he says, νῦν . . . ἀντὶ δὲ τοῦ δέλτα ζῆτα (μεταστρέφουσιν), ὡς δὴ μεγαλοπρεπέστερα ὄντα, referring to those Athenians in his day who tended to pronounce Δ as Z *as [it] must be [considered] more grandiose* (*Kratylos*, 418c). First, Plato does not see Z as a double sound; and second, his reference to a third party's pronunciation peculiarities clearly indicates that he himself did not pronounce Δ as Z . A lisped Z(ζ) at any rate will sound like Δ(δ), hence Δεύς for Ζεύς, and ζόρξ for δορκάς.[124] Plato obviously viewed Z as a simple sound distinct from Δ and Σ.

---

"natural" tendency at conversational speed is for σ/ς before a voiced consonant to euphonically turn into a "voiced s," i.e., [z].

119. Davidson, *Dionysios Thrax*, 6.

120. Bekkeri, *Anecdota Graeca*, 780.

121. Timayenis, *Modern Greek*, 178.

122. Jannaris, *Historical Greek Grammar*, 62.

123. Geldart, *Modern Greek Language*, 32.

124. Geldart, *Modern Greek Language*, 31.

But Plato's comment reveals one more thing: in order for Z to be used in place of Δ, Δ had to be of the same manner of articulation as Z (8.12). Thus, with Z being a continuant, Δ had to be a continuant as well, that is, [ð] as in *the*, not a stop—not the Erasmian [d]. And that is how Z and Δ are treated in Neohellenic.

## 2.21 IN RETROSPECT

The main focus in the foregoing study has been the development of Κοινή and the similarity between Κοινή and Neohellenic sounds. As it became obvious from the very start, the ground Κοινή and Neohellenic share in the area of vowel sounds, where variant spellings (spelling errors) occur, encompasses Attic. It was therefore necessary to trace these variant spellings to their pre-Hellenistic origins, especially to the adoption of the Ionic alphabet in 403 BC, an event that brought about an increase in the diversity of variant spellings. Orthographical rules that were consequently laid out by the Athenians effectuated the distinction of grammatical forms in a manner hitherto not possible (1.11), with acoustically interchangeable variant spellings now coming under the jurisdiction of stringent orthography.

**The 403 BC Eucleidean event marked not the formation of a more phonetic alphabet for a changing sound system, but the adoption of a script that would more efficiently express the grammatical distinctions of the language.**

But how did the semiliterate Attic inscriptionist view acoustically interchangeable variant spellings? Apparently, "variant" to him meant that he could rely on his ear to choose now this spelling for a given ι-sound, ε-sound, or ο-sound, now an alternative spelling, regardless of whether he was aware that his spelling was grammatically wrong. As for the literate inscriptionist, a variant spelling was a grammatical discrepancy. Similarly, a semiliterate speaker of Greek today may use ι or η for ει because he regards these acoustically as variants of [i], while a more educated person considers an ungrammatical use of a variant an error.

This standard can be applied diachronically from the mid-5th c. BC onward, especially from 403 BC, when the post-Eucleidean writing system was crystallized, a system fully operative in Neohellenic. Thus, in numerous cases what is considered a spelling error today was likewise considered a spelling error in Paul's time as well as in Aristotle's. ΛΕΓΕΙΣ, for instance, whose personal ending -ΕΙΣ in Neohellenic indicates second person singular present active indicative, was so spelled and read and grammatically understood in NT times and in the 4th c. BC;[125] and ΧΑΡΙΤΟΣ today is understood as a genitive singular feminine noun and was so spelled and read and grammatically understood in NT times and in the 4th c. BC. By contrast, the spelling ΛΕΓΙΣ, with I in place of EI, and ΧΑΡΗΤΟΣ, with H in place of I, are just as incorrect in Neohellenic as they would have been in AD 50 or in 403 BC.

125. As of about 1976, Dimotiki uses -ει, -εις, -ομε/-ουμε in the present indicative and subjunctive alike, whereas literary Katharevousa still uses the traditional subjunctive endings -η, -ης, -ωμεν.

Such diachronically observable grammatical and phonological features of the Greek language are not a rarity; for the same features hold true with respect to a great number of Classical Attic and NT words in Neohellenic that are still spelled, read, inflected, and understood the same way (except where morphosemantic changes occur) and according to the same grammar rules and the use of the same historical twenty-four-letter alphabet.

In short, faulty readings of the classical period were not variant spellings which later (in Hellenistic times) "evolved" phonologically and were further subjected to modern whims and ideas, but rather the result of a practice prevalent among the less educated, as has uninterruptedly been the case from classical times down to the present. It is thus such readings that furnish us with ample evidence of what the historical sounds of Greek were more than twenty-four centuries ago. That is why in the midst of the transition from the old Attic writing system to the Ionic we hear Plato say that the Athenians would use EI or H in place of I, and Ω in place of O, his observation sounding no different from that of a modern-day academic.[126] This situation of spelling mistakes is summed up thus:

> The study of the pronunciation of Greek from classical times on was based on the study of faulty readings in the inscriptions, particularly the Attic ones. . . . The mistakes of the stone cutters, which have come down to us unaltered, are the best proof of the actual pronunciation of Greek in those early periods. Those same mistakes we find repeated in the papyri from the IV$^{th}$ century B.C. on. This circumstance shows the unbroken continuity in the tradition of faulty readings, first in the inscriptions and later in the papyri, i.e., from around 600 B.C. to the end of the papyri period, the VIII$^{th}$ century A.D.[127]

In retrospect, it may once again be pointed out that reading and pronouncing Biblical Greek the Neohellenic way according to which, for instance, the sound [i] may be represented by ι, η, υ, ει, οι, or υι, can scarcely be considered a Modern Greek invention (2.2); rather, it is the result of developments traceable to classical or pre-classical Athens. The 403 BC Eucleidean event therefore marked not the formation of a more phonetic alphabet for a changing sound system, but the adoption of a script that would more efficiently express the grammatical distinctions of the language.

126. Such changes are not changes in pronunciation, as they reflect allographic variations (variations in spelling). The change in pronunciation of the primordial diphthong EI [e-i] into the monophthong I [i] had no bearing on the phonemic inventory of the Greek vocalic sounds, for as a "diphthong" EI consisted of two contiguous but distinct syllabic vowels, E and I, both part of the five-phoneme vowel inventory of Greek: /i e a o u/.

127. Caragounis, *Development of Greek*, 496–97.

## 2.22 SUMMARY AND CONCLUSIONS

The foregoing cursory study of the development of Κοινή and its phonology shows the many features Κοινή and Neohellenic share, which may be summed up as follows:

1. an identical 24-letter Classical Attic alphabet
2. a virtually identical orthographical system
3. the iotacization of ει = οι = υι = η = ῃ = υ = ι
4. the equalization of αι = ε and ῳ, ω = ο
5. the monophthongal pronunciation of ει, οι, υι, αι, ου, ᾳ, ῃ, ῳ
6. an orthophonically isochronous vocalic system /i, e, a, o, u/
7. the pronunciation of fricativized υ in αυ, ευ, ηυ as β/φ
8. the identification of β, δ, γ, φ, θ, χ as fricatives
9. the dimorphic (formal/informal) use of π/φ, τ/θ, κ/χ, νδ/ντ, η/ε
10. the use of combinatory variants for euphonic, nonphonemic [b, d, g]
11. euphonic medial or final ν [n] as [m]/[ɱ] or "nasal γ" [ŋ]
12. the sound of ζ as [z], and assimilation of σ/ς into [z] before voiced consonants
13. the nonuse of aspiration
14. phonetically interchangeable allographs that cause diachronically identical misspellings among the less literate
15. pitch-accent patterns tied to trisyllabotony
16. application of intonational patterns for the formation of questions

The likelihood therefore is high that the Κοινή of the NT and Neohellenic share the same orthophonic pronunciation and in fact overall phonological system. Additionally, and most notably, if we consider one by one the features listed above, we are struck by the brow-raising cognizance that there is hardly any feature listed—in fact, none—that would not apply as well to the daily use of the Attic speech in Alexander and Aristotle's day (3.4).

## 2.23 CLOSING REMARKS

The phonology of Κοινή and its relation to Neohellenic was presented on two parallel evidentiary tracks. One track concerned vowels and vowel digraphs on the premise that faulty readings of an acoustic nature are telling of pronunciation. The origins of those errors coincided chiefly with the transition from the older Attic writing system to a new system known as the post-Eucleidean grammar. This unbroken track of repeated spelling errors, gauged by the same diachronic standard—the same writing system *and* orthography—indicates that the spelling, reading, and pronouncing method Κοινή and Neohellenic share was in place, or originated, in Classical Attic.

The second evidentiary track, gauged by the same standard, concerned consonants that accounted for such diachronic peculiarities as dimorphic and euphonic pronunciation, the nonuse of aspiration, and other findings such as listed above (2.22), with their origins also being traceable to Classical Attic or earlier. These findings point to Attic sounds entering Κοινή in their definitive value and form and developing into what will henceforth be collectively referred to as the *Historical Greek Pronunciation* (HGP), discussed next.

# Chapter 3

# The Historical Greek Pronunciation

## 3.1 INTRODUCTORY

THE DESCRIPTION IN CHAPTER 2 of the development of Κοινή phonology and its similarities to Neohellenic of necessity led to an investigation of the origins of Κοινή sounds, which were traced back to classical and pre-classical times. Chapter 3 now takes sort of a reverse diachronic approach. First, it focuses on the significance of the sounds of Attic Greek (due to the time period in which they emerged), then on their impact on Κοινή, and finally on their relation to Neohellenic.

## 3.2 FORMATION OF THE HISTORICAL GREEK PRONUNCIATION (HGP)

Written records from the beginning of the inscriptional period in 600 BC—there are just a few from around 725 BC—all through classical times show that the various letters, particularly vowels, are confused. This means that the evidence of misspellings we see in the Hellenistic papyri is already present in the earlier inscriptions. This unbroken chain of evidence helps us trace the development of the Historical Greek Pronunciation (HGP),[1] a pronunciation that took several centuries to develop and which we first meet in the 6th c. BC, when digraph EI(ει) is first read and pronounced as I(ι) [i].

The particular time a new pronunciation pattern such as EI = I is first detected becomes of paramount significance in the diachronic study of the historical Greek sounds. For one thing, we know that this type of change could not have taken place abruptly but over a period of time during which the old spelling was used along with

1. The name is credited to Prof. Chrys C. Caragounis. It comprises the Greek sounds represented by their respective post-Eucleidean graphemes and whose initiation or formation is traceable to Classical Attic or beyond.

the new pronunciation, with the sounds probably passing through several intermediary stages while no intermediary letters were used to record their phonetic progress. Therefore it is the time of the formation of the historical Greek sounds, rather than their completion, that first and foremost concerns us.

Tracking the emergence of such changes helps us not only in following the origin and development of the Classical Attic sounds through the unbroken epigraphical and papyrical record, but also in identifying them in their later developments and tracing them back to their historical origins. And that is what lies at the heart of the matter: tracing the time of the emergence of that forward-looking force, the HGP of mainline Classical Attic.

We are thus interested in the recorded origins and new developments of the Classical Attic pronunciation, developments that determine the course of the future, not in the relics in some isolated dialectal regions, of whose exact sound we cannot be certain. We may not be in a position to confirm by documentary evidence any later developments of the pronunciation of Greek in Spain, Crimea, Bactria, Afghanistan, or India; for, granted, some Attic Greek sounds, having spread later throughout the Hellenized world, must have undergone in isolated regions a leveling process that was presumably completed sometime around NT times, though they were still very similar to the Athenian pronunciation, since they reflected the Attic-based pronunciation used in Alexander's empire. This is of no consequence, however, for the issue, again, is not any regional or peripheral application of sounds to Greek, but the Attic sounds of classical Athens, the mainline Hellenic speech sounds that formed the HGP. For once the Attic pronunciation gradually emerged and developed, it became the force that eventually succeeded in prevailing over all other dialectal or peripheral ways of pronouncing Greek.[2]

## 3.3 THE HGP IN KOINH

Scholars typically view Alexander's campaigns as the launching pad for every sound change Attic Greek presumably underwent following the classical period. They allege that exporting the Attic sounds to foreign lands—as though no Attic sounds were left behind—exposed the Attic pronunciation to external linguistic elements and forces that caused it to change and form into a distinct sound system, that of Κοινή. Impressionable students envision Classical Attic sounds being swiftly exported from Athens alongside Alexander's Bucephalus as plosives begin to crunch under friction, tonal harmony succumbs to stress, long vowels become short-lived, and aspiration expires.

2. The Doric dialect resisted the infiltration of Κοινή more than any other Greek dialect in various parts of the Greek world (Peloponnesos, Crete, Kyrene, Rhodes, parts of Asia Minor, some islands in the southern Aegean Sea, and a few other isolated regions), its persistence fading by the 2nd c. AD. Today Tsakonian, a dying form of Doric, is spoken by a handful of people in isolated towns and villages in and near Laconia (Ancient Sparta).

However expressed, such unsubstantiated notions sound logical to the inexperienced seminarian, lending credence to the theorists' regurgitated "explanations" of how Κοινή took form on foreign lips in conquered lands.

Such assertions lack evidence. First, there is no evidence that φ, θ, χ were plosives in Aristotle's day, nor when and where they began to turn into fricatives, for that matter. Comparative linguistics assumptions (such as Allen's) that in Classical Attic these were plosives to begin with do not amount to evidence (2.10.1). And there are no grounds for treating Attic β, δ, γ as the English plosives b, d, g[3] (2.11). No one can explain how six Attic plosives could have turned into fricatives (φ, θ, χ, β, δ, γ) between the 3rd c. BC and 2nd c. AD so uniformly throughout the immense empire, yet for a disproportionately much longer period—two millennia!—could remain fricatives. The very longevity of these fricatives to date evinces the tenacity of the intrinsic properties with which they entered Κοινή.

**Κοινή should be compared with the Attic vernacular, not Attic verse.**

Second, no evidence has shown on what basis and according to what processes and criteria Classical Attic metamorphosed from a tonal and lyrical speech into a stress language. In fact the strongest evidence available to date amounts to no more than Allen's speculation, who says, "The eventual change from a melodic to a stress-accent in Greek cannot be precisely dated."[4] Doubtless, such a factual statement rests on the assumption that a change of this type did occur; therefore, that Greek once was melodic and eventually ceased being melodic now appears to be a mere fact. It must be remembered that Κοινή is chiefly the continuation of the Classical Attic vernacular, the everyday speech of the common Athenian, not of the highly refined artificialities applied to metrical verse or to other literary masterpieces of the Golden Age of Athens, although in either case the phonology was one and the same (1.10). Κοινή thus ought to be compared with the Classical Attic vernacular, leaving rhythm, tone, and length related to melodic versification outside the purview of an otherwise unfounded phonological comparison.

Third, there is no evidence that Classical Attic had sixteen to eighteen English-like vowels and diphthongs (6.5.2) rather than the five vowels of Κοινή, the same as the five Mycenaean as well as Neohellenic vowels /i, e, a, o, u/ (1.11; 2.5); for there can

3. Attempts to impose on Greek, an Indo-European (IE) language, across-the-board phonological changes noted in other IE languages based on Grassmann's Law will find oneself on a treadmill of skewed speculation. A surer perspective of the development of Greek sounds, based on the *written* record, can be gained from the fact that the HGP has survived for nearly twenty-five centuries as opposed to the sweeping transformations all Germanic and Romance IE languages have undergone in a fraction of that time. Moreover, one should not theorize how Attic Greek was pronounced while leaving Neohellenic out of the loop. Without Neohellenic as a reference point we would probably have no reliable basis for assuming what sounds were represented by what symbols even in Byzantine times, let alone the classical period (1.13).

4. Allen, *Vox Graeca*, 130. Worth noting is that following this opening statement, Allen looks for signs of evidence based not on regular speech but on metered verse and rhythm, especially hymns composed in the 4th c. AD.

be no phonological process whereby the five phonemic vowels of the language of a city-state can possibly increase to such a prodigious English-like vocalic system and within a couple of centuries of being spread over distant lands revert to their original status.

Finally, there is no proof that Aristotle used aspiration in speech any more than speakers of Neohellenic just because they use(d) aspiration marks in writing (2.18.1). In short, there is no *hard* evidence that the phonemic sounds of Κοινή, first and foremost in Athens, became different from those of Classical Attic. For just as in pre-Hellenistic times Attic prevailed over all other Greek dialects as the leading speech of the Greek world (1.3), so did Athens serve throughout pre-NT times as the linguistic epicenter that emitted to the Hellenized world waves of her historical sounds. Those were the sounds Alexander and his soldiers took to Egypt and Asia, the HGP, the pronunciation that emanated from Athens during Alexander's time and beyond, as the stark evidence of the inscriptional and papyrical record of repeated spelling errors attests.

## 3.4 FROM SEPTUAGINT TO NEW TESTAMENT

**How different were the Κοινή sounds of the Septuagint translators from Aristotle's Classical Attic sounds?**

As already seen, the translation of the Septuagint, initially the Pentateuch, commenced around 285 BC (1.5), while the original NT writings were all completed by the end of the first century. Numerous direct quotations from the Septuagint were incorporated into the NT text without the need for any morphological, syntactic, semantic, orthographical, or other linguistic adjustment by the NT authors.

Thus, however one slices the pie, the Κοινή of the Septuagint and the Κοινή of the New Testament are one and the same language and share one and the same writing and orthographic system, the post-Eucleidean. Distinctions such as "Jewish Koine," "Egyptian Greek," "Alexandrian Koine," or "Christian Greek" regarding Κοινή (1.6) are nothing more than fanciful names, dear though they are to grammarians, lexicographers, and exegetes. Besides, our premise concerns the mainstream Κοινή phonology, not arbitrary descriptions of Κοινή or isolated peculiarities of any Κοινή expression.

Our premise then triggers the question: Since the Septuagint and the New Testament were written in Κοινή, and while the Κοινή sounds were supposedly different from the Attic Greek sounds of classical Athens, how different were the Κοινή sounds of the Septuagint translators in 285 BC from Alexander and Aristotle's Attic Greek sounds in 325 BC, or roughly forty years earlier? The chart below is meant to add some visual perspective to this question:

### From Classical Attic to Κοινή

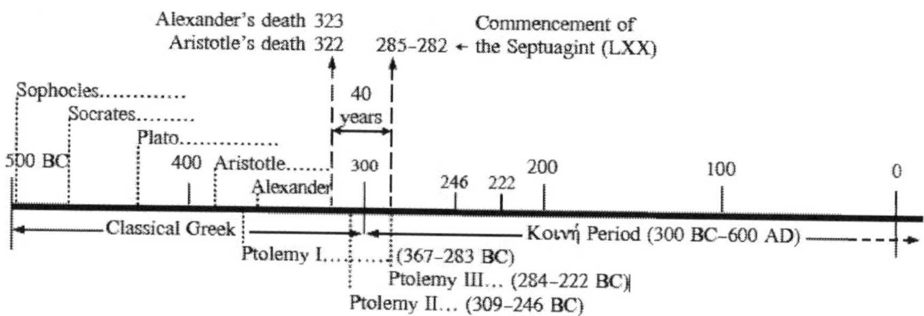


As the above chart shows, Alexander and his private tutor, Aristotle, died within a year of each other, their death coinciding with the close of the classical period (500–300 BC) and the beginning of the Hellenistic (300 BC–AD 300).[5] If Aristotle's (or Alexander's) Attic was now to turn into the Κοινή of the Septuagint, there was barely a forty-year window between his death and the commencement of the translation of the Septuagint in order for classical η, ῃ, υ, ει, οι, υι to be read as ι [i], αι as ε [e], ᾳ as α [a], ῳ and ω as ο [o]; for φ, θ, χ, β, δ, γ and the υ of αυ ευ ηυ to become fricativized; for aspirate [h] to go into disuse; for biphthongal ζ [dz]/[zd] to turn into monophthongal [z]; for the long-short vowel distinction to disappear; and for the tonal features of the language to give way to stress.[6]

Such preposterous notions laid aside, it is highly likely that at least some of the seventy-two Jewish emissaries assigned to the task of translating the Hebrew Scriptures into Κοινή were old enough to have been educated in Greek even while Aristotle was still alive.[7] These Jews therefore spoke Κοινή using the historical sounds of Attic Greek as did Aristotle, Alexander, and the Ptolemies, and wrote according to the same standardized post-Eucleidean orthography of contemporary Athens—irrespective of whether or not any of them spoke flawless Athenian or with some Semitic accent.

5. Some authorities view the year of Alenxander's death (323 BC) as the beginning of the Hellenistic period.

6. If so, the Κοινή of Ptolemy III, king of Egypt, would have sounded nearly unintelligible to his grandfather, Ptolemy I, one of Alexander's generals and for forty-four years a contemporary of Aristotle, also a contemporary of the Jewish translators; and, alas, the Κοινή of Atticist Dionysios Thrax (170–90 BC), like a foreign tongue.

7. As the diagram shows, Sophocles died at age ninety, Plato at eighty-two, Aristotle at sixty-two. The average lifespan of these men, including Socrates' premature death at seventy, was seventy-six years. It was therefore not unusual for a person born in that period, whether in Athens, Rome, Jerusalem, Alexandria, or elsewhere, to live well past the age of seventy. In that the translation of the Septuagint began in Alexandria around 285 BC, that is, within forty years of Aristotle's death, it follows that any of the Septuagint translators enjoying a higher lifespan were educated in Greek when Aristotle was still living, while the younger ones were educated by teachers who had been contemporaries of Aristotle. In either case, the Greek speech sounds of those emissaries were doubtless the HGP sounds of Aristotle's day. And while parts of the Septuagint were completed in later years, they were written in the same Κοινή, also the Κοινή of the New Testament.

From the very outset these erudite men knew, for instance, that ευ was not Erasmian [ju] as in *feud* but fricativized [ev] as in Λευιτικόν [levitikón] *Leviticus*; and that αυ was not Erasmian [a$^{ʊ}$] as in *sauerkraut* but [av] as in Δαυίδ [ðavíð] *David*. For by then the processes of fricativization and other linguistic changes, such as already discussed, had long been in place by classical times, with the Attic Greek vernacular and its HGP sounds, historical alphabet, and orthography entering the Κοινή period in their definitive form.

Between the generation of the seventy-two translators and the NT era the vast Hellenized world was ethnically and culturally too diversified and too complex for any drastic pronunciation changes of Attic Greek (such as delineated above) to have been initiated, developed, and spread uniformly. Such changes naturally presuppose lengthy periods of time during which the first vowel of a diphthong, for instance, must have struggled to overtake the second vowel, while some plosive turned into a fricative earlier than other plosives, and so on. Had any such radical changes emerged and been established within the three-hundred-year time frame of the pre-NT Hellenistic period, by NT times there would have been multiple pronunciations of Κοινή at different stages of their development throughout the empire and with slurred changes and differences from region to region grave enough to inhibit the free flow of oral communication in Greek.

That was obviously not the case, for what we see instead speaks of a general uniformity in the pronunciation of the *lingua franca* throughout the Hellenized world. We see, for instance, Paul of Tarsus communicating uninhibitedly with Greek-speaking "Gentiles" in distant cities within the Roman Empire, including the city of Athens. It is in fact Paul's message to pronunciation-sensitive Athenians in AD 50 that speaks of an established general pronunciation of Κοινή in NT times. Paul was not Greek, yet to the Athenians he sounded like one of their own. No heckler ridiculed his pronunciation, no one complained about not being able to fully understand him. On the contrary, some became converts, including Dionysios the Areopagite, a member of the Areios Pagos court (Acts 17:34).

But the bigger linguistic picture is more than just the fact that Paul spoke Greek like an Athenian. It is a picture of the tenaciousness of the Attic Greek HGP, the force of the sound system that emanated from Athens until it prevailed over all other potential pronunciations of Greek in the Hellenized world. Let us then take a look at HGP's tenacity.

## 3.5 THE TENACITY OF THE HGP

Language change can occur in sundry ways and forms. It may encompass phonological but also grammatical, semantic, syntactical, morphological, lexical, orthographical, idiomatic, and other conventional changes. Neohellenic, the latest phase of Classical Attic, in addition to preserving the HGP, has preserved all the basic grammatical categories. This fact speaks of the tenacity of the Greek language and its resistance to change (1.9).

Today a number of scholars among those who are probably appreciably familiar with the phonological development of Κοινή (but perhaps unwilling to accept the verdict of the historical evidence that Κοινή is a continuation of Classical Greek) give the impression that Κοινή emerged virtually as a new language: "Just as a newborn baby does not immediately speak," says Wallace, "it took some time before Koine took shape."[8]

On the other hand, scholars unfamiliar with the historical development of the Greek pronunciation seem to be under the impression that the Greek language evolved in the same general way as the Germanic and Romance dialects, measuring in other words presumed changes simply by the yardstick of time. Fee and Strauss, for instance, claim: "For contemporary Israelis and Greeks reading the Bible in their original languages is like our reading the English of its earlier writers, such as the fourteenth-century Chaucer. We recognize many of the words, but many we do not, and the grammar is especially strange to our ears."[9]

**Of the 4900 words in the NT over 92% are either used or understood well today.**

It is not just words and grammar these scholars are alluding to but also to pronunciation, since the difference between Chaucer and Modern English unquestionably entails both. In any case, their claim is not valid as far as Greek is concerned. Compare their claim with another scholar's view, a view that bears repetition:

> Ancient Greek is not a foreign language to the Greek of today as Anglo-Saxon is to the modern Englishman. . . . Perhaps connected with this continuous identity over some three and a half millennia is the slowness of change in Greek. . . . Earlier stages of the language are thus accessible to speakers of later stages . . . [a] peculiar situation created by a long and continuous literary tradition which makes all elements of Greek from antiquity to the present day in a sense accessible and "present" to any literate Greek.[10]

Indeed, it is estimated that of the 6,844 Homeric words, about 53 percent were used in classical times, and over 30 percent are used in Neohellenic (not including words that have changed in meaning or spelling or are found in compound words). Also, of the 4,900 words in the NT (not counting inflected forms, which would bring the total to a much higher figure), over 92 percent are either spoken or understood well today.[11]

Thus the average Greek person today can read and understand many parts of the original Greek New Testament (e.g., nearly all parts of the gospels, John, and

8. Wallace, *Beyond Basics*, 18.

9. Fee, *Choose a Translation*, 20.

10. Browning, *Medieval and Modern Greek*, vii, 2–3, 13.

11. Percentages are based on figures given by Caragounis, *Development of Greek*, 85–86.

Revelation; most of Acts, Paul's writings, Peter, James, and Jude; and much of Hebrews), while only well-educated Greeks can understand the more literary parts in Hebrews, Paul's epistles, Acts, Peter, James, and Jude, the degree of comprehension depending on one's educational, occupational, and intellectual levels as well as exposure to and familiarity with the NT Scriptures.

But beyond this fact, the eyebrow-raising truth is that today a Greek person reading out aloud orthophonically a part of the original Greek New Testament would have been understood by its author; and Aristotle's writings, by Aristotle himself—all because of the tenacious, diachronically recognizable historical Greek sounds and the support they get from an equally tenacious historical alphabet and consistent post-Eucleidean orthography.

**"Modern Greek is closer to Ancient Greek than is any other Modern Language to an ancient predecessor of even a few centuries."**

The persistent qualities of the HGP tradition can be seen through a simple comparison of the changes English and Greek underwent in the past five centuries. Allen, for instance, describes the Great English Vowel Shift (in England),[12] a sound change in the English long vowels that had long-term implications on English spelling, reading, and the understanding of any English text written before or during the shift. It so happened that the process of this massive English change in the sixteenth century coincided with the effects Greek learning had in Renaissance Europe following the fall of Constantinople in 1453. Allen's discussion of the circumstances surrounding the Great English Vowel Shift is preceded by a list of the characteristic features of Greek around that time as follows:[13]

β, δ, γ (as well as φ, θ, χ) pronounced as fricatives;

ζ pronounced as a single sound [z];

κ, χ, γ, λ, ν palatalized before front vowels;

π, τ, κ voiced after nasals;

υ in αυ, ευ pronounced as [v] or [f];

αι pronounced as a monophthong [e];

and, above all, the single value [i] accorded to ι, η, υ, ει, οι, υι.

What Allen is coincidentally showing here is that, whereas English underwent profound pronunciation changes over the last five hundred years, the pronunciation of Greek during the same period has remained unchanged. This tenaciousness of the Greek pronunciation system speaks as well of the tenaciousness of the HGP five hundred years before the fall of Constantinople, the millennium before then, and the

12. Allen, *Vox Graeca*, 146.

13. Allen, *Vox Graeca*, 140. Here Allen's list is nearly complete and basically correct, except his across-the-board "rules" regarding palatalization do not particularly apply to λ and ν (e.g., βασιλεία [vasilia] *kingdom*, κοινωνία [kinonia] *communion*). Palatalized λ and ν in such examples is considered substandard pronunciation (see 8.10, fn.). For the voiceness of π, τ, κ after nasals, see 2.12; 8.8.

three pre-Christian Hellenistic centuries leading back to Alexander and Aristotle's day. As Brown points out:

> Our much vaunted Erasmian, or so-called ancient, pronunciation of Greek [cf. 5.2] is partly to blame for the misconception that Modern Greek is entirely different from Ancient [Greek] . . . Modern Greek is closer to Ancient Greek than is any other Modern Language to an ancient predecessor of even a few centuries.[14]

Within the context of linguistic change alluded to earlier in this section, it may be parenthetically noted here that English phonology, with a comparatively high number of vocalic and consonantal phonemes (about twice the number of Greek phonemes), is more prone to change and to variations in pronunciation than Greek. In contrast, Greek phonology, with only five vocalic and fifteen consonantal phonemes, and aided by a centuries-old writing and spelling system, is a key contributor to the tenacity and preservation of the historical Greek sounds. (For a comparison of the Greek and English phonemes, see 5.4.)

## 3.6 "MODERN GREEK PRONUNCIATION" A MISNOMER

The pronunciation characteristics of Neohellenic coincide with the emergence of the HGP from the beginning of the inscriptional period around 600 BC. Thus no part of the phonemic sounds of Neohellenic is "modern." Such a label implies a new pronunciation, one developed in recent times, whether naturally evolved or artificially concocted. The phonemic sounds of Greek are historical, ancient. They are of a pronunciation formed naturally by the people of ancient Greece, especially the Athenians. That is why it is called *historical*.[15] There may well have been variations in the HGP among ancient speakers—variations exist today, too; not all Greeks, for example, share the same intonational patterns. Since we have no recordings from ancient Athenian authors, we do not know their exact intonation, thus we will never know exactly how they sounded, whether in daily conversation or in artistic expression. However, we do know what values they assigned to the alphabet letters and digraphs. And there is no evidence since mid-classical times (403 BC) that there has ever been a separation between the Attic Greek alphabet and the HGP sounds it supports. From the beginning both looked forward, and within a few decades later (from 334 BC on) they began to spread and become common throughout Alexander's Hellenized world. By NT times all the characteristics of the HGP in the established Κοινή are reflected in Neohellenic. And that is what proves that Neohellenic continues that HGP tradition

14. Brown, *Classical Weekly*, 84.

15. *Historical* characterizes the nature and diachronic applicability of the Greek phonemes from classical times to the present, including the traditional value assigned to the historical alphabet letters and digraphs.

of almost twenty-five hundred years. In that sense, then, i.e., for purely factual and scientific reasons, we cannot speak of a "Modern Greek pronunciation" (1.2).

## 3.7 APPLYING THE HGP TO NT GREEK

Pronunciation in a broad sense consists of pitch, juncture, rhythm, length, and voice quality, all features of oral communication. In a narrow sense, and as already seen, pronunciation is the orthophonic articulation of an isolated sound segment, syllable, or word (1.13). The significance of the latter is twofold: (a) it is possible for the learner of NT Greek not familiar with Neohellenic to practice applying the HGP orthophonically to NT Greek words or phrases and progressively to strings of words and sentences; and (b) the learner's pronunciation will sound intelligible from the very start, not just to an instructor and perhaps a handful of classmates, but universally to millions of speakers of Greek and to those who likewise apply the HGP. And as is the case with learning the pronunciation of any language, the HGP cannot be learned from charts and tables; it is learned from native speakers and those who sound like them (7.5).[16]

Of course it is not solely the application of the HGP to NT Greek that we should be concerned about, but how the HGP can help in viewing the Greek language as a whole. "If the language is approached as a unity and with the right pronunciation," says Caragounis, "then it will certainly be realized that a greater portion of Greek is necessary . . . for an exodus from the restricted area of the NT into the panoramic vistas of the Greek language and its literature."[17]

For those to whom the thought of trying the HGP plucks a string of concern, here are words of assurance:

> "There are a number of advantages associated with the historical Greek pronunciation system," says McLean, whose work on NT Greek grammar signals a growing HGP presence in the classroom. "In contrast to the Erasmian system, . . . [it] is a *real, euphonic* system . . . [and] not very difficult because it is *entirely regular*."[18]

## 3.8 TESTIMONIALS

Below are sample testimonials of individuals who switched to the HGP.

> As I studied Scripture as a young man, I became aware of the need to adhere faithfully to the biblical text. At Moody Bible Institute back in the 1950s, I was introduced to Greek in the classroom of Kenneth Wuest where we learned the Erasmian pronunciation. This was all I knew about the pronunciation of

16. For the HGP sounds, see 5.4.
17. Caragounis, *Development of Greek*, 582.
18. McLean, *New Testament Greek*, 4–5.

Greek and used it for many years, until I discovered Dr. Zachariou's work on the historical development of the Greek language. So I decided to make the switch to the historical pronunciation. I must say that the switch wasn't too difficult. After about six months, I even began thinking in the historical pronunciation as I spent time each day reading the Greek text. Now I read the text with no trouble.

—Dr. Taylor Williams, Schertz, Texas

One of the requirements for the Greek component of my studies at Christian college here in New Zealand was to attend a reading group with our professor of Greek. This was the first time I read Greek out aloud with the modern pronunciation, which I learned from Philemon Zachariou. Upon hearing me read, my Erasmian-trained professor said, "Wow, that's better [Greek] than mine!" When it was my turn again, he said, "Okay, Jim, let's hear some more of that beautiful Greek of yours."

—Jim Kerr, Aukland, New Zealand

I have started to read your book. It is excellent. I am hoping with resources such as what you provide, as well as computer technology as the enabling foundation, I will be able to achieve fluency in Greek and be able to read the New Testament as well as various ancient authors.

—Donald D. Derkacht, Toledo, Washington

I have learned a lot from [your work]. Of great value is the fact that New Testament Greek is not treated as a dead language or one that survives only in the New Testament and the classical writings but as a living language, with most New Testament words being used or understood in Modern Greek today. I also found it helpful to know that New Testament and Modern Greek share many similarities not only in terms of pronunciation alone, but also in terms of vocabulary, syntax, morphology, and general grammar.

—Jordan Rabideau, Ontario, Canada

When a Greek friend of mine made me aware that my Erasmian pronunciation of Greek sounded "funny," I realized that I pronounced Greek the wrong way. So I decided to learn the Modern Greek pronunciation. I found the switch to be not too difficult and Zachariou's material helpful in making the switch. Through communication with him, I now also understand that "modern" does not mean that today's Greek sounds are not historical.

—Roland Floyd, Tallahassee, Florida

Here's why I find Phil Zachariou's work [on the HGP] so important. When you read an ancient text in the mnemonic style of an author writing for an oral audience, and you do so in the pronunciation peculiar to the time, you can actually find yourself "in the head" of that author. I first felt this years ago while reading Paul's "love song" in 1 Corinthians 13:1–13. This cannot happen if you voice it in your head to a phonemic scheme invented as a joke on Erasmus by Henricus, which has become a joke on Greek scholarship for over 480 years. Zachariou is not just teaching Greek phonology: he is introducing students to Paul of Tarsus, Mark, Luke, John of Ephesus—some for the fist time.

—Jack Kilmon, Houston, Texas

I highly recommend Dr. Zachariou and his book, *Reading and Pronouncing Biblical Greek*. His book is easy to read and understand. The material is presented in an interesting, even an entertaining, manner. If you are even mildly interested in the history of the Greek language, read this book.

—Robert E. Smith, La Puente, California

PART TWO

# The Erasmian Influence

# Chapter 4

# Origins and Nature of the Erasmian Pronunciation

## 4.1 ORIGINS OF THE ERASMIAN PRONUNCIATION

After the fall of Constantinople in 1453, many Byzantine scholars emigrated and settled in Europe, particularly in Italy, bringing with them invaluable knowledge and treasured texts of Greek learning. These scholars taught Greek at various universities in Italy and other parts of Europe according to the historical sounds preserved in Greek speech in Byzantium for well over a millennium—in fact, since Hellenistic times. Their advent in Italy helped initiate the Renaissance there, and their teaching expanded Greek learning and the study of Classical Greek throughout Europe. Learners of Greek such as Johannes Reuchlin (1455–1522), a German scholar, studied Greek under Byzantine scholars and passed on the Byzantine pronunciation of Κοινή to much of Western Europe.

In Reuchlin's day, certain eminent scholars (Jerome Aleander in France, Aldus Manutius in Italy, and Antonio of Lebrixa in Spain) postulated that the Byzantine scholars did not use the Ancient Greek pronunciation because they mispronounced the vowels and diphthongs and sacrificed vowel quantity to accent.[1] Additionally, they did not use aspiration, nor did they transliterate or pronounce certain Greek letters according to their Latin counterparts.[2] These men shared their ideas about the pronunciation of the Byzantines with Desiderius Erasmus of Rotterdam, a learned and influential Dutch scholar at the forefront of his age.[3]

1. Bywater, *Erasmian Pronunciation*, 12.

2. Jannaris, *Historical Greek Grammar*, 31.

3. Born Geert Geerts (also known as Gerhard Gerhards), Desiderius Erasmus (1466–1536) was born in Rotterdam, Burgundian Netherlands. He was a Dutch Renaissance humanist, Roman Catholic priest, theologian, social critic, and teacher. He studied at the university of Paris. His adopted Latinized Greek name *Erasmus* (from ἐράσμιος "desirable") is more accurately rendered *Erasmius.*

In 1528 Erasmus, at the suggestion of the illustrious Swiss scholar Henricus Glareanus, and eager to be credited with a novelty, published a work titled *De Recta Latini Graecique Sermonis Pronuntiatione Dialogus* (Basel, Switzerland), a literary squib in the form of a dialogue between a lion and a bear. Erasmus' satire introduced a customized, non-Byzantine pronunciation of Ancient Greek, though allegedly Erasmus himself did not use the pronunciation named after him nor did he propound its application—ironically, he continued the Byzantine pronunciation to the end of his life.[4] However, his publication, used by future scholars as the authority for linguistic innovation, tied a deviant academic knot around the pronunciation of Greek, inadvertently creating a problem that has been knotty ever since.

While the Greeks were engaged in a life-and-death struggle against their Turkish oppressors[5] and therefore no national Greek voice could be heard in defense of the language of Ἑλλάς (Greece), an intellectual battle erupted among non-Greek scholars in Europe to essentially determine the fate of the Greek language as if at the toss of a die. In 1542 Stephen Gardiner (1493–1555), Bishop of Winchester and Chancellor of the University of Cambridge, issued a decree in which the Erasmian pronunciation was interdicted. "A professor who should teach the system was to lose his chair; a candidate who favored it was to be excluded from all academic degrees; and a student who used it was to be banished from the school."[6] Gardiner categorically forbade distinguishing the pronunciation of αι and ε, and of ει, οι and ι under penalty of expulsion from the Senate, exclusion from the attainment of a degree, rustication for students, and domestic chastisement for boys.[7] Though the continental pronunciation of Ancient Greek was "Erasmian," at Cambridge and Oxford the "Reuchlinian" (i.e., Byzantine) prevailed.[8]

Meanwhile, the growing presence of Byzantine scholarship in Europe carried political undertones that evoked centuries-old antagonistic threats exchanged between the (Western) Catholic Church and the Byzantine (Eastern) Orthodox Church, which the Catholics considered heretical. Erasmus, Europe's most influential humanist, could undoubtedly help turn the tide. The goal now was to steal away the New and Old Testaments from Orthodox scholarship under the pretense that the Orthodox Church must have transmogrified the true Greek language, and it would therefore be an unprincipled practice to follow the "degenerated" pronunciation (*pronuntiatio depravata*) of Byzantine Greek.[9]

4. Jannaris, *Historical Greek Grammar*, 32.

5. Constantinople fell into Turkish hands in 1453. The Turkish occupation of Greece lasted for four hundred years.

6. Scomp, *Manual of Romaic*, 9.

7. Blass, *Ancient Greek*, 3.

8. Robertson, *Grammar of the Greek New Testament*, 237.

9. Angelopoulos, "Sound of Greek."

The Reuchlinians, galled by the taunts of the Erasmians, amassed historical proofs in support of their position. But those in favor of the genuine Greek pronunciation were no match for the authority of the Dutch scholar whose influence and success was shown by the many reprints of his *Dialogus* that issued from the presses of France and Germany.[10] By now Erasmus' influence had spread even to Cambridge, where Sir John Cheke (1514–1557) and Sir Thomas Smith (1513–1577), having confronted Gardiner, introduced an Erasmian-like pronunciation there. It was tacitly assumed, after all, that because of the Turkish occupation of Greece, the pronunciation of Greek was of no very great importance since it was that of a language that was clearly moribund.

The heroic struggle of the Greeks to throw off the Turkish yoke (1821–27) rekindled scholarly interest in the Greek language. But by then the Erasmian pronunciation was deeply ingrained into the European academic fiber. Besides, a circumstance favorable to the growth of the Erasmian pronunciation was that it agreed very much with the sound system of German, so Erasmian ultimately became widely accepted (Germanized) among the Germans.[11] Following is a glance at what lies at the foundation of this customized pronunciation of Ancient Greek.

## 4.2 LATIN TRANSLITERATION OF GREEK

The pronunciation of Ancient Greek in the manner of Neohellenic had been accepted prior to and through Byzantine times as a matter of incontestable fact. Objections to it were first raised by Renaissance scholars, chiefly Erasmus, who noted its incongruity with the pronunciation of Latin, the then academic language of Europe. It must be borne in mind that by Erasmus' time Latin had long metamorphosed into several European languages; therefore, Latin's questionable pronunciation in Erasmus' time could not be relied upon as a guide for the pronunciation of Greek. Shown below are some of the types of concerns one would encounter in converting Greek letters into Latin and vice versa.

a. Latin adopted the Chalcidic Greek alphabet (7th c. BC), but its letters were not necessarily assigned one by one the phonetic value of Greek counterparts. This accounts in part for earlier and later variations in the Latin transliteration of Greek.

b. Latin transliteration both of η and ε as *e* does not mean that η and ε are the same sound any more than the *i* in *Virgilius* and the *e* in *Vergilius*. Because Latin already used Chalcidic H, which was familiar to Romans as *h*, it could not invent a special symbol for the H(η) vowel which Attic adopted, the more so as this symbol shifted among the Greeks themselves. Latin continued to adhere to the old familiar use of E, which prior to mid-5th c. BC stood for Attic [e] and [i]

10. Bywater, *Erasmian Pronunciation*, 7.

11. Scomp, *Manual of Romaic*, 8.

sounds (2.17, A13). Thus ζωή is rendered *zoe* and ἀγάπη *agape*, where *e* leads to the mispronunciation of η as [e]—or even to diphthongized "long" *ay* [eˈ]!

c. Latin transcribed initial E(ε) as E (Ephesus, Europe), but "aspirated E" (whether E = ε or E = η) as HE (Ἕλληνες > HEllenes, Ἡρόδοτος > HErodotus).

d. Digraph αι was originally AE(αε) (2.14), hence Latin Æ(æ) [e] as in *Caesar* [kesar]. Erasmian sees αι as [aˈ], mispronouncing the name Καίσαρ as [kaˈzər]. Spanish *e* in *Cesar* [sesar] adheres to original [e] in Καίσαρ [kesar].

e. After the 2nd c. BC, Latin OI(oi) for OI(οι), probably influenced by *ae*, changed to OE(œ). The *oe* = [i] in *Phoenix* [finɪx], *Phoebe* [fibɪ], *amoeba* [əmibə], *oedema* [ɪdimə], from Φοίνιξ, Φοίβη, ἀμοιβάς, οἴδημα shows the retention in English of the sound of OI(οι) as [i], while the οι of Κοινή as [ɔˈ] betrays Erasmian.

f. Latin rendered ου as *u*, but ος as *us* rather than *os* (Cratylus for Κρατύλος). Pre-Eucleidean O = [o] or [u] (2.17), e.g., Νεοκλέος = Νεοκλέους, thus Latin converted both -ος and -ους to its name-ending suffix *-us*.

g. After Attic replaced ΠΗ, ΤΗ, ΚΗ with the Greek-invented letters Φ, Θ, Χ, Latin switched from the use of PH for Φ to F, but for Θ and X it continued to use TH and CH respectively, because it had no equivalents for the monoliteral fricatives Θ, X (2.10). But under Erasmian influence, F for Φ (*fantastic*) gave way to PH (*phantom*).

h. Around the time of Julius Ceasar (1st c. BC), Latin reintroduced Z and adopted Y to represent Greek words and loanwords containing them. To differentiate between I and Greek-invented Y, the Romans named Y *i Graeca* "Greek [i]"—not [ü]!—a name still used among Romance languages today; for at the time of its adoption into Latin, Υ(υ) had long been confused with I(ι), e.g., CIGNVS *cignus* for κύκνος.[12] At the time Latin reintroduced Greek Z into its alphabet, it already had the sound [z], for which it used *s* or *ss*. Latin borrowed Z, the Greek equivalent of Latin [z], not because it needed to adopt a new sound but because it used Greek words containing Z.[13]

## 4.3 ERASMIAN "CLASSICAL GREEK" SOUNDS APPLIED TO BIBLICAL GREEK

Below is a list of the Attic Greek letters and digraphs which Erasmians dispute yet apply to Biblical and Classical Greek alike. Because α, ε, ι, ου, κ, λ, μ, ν, ξ, π, ρ, σ/ς, τ, ψ, γγ, γκ, γξ are usually not in dispute, they are not included here. For γχ, see γ and χ.

12. Lindsay, *Latin Language*, 36.

13. "There is no doubt that this was the pronunciation of ζ at the time when z was introduced into the [Latin] alphabet." Hahn, "Quintilian on Greek Letters." (See also 2.20.)

| Greek letters | "Standard" Erasmian pronunciation | Greek pronunciation | Difference seen in IPA: Erasmian | Greek |
|---|---|---|---|---|
| η | obey | feet | [eˈ] | [i] |
| ο | not | for | [ɔ] | [o] |
| ω | tone | for | [oᶷ] | [o][14] |
| υ | German ü, French u | feet | [u] | [i] |
| υι | suite | feet | [ui] | [i] |
| οι | oil | feet | [ɔˈ] | [i] |
| αι | aisle | end | [aˈ] | [e] |
| ει | eight | feet | [eˈ] | [i] |
| αυ | sauerkraut | bravo/pilaf | [aᶷ] | [av]/[af] |
| ευ | feud | ever/effort | [ju] | [ev]/[ef] |
| ηυ | feud | evil/reef | [ju] | [iv]/[if] |
| β | b (stop) | very (continuant) | [b] | [v] |
| δ | d (stop) | that (continuant) | [d] | [ð] |
| γ | g (stop) | γ (continuant) | [g] | [ɣ] |
| φ | ph (aspirated stop) | far (continuant) | [ph] | [f] |
| θ | th (aspirated stop) | thin (continuant) | [th] | [θ] |
| χ | kh (aspirated stop) | χ (continuant) | [kʰ] | [x] |
| ζ | zd/dz (affricate stop) | daze (continuant) | [zd]/[dz] | [z] |
| ( ʽ ) aspiration | h | — | [h] | — |

## 4.4 ERASMIAN INCONSISTENCIES

The above table shows the main differences between the two pronunciation systems, Erasmian and Greek. Of the total of thirty-four single letters, digraphs, and one breath mark, at least nineteen (listed above) are in dispute, a deviation of nearly 56 percent from the Greek norm. In addition, inconsistencies are noted in the pronunciation of Erasmian from speaker to speaker. For instance, ζ is pronounced [dz] as in *adz* by Black,[15] but [z] as in *daze* by Mounce[16] and [zd] as in *wisdom* by Allen;[17] υ is pronounced [u] as in *boot* or as the German ü by Black, [ju] as in *universe* (also [ʊ] as in *book* or as the German ü by Mounce,[18] or even [ʌ] as in *hut* by Drumwright;[19] ει is pronounced [eˈ] as in *eight* by Mounce and Stevens,[20] but [i] as in *seize* by Rife[21] and

14. Greek ο and ω are pronounced alike as [o] and are distinct from English [oᶷ]. Porter is incorrect in saying that in Modern Greek these are pronounced as the *o* in *go* [goᶷ]. Porter et al., *Fundamentals*, 2.

15. Black, *Linguistics*, 33–37.

16. Mounce, *Basics of Biblical Greek*, 8–10.

17. Allen, *Vox Graeca*, 177.

18. Mounce, *Basics of Biblical Greek*, 9.

19. Drumwright, *Introduction*, 10.

20. Stevens, *New Testament Greek*, 4.

21. Rife, *Beginning Greek*, 2.

[aᴵ] as in *height* by Summers;[22] ευ is pronounced ε+ου [eu] by Rife, but [ju] as in *feud* by Black and Mounce; ηυ is pronounced [eu] (as in *care+soup* or *met+moon*) by Rife and Smyth,[23] but [ju] as in *feud* by Black and Mounce, neither of whom differentiates between the pronunciation of ευ and ηυ; η and ει are pronounced alike as [eᴵ] (*late*) by Paine, Mounce, and others, while η is correctly pronounced [i] as in *deep* by Jay.[24] Dobson, on the other hand, gives two pronunciations for η: "ai" as in *air*, and "ay" as in *say*[25] but with no explanation as to which to use when, while Allen treats it as a long ε. White suggests [aᵁ] as in *hour* for αυ,[26] but Green and Harkness, like Moulton, apparently by association with English spelling, suggest [ɔ] as in *naught*. Furthermore, they suggest [waᴵ] as in *wine* for υι (but [wi] as in *suite*, [wɪ] as in *quit*, or [u:ɪ] as in *ruin* by others); and, surprisingly, [aᵁ] as in *out* (the same as the αυ by White) for the normally undisputed ου [u].[27] Some consider "long" α to be the *a* in *late* (in which case α and η are the same as ει), but for Goodwin, Smyth, and others it is the [ɑ] in *father*—which is "short" for others. Allen, on the other hand, pronounces α [ʌ] as in *cup* if short—the same as the pronunciation of υ by other speakers, as noted—but [ɑ] as in *father* (though [æ] as in *pass* by Jay) when long.[28] Most scholars pronounce "short" omicron ο [ɑ] as in *cot* (the same as α by Smyth), but Balme and Lawall pronounce it [ʌ] as in *but*,[29] the same as the α by Allen or υ by others, while Thornhill pronounces it [oᵁ] as in *oval*, with an alternative pronunciation of [ɑ] as in *hot*;[30] and "long" omega ω [oᵁ] as in *tone*, except some, like Allen, who pronounces ω [ɔ] as in *saw*,[31] the same as Green's αυ (above). As for ι, it is pronounced by some [ɪ] as in *pit* when "short,"[32] but [i] as in *ski* when "long," while Jay treats it as the *i* [aᴵ] in *pile* when "long."[33] Nondistinction of οι ~ οϊ, αι ~ αϊ, αυ ~ αϋ by Erasmian adherents betrays Erasmic mishandling of οι, αι, αυ. With regard to ψ, χ, θ, Mounce says that "technically [they] are not stops but . . . it is easier to view them as stops."[34] This designation is an arbitrary misnomer, for ψ is stop π + continuant σ; and χ and θ are not stops but continuants.[35]

22. Summers, *Essentials of New Testament Greek*, 1–3.

23. Smyth, *Greek Grammar for Colleges*, 13.

24. Jay, *Introductory Grammar*, 4.

25. Dobson, *Learn New Testament Greek*, 1.

26. White, *First Greek Book*, 3.

27. Samuel Green, *Brief Introduction*, 10.

28. Allen, *Vox Graeca*, 179.

29. Balme, *Athenaze*, xii.

30. Thornhill, *Greek for Everyone*, 5.

31. Allen, *Vox Graeca*, 63, 177

32. Argyle, *Introductory Grammar*, 1.

33. Jay, *Introductory Grammar*, 4.

34. Mounce, *Basics of Biblical Greek*, 83.

35. Most authors treat α, η, ω and ᾳ, ῃ, ῳ alike. Stevens transliterates α = a, η = e, ω = o, ᾳ = āi, ῃ = ēi, ῳ = ōi (Stevens, *New Testament Greek*, 11). This obviously leads to a spelling pronunciation that confuses ᾳ with αι, ῃ with ει, ῳ with οι.

## 4.5 CUSTOMIZED PRONUNCIATIONS OF GREEK

The table below summarizes pronunciation inconsistencies of NT Greek among various authors, none of which reflects the undisputed evidence of iotacization or fricativization. The table shows that within this hodgepodge of arbitrary pronunciation styles the letter ι (*pile*) for one author is αι (*aisle*) or ει (*height*) for another, or that one's α (*cup*) is another's υ (*nut*) or ο (*but*), or one's η (*fate*) is another's α (*hate*) or ει (*weight*), or one's αυ (*out*) is another's ου (*count*), or one's ω (*broad*) is another's αυ (*naught*); and that individual letters are pronounced differently by different authors—e.g., α, like υι, is pronounced four different ways.

**"No one is consistent in the use of the theoretical pronunciation."**

### 4.5.1 Summary of Erasmian Pronunciation Inconsistencies

| Greek letter(s) | Pronunciation examples | | | | # of ways |
|---|---|---|---|---|---|
| α | hat | hate [1] | father | cup [2] | 4 |
| η | hair | fate [1] | deep [3] | | 3 |
| ι | hit | keen [3] | pile [4] | | 3 |
| υ | nut [2] | goose [5] | put | | 3 |
| ο | cot | but [2] | | | 2 |
| ω | note | broad [6] | | | 2 |
| αι | aisle [4] | | | | 1 |
| αυ | out [7] | naught [6] | | | 2 |
| ει | weight [1] | seize [3] | height [4] | | 3 |
| ευ | feud [8] | get+wet | | | 2 |
| ηυ | feud [8] | fate+food | | | 2 |
| ου | food [5] | count [7] | | | 2 |
| υι | we | wine | quit | ruin | 4 |
| ζ | daze | wisdom | adz | | 3 |
| 14 | | | | | 36 |

| Pronounced alike | | |
|---|---|---|
| [1] α | η | ει |
| [2] α | υ | ο |
| [3] η | ι | ει |
| [4] ι | αι | ει |
| [5] υ | ου | |
| [6] ω | αυ | |
| [7] αυ | ου | |
| [8] ευ | ηυ | |

Results vary depending on authors compared

Transmission of inconsistencies is ongoing. Says Jay, "In England several different systems of pronouncing the vowels and diphthongs are in use. The student will do well to follow the guidance of his teacher."[36] "The instructor's pronunciation . . . should be imitated," echoes Goethius.[37] Conversely, Buth places the onus of choice on the student by suggesting a menu of pronunciations including his own customized "imperial" version.[38] Rife admits that "no one is consistent in the use of the theoretical pronunciation,"[39] while Moulton's audacious admission that the pronunciation is "based on the treatment of Greek words as if they were English"(!) comes also with the caveat: "Hardly any of these pronunciations are even nearly right."[40] "Personally I

36. Jay, *Introductory Grammar*, 4.
37. Goethius, *Language of New Testament*, 7.
38. Buth, "Koine Pronunciation."
39. Rife, *Beginning Greek Book*, 138.
40. Moulton, *Introduction to New Testament Greek*, 11.

use . . . [an Erasmian] system," admits Decker, "freely acknowledging that it is not an accurate representation of exactly what Jesus and Paul sounded like when they spoke Greek."[41] Does admission right the wrong?

Such inconsistencies would not be present if the phonology of Greek were followed. Greek does not support the English [i]~[ɪ] (*feet/fit*) or [oʊ]~[ɑ] (*note/not*) distinction, nor the environmentally-determined phonetic difference between long and short vowel sounds (*bead/beat, had/hat*) (8.3), nor the long-short phonemic distinction as in Latin *mālum* [ma:lum] "apple" and *malum* [malum] "bad": for all Greek vowels are isochronous (equally-timed); and Greek has no diphthongs, only digraphs.

## 4.6 MISPRONUNCIATION COMPOUNDED BY TRANSLITERATION

A key contributor to the mispronunciation of Greek is the Erasmian rendering of υ [i] as *u* [u]. The word ψυχή *soul*, for instance, in Erasmian is *psuche*. Additionally, because English drops the initial *p* of words beginning with *ps*, *psuche* is pronounced "Sue-Kay," while the traditionist rendition *psyche* in *Merriam-Webster's Dictionary* leads to the pronunciation "sigh-key." Either pronunciation is a far cry from Greek [psihí].[42] The transliteration of υ as *u* reflects in part the tremendous influence Erasmian has exerted on English borrowings from Greek since the fourteenth century.

The sample list below compares the Erasmian and the traditionist method of transliterating Greek words that contain υ or ευ. The English rendering of υ properly as *y* (*hymn*) and of ευ properly as *ev* (*evangel*) generally indicates a loanword's entry into English prior to the beginning of the Erasmian influence in the 1520s. This probably set a precedent for later lexical borrowings or hybrids in which υ = *y* (ἀνάλυσις *analysis*, διάλυσις *dialysis*, πολύγραφος *polygraph*), with *y* being closer to the Greek ι-sound υ. Apparently ευ came under direct Erasmian influence as indicated by its transliteration as *eu* in numerous Greek loanwords in English, including later entries (πνευμονία *pneumonia*, εὐφορικός *euphoric*, νεύρωσις *neurosis*), with ευ seen as *ev* chiefly in older borrowings such as *evangelize*, *evangelist*, and a few other cognates.

41. Decker, *Reading Koine*, xxi.

42. It must be strongly pointed out that the traditionist spelling and pronunciation of Greek loanwords in English is of no consequence in this study whatsoever, for that is the way native speakers of English learn those loanwords "naturally" as part of their mother tongue.

| Greek word | Erasmian transliteration | Traditionist transliteration and first use in English[43] |
|---|---|---|
| εὐχαριστία | eucharistia | Eucharist (14th c.) |
| πνεῦμα | pneuma | cf. pneumonia (1603) |
| εὕρηκα | heureka (with aspiration) | eureka (no aspiration) (1603) |
| εὐαγγέλιον | euangelion | evangel (14th c.) |
| ὑποκριτής | hupokrites | hypocrite (13th c.) |
| φυσικός | phusikos | physical (1580) |
| δύναμις | dunamis | cf. dynamic (1827) |
| ἀποκάλυψις | apokalupsis | apocalypse (13th c.) |
| ὕμνος | humnos | hymn (12th c.) |

## 4.7 THE CONSISTENCY OF GREEK

The table below shows that there is absolute consistency in the way the Greek vowels, vowel digraphs, and consonants are pronounced:

| | |
|---|---|
| ι, η, υ, ει, οι, υι | are always [i] and there is no short-long distinction in pronunciation[44] |
| αι, ε | are always [e] and there is no short-long distinction in pronunciation |
| ο, ω, ῳ | are always [o] and there is no short-long distinction in pronunciation |
| α, ᾳ | is always [ɑ] and there is no short-long distinction in pronunciation |
| ου | is always [u] and there is no short-long distinction in pronunciation |
| υ of αυ, ευ, ηυ | is always [v] before voiced sounds and [f] before voiceless sounds or at the end of words |

The distinction of οι ~ οϊ, αι ~ αϊ, αυ ~ αϋ by the use of dieresis ( ¨ ) is consistent.
The sound of each consonant **β γ δ ζ θ κ λ μ ω ξ π ρ σ ς τ φ χ ψ** is consistent.
Allophonic γ as [ŋ] in γγ γκ γχ γξ is consistent.

## 4.8 CONCLUSION

Erasmus' unprecedented pronunciation of Greek was founded on a mix of ignorance and circumstance: the Greek language was defenseless, the ancient stones were mute, the papyrical evidence remained buried, and Byzantine Orthodox scholarship was viewed by the Catholics as a political threat.

Thrown into the mix was the right bonding agent: personal gain. Regardless of whether Erasmus was induced into publishing his volatile *Dialogus*, the fact remains that he did nothing to defend the pronunciation of the language he had studied under Byzantine scholars—and which he allegedly applied the rest of his life[45]—thereby allowing his infamous novelty to crystallize his self-proclaimed authority on Greek.

43. Morris, *American Heritage Dictionary*.

44. Vowel length in speech is arbitrary and depends on one's own intonational patterns. However, all vowels or syllables pronounced orthophonically (in isolation) are isochronous "of equal length" (1.13).

45. In a letter to Johannes Lascaris in 1518 in connection with the appointment of an instructor of

In a similar vein of personal pursuit the defiant confrontation of John Cheke and Thomas Smith with Stephen Gardiner at Cambridge was hardly over the correct pronunciation of Greek. Since then, Greek has been kept at bay by generations of Chekes and Smiths who safeguard the preservation of an unrestricted, accountability-free comfort zone among Erasmian associates and peers (7.5). This scenario is bluntly summed up in Scomp's words:

> [The Erasmian pronunciation] is rather an attempt of a theory to maintain itself in defiance of the actual pronunciation daily used by a great people.[46]

## 4.9 ADDENDUM: GENESIS OF THE ERASMIAN DOCTRINE

The following account, deemed necessary for a clearer understanding of the events and circumstances that gave rise to the Erasmian pronunciation of Greek, is taken in its entirety from Jannaris' work, pp. 31–32.

> The Erasmian pronunciation was not propounded but tentatively suggested by Erasmus in a dialogue between a bear and a lion, entitled *De Recta Latini Graecique sermonis pronuntiatione*, published first at Basle (also Paris) in 1528, and the origin of the doctrine receives a curious illustration in the account given by Gerald Jan Voss (or "Vossius" 1577–1649), a leading Dutch professor and zealous promoter of Erasmianism. In his *Aristarchus sive de Grammatica* (Amsterdam, 1635), this earnest scholar explains how Erasmus came to write his now famous dialogue (*quo modo Erasmus scripærit dialogum de recta pronuntiatione*) by the following narrative:
>
>> I believe that it is known to few in what circumstances Erasmus was induced to write on the correct pronunciation. Therefore I have deemed it best to subjoin the account which I possess written, some time ago, on a piece of paper by the hand of Henricus Coracopetræus, a most learned man and well known to scholars. It reads as follows:—
>>
>> "I have heard M. Rutgerus Reschius, who was professor of Greek in the Busleidan (Buslidiano) College at Louvain, and my preceptor of severed memory, relate, that he was in the Liliensian School for about two years at the same time as Erasmus, who occupied an upper room, while he had a lower one; that Henry Glareanus [Henricus Loritus, a Swiss scholar, born at Glarus (1488–1563), whence his surname Glareanus], having arrived at Louvain from Paris, was invited by Erasmus to dine at the College; and on being asked what news he brought with him, he said—which was a story he had made up on the journey, inasmuch as he knew Erasmus to be

Greek at a new college at the University of Louvrain, Erasmus wrote: "My advice has always been that we should secure a native Greek, from whom his audience could acquire the true pronunciation of Greek at first hand. . . . Louvrain, morrow of St Mark 1518." Mynors, *Correspondence of Erasmus*, 414.

46. Scomp, *Manual of Romaic*, 11.

inordinately fond of novelties and wondrously credulous—that some native Greeks had arrived in Paris, men of marvellous [*sic*] learning, who made use of a pronunciation of the Greek tongue entirely different from that generally received in these parts; for instance, they called β, instead of *Vita*, Beta, and η, instead of *Ita*, Eta; αι, instead of œ, ai; οι, instead of *i*, oi; and so on; that on hearing this Erasmus wrote soon afterwards the *Dialogue* on the right pronunciation of the Latin and Greek tongues, *in order to appear himself the inventor of the matter* (ut videretur huius rei ipse inventor), and offered it to the printer, Peter of Alost, for printing; but, as the printer declined, either because he was engaged in other work, or at any rate because he said he was not able to produce it as soon as was desired, Erasmus sent the treatise to Froben of Basle, by whom it was immediately printed and published. Erasmus, however, having found out the trick (practiced upon him), never afterwards used that method of pronouncing, nor did he direct those of his friends, with whom he was more familiar, to follow it. In proof of this M. Rutgerus used to show a scheme (*formulam*) of pronunciation written by the hand of Erasmus himself—a copy of which is still in my [Voss's] possession—for the use of Damian de Goes, a Spaniard, which in no way differed from that which learned and unlearned use everywhere for that language.

"(Signed) Henricus Coracopetræus Cuccensis [Henrik Ravensberg van Kuik] Neomagi [Nijmegen] 1569, the eve of St. Simon and St. Jude [27th of October]."

This incident then explains on the one hand why Erasmus did not treat the subject in a direct and earnest manner, but put the discussion into the mouth of animals, and on the other accounts for the fact that he continued to abide by the traditional (or Modern Greek) pronunciation of Greek to the end of his life. The whole thing bearing on the genesis and history of the Erasmian doctrine is ably and lucidly set forth by JGennadios in the *Nineteenth Century* (vol. xxxviii f.), to whom I am indebted for the above extract.

# Chapter 5

# Erasmian Misconceptions

## 5.1 TWO MISCONCEPTIONS ABOUT NEOHELLENIC

Before and nearly throughout the medieval period, the pronunciation of Ancient Greek in the manner Greeks had traditionally pronounced their language was never a questionable issue. The first objections to it were raised early in the fifteenth century by a handful of non-Greek European scholars. One of their objections was that the Byzantines pronounced certain letters alike: η, υ, ει, οι, υι = ι; αι = ε; ο = ω, a far cry, that is, from the way these letters were supposedly pronounced in ancient times. For five hundred years now Erasmian scholars have viewed the Byzantine pronunciation of these letters as a modern development. But while many Erasmian scholars today would probably concede that NT Greek sounded much like Neohellenic, they paradoxically continue to apply to NT Greek what they claim to have been the pronunciation of Classical Greek, arguing at the same time that the Modern Greek method poses pedagogical difficulties. Another argument Erasmians raise is that Modern Greek and NT Greek words are dissimilar, so Neohellenic offers no help in learning NT words. This chapter shows that these two arguments are misconceptions.

## 5.2 MISCONCEPTION #1—DIFFICULT PRONUNCIATION

Black says,

> The fact that certain diphthongs became monophthongs in the history of Greek creates a problem—that of the pronunciation of NT Greek. The pronunciation commonly used in American colleges and seminaries is an attempt to approximate that used by an Athenian during the classical period in Greece (fifth and

> fourth centuries B.C.). The pronunciation now used in modern Greece differs greatly from this and is much more difficult for English-speaking students.[1]

Black apparently believes (a) that the Erasmian method of reading and pronouncing NT Greek is much like Classical Attic, whereas Neohellenic is very different; and (b) that the Neohellenic method is difficult for English-speaking students. The latter notion is discussed next, while the former is taken up in chapter 6.

Thus the focus here will be on how *difficult* it is to pronounce NT Greek the Neohellenic way. Since Erasmian authors typically Anglicize (or Germanize) Greek phonology, for a clearer perspective we will make a comparison of the Greek and English phonological and orthographical systems. The aim is (a) to demonstrate that reading and pronouncing Greek the Neohellenic way is much simpler than Erasmians suppose; (b) to point out that English-speaking college students are already familiar with a comparatively much more complex reading and pronunciation system—and what that could mean in terms of their ability to handle the much simpler Neohellenic system; and (c) to assess the judiciousness of the concern regarding difficulties in language learning in the first place.

## 5.3 ENGLISH SPELLING AND PRONUNCIATION

The list of words below (list 1) shows the variety of ways in which conventional spelling represents the sounds of "standard" American English.[2] The list is basic: except for a dozen words or so, it comprises words English learners encounter at the beginning level. Pairs of consonants (ss, ll, rr / σσ, λλ, ρρ, etc.) are not included, nor are homonyms or minimal pairs. Two other lists follow. The lists are not exhaustive.

### List 1. One Sound, Multiple Spellings

| | |
|---|---|
| [i][3] | amoeba, belief, Caesar, debris, he, key, lazy, people, receipt, receive, sea, see, ski, quay |
| [ɪ] | Aegean, been, build, buoy, busy, chamois, English, exhibit, gear, gym, it, marriage, message, Monday, tier, weird, women |
| [e] | berry, bread, bury, care, heir, leopard, said, their |
| [æ] | half, hat, laugh, meringue, plaid |
| [a] | father, heart, honest, John, not, sergeant |

1. Black, *Linguistics*, 38. Black's book is an excellent source of Erasmian views as this quotation indicates.

2. The pronunciation of the words on this list is based on Kenyon's *Pronouncing Dictionary of American English*.

3. At the basic level of English, one may encounter twenty-two i-sound spellings. At the higher levels the inclusion of less common words such as *amoeba, Aegean* [ɪdʒíən], *buoy, Caesar, chamois, quay*, etc. increases the total to thrity. Similar observations may be made with regard to other vowels and consonants.

[ɔ] awe, broad, call, cost, exhaust, George, haul, law, ought, talk, taught

[ʊ] book, could, pull, statue, wolf

[u] beautiful, fruit, glue, lieutenant, new, pneumonia, shoe, super, through, to, too, two, you

[ə] answer, banana, bus, early, father, flood, guerilla, gorgeous, jealous, Michael, mountain, nation, physician, pigeon, religious, stir, tortoise, word

[e$^{\text{I}}$] buffet, date, day, dossier, entrée, gauge, rain, reign, résumé, sleigh, they, vein

[a$^{\text{I}}$] aisle, aye, buy, by, bye, choir, eye, geyser, guide, height, heist, high, isle, lie, maestro, ride

[a$^{\text{ʊ}}$] bough, hour, house, how, sauerkraut

[ɔ$^{\text{I}}$] boy, oil

[o$^{\text{ʊ}}$] coal, depot, owe, plateau, sew, so, sow, soul, though, toe, yolk

[b] boy, babe

[d] dog, made

[f] if, life, off, often, phone, tough

[g] ago, dialogue, ghost, guarantee

[hw] where

**Learners of English, unlike learners of Greek, have to memorize the pronunciation of virtually every word.**

[w] one, won

[h] he, who

[j] beauty, few, use, William, yes

[k] ache, cake, cat, Christmas, khaki, kite, liquor, neck, racquet, unique

[l] isle, lion, male

[m] dumb, hymn, mom, palm, same

[n] know, mnemonic, on, one, pneumonia, sign, Wednesday

[ŋ] going, tongue

[p] pig, pipe

[r] care, colonel, corps, iron, rhinoceros, run, write

[s] case, ice, listen, psychology, scent, send, sword

[t] doubt, late, receipt, top, stopped

[v] of, save, Stephen, very

[z] his, realize, rise, xylophone, zero

[ʒ] azure, beige, equation, pleasure

[dʒ] adjust, age, cordial, gym, just, pledge

[ʃ] anxious, cache, conscious, machine, nation, ocean, sure, wish

[tʃ] furniture, switch, teacher

[ð] bathe, that

[θ] thin

### List 2. Same Single Letter, Different Sounds

(a) above, call, care, father, have, late, wash; (b) be, numb; (c) cat, cure, ice, ocean; (d) loved, stopped; (e) crepe, here, permit, red, sergeant, she; (f) fire, of; (g) go, imagine, sign, sing; (h) honest, hot; (i) it, family, girl, machine, meringue, ride; (k) kit, know; (l) lot, palm; (o) above, do, note, office, thorough, wolf, women; (p) pen, psalm; (s) isle, laser, see, sure, vision; (t) equation, furniture, listen, top; (u) bury, bus, busy, buy, guard, hurt, put, super, use; (w) cow, wear; (x) exit, tax, xylophone; (y) physician, myth, toy, type, yes.

### List 3. Same Pair of Letters, Different Sounds

(ae) aerial, Caesar, maelstrom, maestro, (ai) again, aisle, bargain, maid, plaid; (al) palm, salt; (au) aunt, gauge, kraut, pause, (ch) chef, chemistry, chew, (ea) break, breath, breathe, ear, European, lineage, ocean; (ee) been, entrée, see; (ei) eight, height, heir, seize, weird; (eo) geography, George, leopard, people; (ew) few, flew, sew; (ey) geyser, key, they; (ft) after, often; (gn) sign, signal; (ho) honest, hot; (ia) appreciate, cordial, encyclopedia, familiar, liar, marriage; (ie) believe, conscience, lie, obedient, science, skier, tier, view; (io) lion, onion, criterion; (oa) boa, broad, oasis, road; (oe) Noel, Phoenix, poem, toe, shoe; (oi) boil, chamois, choir, going, tortoise; (ol) colonel, old; (oo) book, flood, food, zoology; (ou) cough, could, court, group, journey, out, though, tough; (ow) cow, grow; (oy) boy, buoy; (ph) Stephen, phone, uphold; (ps) cups, psychology; (st) listen, step; (sw) swing, answer; (th) there, thin; (ua) graduate (v/adj);(ue) duet, dialogue, fuel, guerilla, sue; (ui) build, guide, quit, ruin, suit, suite; (wa) forward, wagon, wall, wash, waste; (we) owe, we, wet; (wi) win, wine; (wo) woke, wolf, won, wore, world.

Lists 1–3 show that (a) the sound represented by individual English letters and digraphs is highly inconsistent, and (b) phonics rules—how to pronounce what spelling—cannot be heavily relied upon for the pronunciation of English words. This means that learners of English have to commit to memory the spelling *and* pronunciation of virtually every word. By contrast, learners of Greek do not need to memorize the pronunciation of any Greek words once they become familiar with the consistent relation between letter(s) and sound.

This difference between English orthography and pronunciation, on the one hand, and Greek orthography and pronunciation, on the other, becomes clearer through a comparison of the Greek and English alphabetic and phonemic systems (see below).

## 5.4 GREEK AND ENGLISH PHONEMES AND CORRESPONDING ALPHABET LETTERS

The table below is a comparison of Greek and English phonemes and variations of the respective conventional alphabet letters that represent them. All Greek variations are listed, including ᾳ, ῃ, ῳ. The English section, based on List 1 (above), is not exhaustive.

| **Phonemes and Letter(s)**<br>**IPA** | | **Phonemes and Letter(s)**<br>**IPA** | |
|---|---|---|---|
| **Greek** | | | |
| /i/ | ι η ῃ υ ει οι υι | /k/ | κ |
| /ε/ | ε αι | /l/ | λ |
| /ɑ/ | α ᾳ | /m/ | μ |
| /o/ | ο ω ῳ | /n/ | ν |
| /u/ | ου | /p/ | π |
| /v/ | β υ | /r/ | ρ |
| /ɣ/ | γ | /s/ | σ, ς |
| /ð/ | δ | /t/ | τ |
| /z/ | ζ | /f/ | φ υ |
| /θ/ | θ | /x/ | χ |
| **English** | | | |
| /i/ | ae ay e ea ee ei eo ey i ie is oe y | /k/ | c ch che ck cqu k ke kh qu que |
| /ɪ/ | a ae ay e ea ee ei hi i ia ie o ois oy u ui y | /l/ | l le sle |
| /e/ | a ai e ea ei eo hei u | /m/ | lm m mb me mn |
| /æ/ | a ai al au i | /n/ | dn gn kn mn n ne pn |
| /a/ | a e ea ho o oh | /ŋ/ | ng ngue |
| /ɔ/ | a al au augh aw awe eo hau o oa ough | /p/ | p pe |
| /ʊ/ | o oo oul u ue | /r/ | l r re rh ro rps wr |
| /u/ | au eu ew ieu o oe oo ou ough u ue ui wo | /s/ | ce ps s sc se st sw |
| /ə/ | a ae ai e ea eo ue eou i ia io iou o oo oi ou we u y | /t/ | bt d pt t te |
| /$e^{ɪ}$/ | a ai au ay e ee ei eig eigh er et ey | /v/ | f ph v ve |
| /$a^{ɪ}$/ | ae ais ay ei ey eye i ie eigh igh is oi ui uy y ye | /w/ | o w |
| /$a^{ʊ}$/ | au hou ou ough ow | /hw/ | wh |
| /$ɔ^{ɪ}$/ | oi oy | /z/ | s se x z ze |
| /$o^{ʊ}$/ | eau ew o oa oe ol ot ou ough ow owe | /ʒ/ | ge s t z |
| /b/ | b be | /dʒ/ | d dge dj g ge j |
| /d/ | d de | /ʃ/ | c ch che s sc sh t x |
| /f/ | f fe ff ft gh ph | /tʃ/ | ch t tch |
| /g/ | g gh gu gue | /ð/ | th the |
| /h/ | h wh | /θ/ | th |
| /j/ | ea e i u y | | |

20 phonemes
33 spelling variations
List is exhaustive.

39 phonemes
248 spelling variations
List is not exhaustive.
(Some variations may be broken down differently.)

## 5.5 GREEK VS. ENGLISH ORTHOGRAPHY

The above table shows that by far the simpler orthographical and phonological system is the Greek. Greek orthography employs twenty-four alphabet letters: seventeen consonants and seven vowels (ι, η, υ, ε, α, ο, ω), six of which are combined to form eight "diphthongs," the digraphs αι, ει, οι, υι, ου, αυ, ευ, ηυ. The pronunciation of these is consistent (4.7).

English orthography employs twenty-six alphabet letters: twenty consonants and six vowels (a, e, i, o, u, y), which are combined to form inordinately long variations that complicate reading and pronunciation. The pronunciation of letters and their combined variations is highly inconsistent, requiring the learner to memorize the spelling and pronunciation of each word.

## 5.6 GREEK VS. ENGLISH PHONOLOGY

Greek has five vowel phonemes /i, e, a, o, u/ and fifteen consonant phonemes, totaling twenty. Overall consistency in the pronunciation of single letters and digraphs facilitates the use of orthography for the phonetic representation of Greek sounds.

English has nine vowels /i, ɪ, e, æ, ɑ, ɔ, ʊ, u, ə/, five diphthongs /e$^{ɪ}$, a$^{ɪ}$, a$^{ʊ}$, ɔ$^{ɪ}$, o$^{ʊ}$/, and twenty-five consonants, totaling (at least) thirty-nine phonemes.[4] The use of English orthography for the phonemic or phonetic representation of English sounds creates numerous inconsistencies in pronunciation and spelling.

## 5.7 CONCLUDING REMARKS AND ASSESSMENT

One might rightly contend that the foregoing comparisons are pointless in that Erasmian pedagogy rarely emphasizes dictation or intensive oral-aural drilling as part of the Greek language learning process. The purpose however of the comparisons is to show that reading and pronouncing NT Greek according to the centuries-old Neohellenic method is much simpler than described by Erasmians. Indeed, one can learn to read and pronounce Greek with notable progress within hours of instruction. This speaks of a comparatively simple and consistent reading and pronouncing system.

But should one be concerned about the difficulty of reading and pronouncing Greek, what should be said about the difficulty of reading and pronouncing English? The Greek ι-sounds—the main complex part of Greek spelling—are spelled six (and with ῃ seven) different but orthographically consistent ways. That number is dwarfed by the thirty inconsistent ways the English i-sounds are spelled, along with nine other sounds spelled ten or more ways each, and another eight sounds spelled six or more ways each.

4. The number of English sounds depends on regional variations. This analysis is based primarily on the sounds of what may be considered standard American English (5.3).

In view of all such peculiarities of English spelling and pronunciation, one could hardly conceive the benefit to English learners if they, for the sake of facility, were instructed to follow the Erasmian practice of pronouncing every letter of a word while supposing that they spoke English!

Simply put, English-speaking students ought to feel superbly equipped to handle the less complex traditional Greek reading and writing system, a system that preserves the HGP.

Should English-speaking students be taught to read and pronounce NT Greek the Neohellenic way now that it has been shown that it is comparatively not so difficult for them after all—or, better yet, that the English way of spelling, reading, and pronouncing is much more complex for learners of English than the Neohellenic way is for English-speaking students? Absurd. The issue is not the level of difficulty in language learning that determines the pronunciation method one must follow (else, for the sake of facility and ease we might as well do away with the Greek NT text altogether by rendering it in some Erasmian form). Rather, the issue is that scholars should direct students' attention to the authentic way of reading and pronouncing Greek, candidly leaving all predilection and self-serving logic outside the bounds of serious scholarship.

Difficulties in language learning are commensurate with one's linguistic background, skills, goals, and determination. But a student's linguistic background and personal history forms no basis for the instructor to apply anachronistic methods in order to facilitate the learner—or, more precisely, the instructor. An instructor's concern about the difficulties English-speaking students would encounter in attempting to read and pronounce NT Greek the "modern" Greek way, abetted by the unscholarly notion that Erasmian makes Greek words easier to read and spell—despite an increasing awareness today that Neohellenic sounds very close to Κοινή—is more than just a misconception: it is an academic travesty.

## 5.8 MISCONCEPTION #2—DISSIMILAR WORDS

In group discussions over the pronunciation of Greek, an Erasmian colleague typically points out that NT and Modern Greek words are very dissimilar, and gives the NT word εὕρηκα [évrika] (Erasmian "heureka" *hue-rake-uh*) as an example. This word, the colleague argues, in Modern Greek is βρῆκα [vrika], its spelling and pronunciation being grossly different from the original. I readily agree, whereupon the colleague appears content that his point is well taken.

But the colleague soon finds that εὕρηκα is used in Neohellenic as it was used in NT (and classical) times, βρῆκα being simply an alternative (simplified) form. In other words, εὕρηκα is used at the literary level (Katharevousa) and even in informal conversation along with other similar forms of the same verb (τὸ γύρευα καὶ δὲν τὸ εὕρησκα, lit. *I was looking for it and wasn't finding it*); and βρῆκα, its alternative (Dimotiki) form, is used informally at the conversational level.

The single articulatory difference between the two forms, the colleague further learns, is the initial epsilon (ε) of εὕρηκα. Dropping the ε of the digraph ευ exposes -υ, here the sound β [v], hence βρῆκα [vrika]. This all the more shows that ευ is pronounced [ev], and that the pronunciation of ευ as *hue* or *you* is not Greek.

The conversation eventually returns to its original spark, which lies at the heart of the issue: Κοινή and Neohellenic share many linguistic features (2.22; 7.2.1). The colleague also learns that of the 4,900 Greek words in the NT, 92 percent are used or understood in Neohellenic (3.5).

The outcome of the dialogue? A skeptical, and perhaps enlightened, Erasmian, yet one who will expediently continue his Erasmian practice.

# Chapter 6

# Erasmian Latitudes

## 6.1 GREEK AND ENGLISH VOWEL DIAGRAMS

Shown below is an exaggerated imaginary vowel diagram that defines the relative tongue positions during the production of vowel sounds. A dot indicates the highest point of the hump of the tongue during the articulation of a vowel. Some works use a rectangle, a triangle, or a rhomboid to illustrate the same.

Based on this image, the two vowel diagrams shown on the next page give a comparative view of the Greek and English vocalic systems. Comparing these two diagrams can set the stage for comprehending the far-fetched latitude of the Erasmian conceptualization of the Greek vowel system.

**The Vowel Diagram Concept**

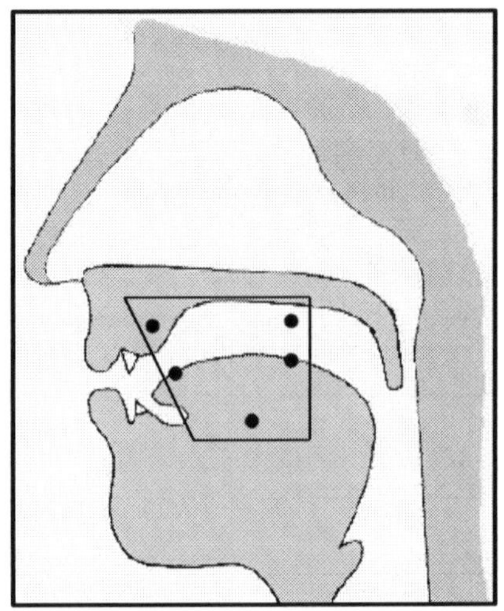

## 6.2 THE GREEK VOWEL DIAGRAM

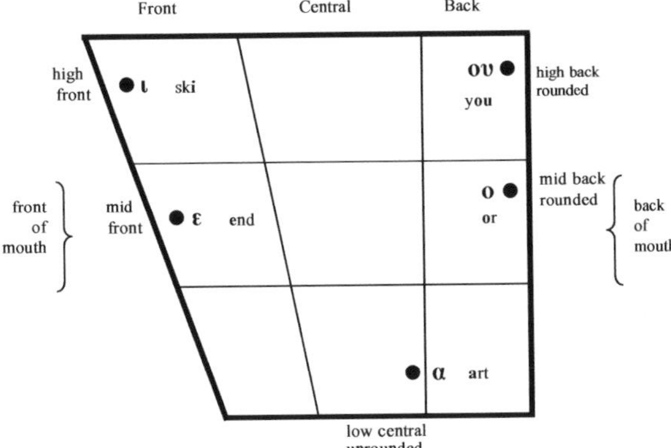


## 6.3 THE ENGLISH VOWEL AND DIPHTHONG DIAGRAM

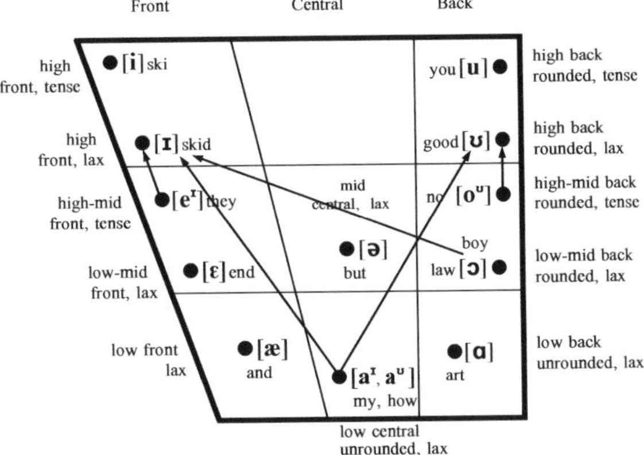


Some linguists use *close* for *high*, *open* for *low*. Tense-lax is relative to the upper/lower position of the tongue within a range: high, mid, low. For example, [i] in *feet* is tense within the high front range compared to [ɪ] in *fit*. Arrows indicate the beginning and ending of the gliding motion of the tongue in the articulation of the diphthongs [eᶦ, aᶦ, aᶷ, ɔᶦ, oᶷ] as in *they, my, how, boy, no*. *Rounded* refers to the rounding of the lips. Note: Greek ι is imperceptibly between *ski* and *skid*, ε between *they* and *end*, and α between *a* in *my* [aᶦ] and *a* in *art*.

## 6.4 AN UN-GREEK VIEW

Black's Erasmian rendition of the Classical Greek vocalic system, presented in a rectangular diagram,[1] is technically a version of the English diagram shown above (6.3). According to Black:

ι is the *ee* in *beet* when long, or the *i* in *bit* when short

η is the *a* in *babe*

ε is the *e* in *bet*

α is the *o* in *pot* when long, or the *a* in *bat* when short

ο is the *ough* in *bought*

ω is the *o* in *bold*

υ is the *oo* in *boot* when long, or the *oo* in *book* when short

Based on the above list, a number of phonological observations can be made:

a. The list suggests that Classical Greek has ten vowel sounds, or twice the number of Classical Greek vowels per the foregoing discussion (2.5).

b. The list suggests long and short vowels. Vowel quantity, however, is a technicality that applies to Attic versification (2.16), not to regular speech.

c. The *a* in *babe* and *o* in *bold* are the English diphthongs [e$^{ɪ}$] and [o$^{ʊ}$] respectively, so η and ω thus pronounced cannot be considered single vowels but diphthongs.[2]

d. The *o* in *pot* cannot be long if the *a* in *bat* is short. Phonetically both are short in that they are followed by voiceless [t], as opposed, for instance, to *pod*/*bad*, where the vowel is followed by voiced [d]—e.g., *pot-pod* [pɑt]-[pɑ:d], and *bat-bad* [bæt]-[bæ:d], " : " signaling length.

e. The same goes for *boot*/*book* where the difference [u]/[ʊ] applies to the tense-lax, not to a long-short, distinction.

Black likewise gives an Erasmian rendition of the Classical Greek diphthongs, suggesting that Classical Greek has eight diphthongs, or three more than the five diphthongs of standard American English [e$^{ɪ}$, a$^{ɪ}$, a$^{ʊ}$, ɔ$^{ɪ}$, o$^{ʊ}$] (6.3). Black's eight Attic diphthongs are as follows:

ει, αι, οι, υι, ου, ηυ, ευ, αυ.[3]

1 Black, *Linguistics*, 36.

2 For a definition of *diphthong*, see 6.5.2, fn.

3 Black, *Linguistics*, 38.

As already seen, however, ει, αι, οι, υι, ου are digraphs that are pronounced as monophthongs, not as diphthongs (2.2–2.5); and postpositive υ in digraphs ηυ, ευ, αυ is fricativized, hence consonantal, not vocalic (2.6).

Add to these Black's description of the Greek r (ρ) as a "retroflex glide"—i.e., typically the American r [ɹ$^{w}$] "as in rear"[4]—plus the consonants described earlier (2.11.1A), and you end up with a kaleidoscopic Erasmian version of a Greek pronunciation system which in classical Athens would have sounded pretty much like American English![5]

## 6.5 A PRISMATIC ERASMIAN VIEW

As Miller points out, the *Linear B* script (1500–1200 BC) indicates that Mycenaean Greek had five vowels: /i, e, a, o, u/.[6] Today, after three and a half thousand years, Neohellenic has the same five vowels (1.11; 2.5). Jannaris concurs: "From its remotest traceable period down to the closing decades of the V$^{th}$ c. B.C., the Attic alphabet shows only five vowel symbols: α ε ι ο υ, which evidently represent (for the earlier antiquity at least) the five normal sounds a e i o u, corresponding to the Latin and the *N* [Neohellenic] sound system."[7] Bearing this point in mind, let us now reassess the "prismatic" Erasmian view of the Classical Greek vocalic system as portrayed by Black.

### 6.5.1 Vowels

According to the above Erasmian view of the Classical Attic vowel system (6.4), and with the five Mycenaean vowels taken into account, between the end of the Mycenaean period (1200 BC) and the beginning of the classical period (500 BC) the Greek vowels doubled in number. The following diagram illustrates this. Double appearance of a vowel indicates Black's long-short distinction suggested above.[8]

Erasmian View of the Classical Greek Vowels

**Mycenaean**

i e a o u

⇩

4 Black, *Linguistics*, 34.

5 It becomes obvious that such an interpretation of Greek phonology is seen through the lens of the American English phonological system.

6 Miller, *Ancient Scripts*, 13.

7 Jannaris, *Historical Greek Grammar*, 27.

8 Some Erasmians might argue that the long-short vowel distinction in Mycenaean cannot be ruled out even though there is no evidence in support of such an argument.

**Classical**

| ι | ι | η | ε | α | α | ο | ω | υ | υ |
|---|---|---|---|---|---|---|---|---|---|

## 6.5.2 Diphthongs

On the same basis, between the end of the Mycenaean period and around the beginning of the classical period, the Greek vocalic system, in addition to doubling the number of its vowels, somehow generated eight diphthongs.[9] Such a phonological metamorphosis translates into a staggering 360 percent increase of the original five-vowel Mycenaean system. Then, from about the end of the classical period this explosive trend is by some counterforce reined in and made to reverse itself. By the end of the pre-NT Hellenistic period (about three centuries later) the vowels and diphthongs fully implode, thereby causing the five Mycenaean vowels to reemerge intact and for the next two millennia remain immune to further change. The following diagram illustrates this:

### A Representation of the Erasmian View[10] of the Classical Greek Vocalic System (Vowels and Diphthongs)

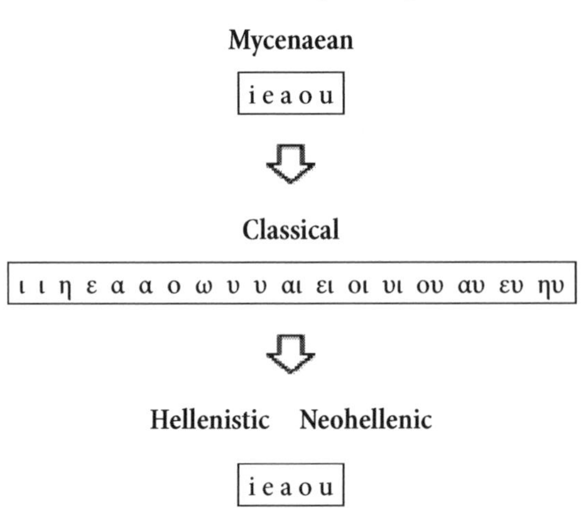


9. An English diphthong may be defined as *a complex speech sound or glide that begins with one vowel and gradually changes to another vowel within the same syllable*—as [e$^{\text{I}}$] in *they* or [a$^{\text{I}}$] in *fine* (not [e-ɪ] or [a-ɪ]). In contrast, no Greek vowel glides into another vowel within the same syllable, for each vowel is a distinct and equally-timed (isochronous) sound segment which is, or belongs in, one syllable (2.14, fn.; 8.6). Greek has five vowel digraphs (αι, ει, οι, υι, ου) or pairs of vowel letters, each pair representing a single vowel sound. Thus, there is no phonological correlation whatsoever between a Greek *vowel digraph* and an English *diphthong*. Each of the digraphs αυ, ευ, ηυ consists of one vowel, α, ε, η, respectively, and one consonant, φ [f] or β [v].

10. This interpretation of Classical Greek vowels is typically Erasmian, though Erasmian scholars do not usually agree on how Greek vowels are pronounced (4.4).

Pondering over this phantasmagoric view of the Greek vocalic system, one may wonder: If by 500 BC the five Mycenaean Greek vowels evolved to such magnitude, how did their evolutionary process reverse itself, and rather than continue to generate further changes—as did all the Romance and Germanic dialects—it caused the original five Mycenaean vowels by NT times to reappear in their original state; and then, for twenty more whole centuries it caused no further changes? The answer is as obvious as it is logical: from Mycenaean times to the present, Greek has always had a five-vowel phonemic system.

## 6.6 SIDNEY ALLEN'S TREATMENT OF THE CLASSICAL ATTIC VOCALIC SYSTEM

A number of points regarding Black's Erasmian view of the Attic vocalic system are found also in Allen's *Vox Graeca*, notwithstanding the fact that a superficial comparison of the two authors' views reveals that their analyses are in major respects different. For one thing, Black suggests ten vowels: seven long and three short (6.4), whereas Allen's "double triangle" diagram (below) shows twelve vowels: seven long (outer triangle) and five short (inner triangle).

Additionally, while Black describes υ as a *back rounded* vowel as in *book*, Allen describes υ as a *front rounded short* vowel as in French *lune*, as well as a *front rounded long* vowel as in French *ruse*.[11] And Black's η and ει are seen on Allen's outer triangle in reverse order, with each author assigning to these symbols different phonetic values. These and other such differences are not surprising given the fact that, as already demonstrated (4.4), there is no consistency in the arbitrary ways Erasmian adherents view the phonology of Classical Attic.

**Allen's Classical Attic Vowels**[12]

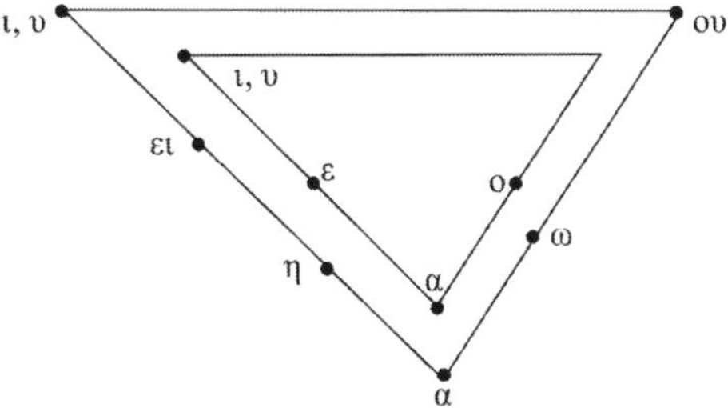


This section examines Allen's views of Classical Attic vowels. A fuller discussion would doubtless be long drawn out and therefore beyond the scope of this study, as Allen's descriptions typically take meandering paths of multifaceted speculation featuring

11. Allen, *Vox Graeca*, 68.

12. Adapted from Allen's *Vox Graeca*, 62.

transliterated words with references to a medley of languages, scant Greek samples, and abrupt personal inferences. Thus Allen's *modus operandi* draws the critic into a maze of interwoven matters that make critiquing difficult. It is hoped nevertheless that the following section will bring about an understanding of the artificial and arbitrary nature of Erasmian or of the so-called "restored" pronunciation of Classical Greek.

## η, ει

While the vast majority of Erasmians pronounce η and ει as the English diphthong [eᶦ] in *say* or *eight*, Allen pronounces η and ει monophthongally, with η being long "open mid" [e] as in French *tête* [te:t], and ει long "close mid" [e] as in German *Beet* [be:t]. The difference between these two "long" [e] vowels is measured essentially in terms of the aperture of the mouth [and relative tongue position] during articulation. In addition to the "long" ει and η [e] vowels, Allen sees *epsilon* ε as a "short mid vowel."[13] In other words, Allen holds that Classical Attic has three /e/-like phonemes: ει, η, ε.

It is perhaps worth quoting Allen's account in its entirety to show how he arrives at a conclusion regarding ει and η:

> There is little external evidence to establish positive values for these symbols in classical Attic. That they were different is shown by the fact that they later develop differently, the sound represented by ει soon becoming a close long front vowel [ī], whereas the sound of η remains for some time in the mid region. These developments further indicate that the sound of ει was always closer than that of η. This situation is reflected in the transcription of Greek words in Latin, where η is represented by ē until a late date, whereas ει is represented by ī (e.g., *sēpia* = σηπία, *pīrata* = πειρατής, and *Aristīdēs* = Ἀριστείδης).
>
> The development of ει to [ī] is revealed by occasional confusion between ει and ι from the late 4 c. B.C., becoming common in the 3 c. But there is no such confusion in earlier times, and the mid value of ει is still indicated by Xenophon's rendering as παράδεισος of an Iranian *par(i)deza*—"garden."
>
> Thus the sounds of both η and ει were long mid vowels in classical Attic, but the former was more open than the latter. Since they had to be accommodated on the front axis between open [ā] and close [ī] (see p. 62), they can hardly have been other than open mid [. . .] (= η) and close mid [. . .] (= ει)—*i.e., approximately the vowels of French tête for η and of German Beet for ει.*[14] (Allen's emphasis)

As mentioned earlier, at the time Attic began to use H as the vowel η around the mid-5th c. BC, the Romans were already using the same Chalcidic symbol H, which was familiar to them as the aspirate *h* (4.2). Latin therefore could not suddenly invent a special new symbol for the Attic vowel H(η); instead, it continued to adhere to the

13. Allen, *Vox Graeca*, 63.

14. Allen, *Vox Graeca*, 69–70.

old familiar way of transliterating H(η) as E, which prior to mid-5th c. BC stood both for [e] and [i] sounds. (See pp. 145–46.) Thus, that H(η) in σηπία was represented by Latin E does not necessarily mean that σηπία was pronounced [sepia] and not [sipia].

Allen says that Classical Attic η and ει were different in that later they developed differently. The evidence, however, points to the confusion of mainstream Attic ει and η from the very beginning of the adoption of η (p. 138), with the two spellings (ει, η) being interchangeable down to the present day. This is how ει and η are treated in Neohellenic and, notwithstanding MSS emendations, in Biblical Greek.

The Attic rendering παράδεισος for Persian παρ[ε]ιδεζα *paradise* was no doubt an attempt to follow the Persian original sound, but is no faithful representation of that sound, hence Allen cannot use it to prove anything. Allen's remark that in Xenophon's time there is no confusion between ει and ι ignores the fact that Plato himself, Xenophon's contemporary, bears witness to the confusion of ει, ι, and η (p. 20). And Allen's position that an "occasional confusion between ει and ι [is seen] from the late 4 c. B.C." actually leads one to doubt that his appended phrase "becoming common in the 3 c." is not an attempt to arbitrarily place iotacized ει outside the time frame of the classical period.

Thus, following some brief speculation involving Latin and Iranian, Allen figures that Classical Attic η and ει "can hardly have been other than" long open mid [e] and long close mid [e]. But in order to make Allen's phonetic distinction between French [e] in *tête* and German [e] in *Beet*, especially with a "short" ε [e] vowel thrown into the mix, it would require actual voice recordings and sound analysis using sophisticated technology—after which it would be incumbent upon Allen to show that his three Attic [e] sounds are also phonemically distinct.

## η, ι

Allen holds that Attic inscriptions begin to reflect the confusion of η and ι in post-NT times: "Confusion between η and ι in Attic inscriptions," he says, "begins around 150 A.D."[15] Here Allen, unwilling to accept the stark historical proof of the initial confusion of η and ι in mid-5th c. BC, audaciously pushes the equation into the future by six hundred years! The evidence clearly shows that the confusion of η and ι is already seen in the 5th c. BC (2.2.2) and increases dramatically by the 3rd c. BC.

At the same time, Allen's footnote reads: "Startling but quite aberrant is the 5 c. B.C. αθινα αρισ αρτεμισ on a slate of a schoolboy signing himself as διμοσοθενισ"[16] for αθηνα αρησ αρτεμισ—δημοσθενης. There is no doubt that the Athenian schoolboy inscribed his text led by his ear. But if this type of writing on an Athenian schoolboy's slate where ι is used in place of η can be startling to Allen, one can scarcely conceive how staggering multiple such samples ought to be. In this light, one may also wonder

15. Allen, *Vox Graeca*, 74.

16. Allen, *Vox Graeca*, 74.

if Allen's placing of the initial confusion of η and ι beyond the NT time frame is not an arbitrary attempt to justify the application of the Erasmian "Classical Attic" pronunciation to the Greek New Testament. It is likely for the same reason that Allen places as well the equation ω = ο in post-NT times.[17]

### υ, ι

Allen's discussion of υ revolves around handpicked transliterated words from Sanskrit, Latin, and Old Persian, with references to Armenian, Gothic, French, and German and a hint of Boeotian and Laconian. It also includes modern Tsakonian, an isolated extant variant of Doric, and alludes to Quintilian xii.10.27, a passage that entails two Greek letters, one being υ, though he gives no further details of the passage probably because of the questionable transliteration variants of two Greek words in the Latin MSS.[18]

While Allen holds that "*the value of Attic short υ was similar to that of e.g. French lune, and of long υ to that of French ruse*"[19] (Allen's emphasis), he does not deny that υ is at times treated as ι. He says, for example, that "the occasional confusion of υ and ι in semi-literate inscriptions (e.g., αριστονιμο beside αριστονυμο on ostraka of 433/2) suggests that υ was by now a front vowel."[20] However, other inscriptions indicate that the confusion of υ and ι in classical times is not "occasional" and that it occurs even earlier than Allen supposes: Λισικλες for Λυσικλης (6th c. BC), δακριον for δακρυον (6–5th c. BC), Τιρινθι for Τιρυνθι (6–5th c. BC), Ηιπότελε for Ηυποτελε (6–5th c. BC), Ηιποκιμενος for Ηυποκειμενος (6–5th c. BC), Διονισος for Διονυσος (5th c. BC), Κρισευς for Κρυσευς (5th c. BC), Διονισια for Διονυσια (5th c. BC), Λισιστρατος for Λυσιστρατος (5th c. BC), Διονισιγενες for Διονυσιγενης (5th c. BC), ημυσυν for ημισυ (4th c. BC), etc. (2.2.2). This suggests that υ was used as a front vowel early on, at any rate prior to the classical period.

Below are examples Allen gives in which υ is treated as ι, but each of which he attempts to explain away. Each of the examples Allen gives is followed by a rebuttal.

17. Allen, *Vox Graeca*, 173.

18. Quintilian's unclear reference to υ does not necessarily mean that in the 1st c. BC he heard υ as [ü]. A Roman rhetorician from Spain, Quintilian was a contemporary of Peter, whom Jesus addressed as Σίμων Ἰωνᾶ, *Simon (son) of Jonas* (John 21:15). Σίμων (Peter) is elsewhere referred to as Συμεών *Symeon* [simeon] (Acts 15:14). It would be absurd to postulate that Quintilian heard Peter's first name Σίμων as [simon] but Συμεών as [sümeon]. As Russell notes, in Quintilian's day υ = ι. Russell, *Quintilian*, 297, fn. 61.

19. Allen, *Vox Graeca*, 68.

20. Allen, *Vox Graeca*, 67.

### Example A. Inscription of 2nd c. BC Indo-Greek coins shows ι for υ.

*Allen's explanation*: "Indo-Aryan had no rounded front vowel, and so rendered it by the equivalent unrounded vowel."[21]

*Rebuttal*: Old Persian, too, had no rounded front vowel, yet used [u] rather than [i] for υ—e.g., Kambusjia for Καμβύσης, Kuruš for Κύρος *Cyrus*—even at a time (5th c. BC) υ and ι already showed signs of confusion. Thus Indo-Aryan in Hellenistic times could have very well opted to emulate that Old Persian practice, but it did not. There is therefore no doubt that the use of ι in place of υ, particularly in government-sanctioned Hellenistic Indo-Greek coins, was intentional and probably aimed at actually circumventing in this case the Old Persian association of υ with [u].

### Example B. 4th c. BC inscriptions show ημυσυ for ἥμισυ, while other inscriptions show βιβλίον for βυβλίον [from βύβλος].

*Allen's explanation*: ημυσυ for ἥμισυ "means only that the unrounded ι [i] was assimilated to the following rounded υ [ü] in this word"; and "the substitution . . . of βιβλίον for βυβλίον simply indicates an assimilation of [ü] to the following [i]."[22]

*Rebuttal*: Whether υ is represented by ι, or ι by υ, Allen resorts to "assimilation" as an explanation. There are inscriptions, however, as shown above, in which υ is substituted by ι in syllables that are neither preceded nor followed by υ or ι, e.g., δακριον for δακρυον (6th–5th c. BC), Ηιποκιμενος for Ηυποκειμενος (6th–5th c. BC), Διονισος for Διονυσος (5th c. BC). Such examples clearly speak not of assimilation but of misspellings through the use of interchangeable letters that stand for acoustically similar or otherwise indistinguishable sounds.

### Example C. Egyptian papyri of the 2nd–3rd c. AD show that υ is confused with ι.

*Allen's explanation*: "This is probably a regional peculiarity."[23]

*Rebuttal*: The countless and well-preserved Hellenistic papyri discovered in Egypt date from the conquest of Egypt by Alexander in 332 BC to the conquest of Egypt by the Muslims in AD 639. These papyri, which display similar and repeated spelling errors (2.2.1), were discovered in various regions in Egypt. Allen's attempt to explain the interchange of υ and ι as "probably a regional peculiarity" is merely conjectural, as it does not show that υ and ι were interchanged in some particular region in Egypt in the 2nd and 3rd c. AD to the exclusion of other regions.

21. Allen, *Vox Graeca*, 67.

22. Allen, *Vox Graeca*, 68.

23. Allen, *Vox Graeca*, 68.

**Example D. υ had still not changed by the 4th c. AD.**

*Allen's explanation*: This is based on "the fact that Wulfila found it necessary to adopt the Greek letter in transcribing the υ of Greek words."[24]

*Rebuttal*: Letter resemblance in transcription does not warrant phonetic equivalency. A number of Greek words in English contain y for υ (i.e., English Y for Greek Y) as in *symbol, physician, hyperbole*. But even though in various cases the y as in *symbol* is within the range of the ι [i] sound, in other cases it is [aˈ] (*hyper*) or [ə] (*physician*). Thus the use of y for υ in such loanwords is not necessarily aimed at preserving the Greek [i] sound. This is also the most likely reason that Wulfila borrowed the Greek Y at the time he sought to translate the Bible into Gothic. Wulfila cared to borrow not an un-Gothic Greek sound but the Greek symbol Y, just as Latin in the 1st c. BC borrowed from Greek not an un-Latin sound but the Greek symbol Y, a letter still identified to this day as *i Graeca* "Greek [i]" (4.2.h).

## E = ε, η, ει, and EI = ει

Allen sees that pre-Eucleidean E is represented later by ε or η, sometimes by ει; and that pre-Eucleidean EI is represented later by ει. The first case involves "contraction" (νεσθε = νεῖσθε) or "compensatory lengthening" (ε'ναι = εἶναι), while the second case involves an original diphthong (τειχοσ = τεῖχος).[25] In the (a) case, ει is not traced to a diphthong, but in the (b) case it is. Allen thus points out that "spurious diphthong" in case (a) is a misnomer, and that in neither case does ει represent a diphthong in classical times. Allen's reasoning is in line with our discussion earlier (2.14; 2.15). He is also correct in saying that "it is virtually certain that by the 5 c. B.C. all words which are now written with ει had the same sound."[26] Allen's reasoning misses the mark, however, when he classifies all three ε, η, and ει as [e] sounds (see triangular diagram above) and does not see ει as ι until the 3rd c. BC despite the strong historical evidence that ει = ι even by pre-classical times.

Whether ει results from *contaction* (πολεες > πολεις, ιπεες > ιππεις, ποιεετε > ποιειτε, φερεεν > φερειν) or from *compensatory lengthening* (ενς > ε'ς > εις, εσναι > ε'ναι > ειναι, χερς > χερ' > χειρ) it is pronounced like monophthongized ει. And as Allen otherwise correctly remarks, "all words which are now written with ει had the same sound."[27]

What Erasmians probably consider as the strongest evidence in support of the pronunciation of η as ε (as Allen does on p. 70) are the two fragmentary lines by

24. Allen, *Vox Graeca*, 68.

25. Allen, *Vox Graeca*, 70–71.

26. Allen, *Vox Graeca*, 71–72.

27. Allen, *Vox Graeca*, 72.

Kratinos and Aristophanes where βηβη and βη respectively represent the bleating of sheep:[28]

Ὁ δ' ἠλίθιος ὥσπερ πρόβατον βῆ βῆ λέγων βαδίζει. (Kratinos)

Θύειν με μέλλει καὶ κελεύει βῆ λέγειν. (Aristophanes)

First, the vowel H(η) cannot belong to Kratinos (520–423 BC) and hardly to Aristophanes (450–386 BC). In Kratinos' case the vowel H had not yet been introduced to the Attic script, and in Aristophanes' case H had not yet been introduced officially. Kratinos, accustomed to the old Attic use of E both for [e] and [i] sounds (1.11), would have written BEBE (βεβε), not BHBH (βηβη), and Aristophanes BE(βε) not BH(βη). Thus it cannot be deduced from these fragmentary lines that Attic H can be interpreted as E[e].[29]

## "Long" Diphthongs ᾱι, ηι, ωι (Allen, 84–88)

As already seen, the adscript of spurious diphthongs AI, EI, OI (later AI, HI, ΩI), from around the 12th c. AD is seen as a subscript, thus ᾳ, ῃ, ῳ. As a compensatory mark, from the beginning of its appearance this adscript (ᾱι, ηι, ωι) or subscript (ᾳ, ῃ, ῳ) was silent, meaning that ᾳ, ῃ, ῳ and α, η, ω have always been pronounced alike. Allen apparently distinguishes between these two sets of symbols, figuring that ᾳ, ῃ, ῳ represent long diphthongs in which the subscript ( ͺ ) is voiced, while α, η, ω are merely long vowels.[30] Pondering over various methods of producing the difference in pronunciation between ᾳ, ῃ, ῳ and α, η, ω, and still not content, Allen finds himself in a quandary.

**Allen's pronunciation of Classical Greek is untenable.**

Suddenly Allen is struck by a popular idea: "*The simplest solution*," he suggests, "*seems to be one which is in fact quite widely adopted, namely to anticipate developments by two or three centuries and to pronounce ᾳ, ῃ, ῳ, as, ᾱ, η, ω, i.e. without their diphthongal element*"[31] (Allen's emphasis).

Thus, in a capricious shift of thought, Allen resorts to what he has all along avoided saying: "Pronounce these the Byzantine way"—just as he did when he found himself in a quandary in connection with the pronunciation of φ, θ, χ when he subtly avoided saying, "the Modern Greek way" (2.10.1). We may then ask, Why not replace

28. Jannaris, "Kratinos and Aristophanes," 46–51.

29. Cries of animals cannot be relied upon as a guide to the pronunciation of language sounds. For if a sheep goes *bεε* in Greek but *baa* in English, one might as well adduce that the same kind of animal, be it a sheep, a dog, a cow, or a lion, must make a different sound in every country where a different language is spoken!

30. Allen, *Vox Graeca*, 84.

31. Allen, *Vox Graeca*, 87.

the whole trumped-up Erasmian story by what is known to have been the pronunciation "by two or three centuries" later, i.e., Modern Greek?

Clearly, this section, along with previous sections on Allen's views regarding Greek sounds (2.10.1; 2.18.1), shows that Allen's pronunciation of Classical Greek is not just arbitrary: it is untenable.

## 6.7 TERRITORIAL INTERESTS

The above representative Erasmian pronunciation systems are much like Moulton's of decades earlier, except Moulton audaciously "qualifies" his by declaring, "We are not generally required to make *our Greek* intelligible to any but Englishmen of the twentieth century"[32] (italics mine). But whether an Erasmian cloaks himself in ancient Athenian garb and steals an anachronistic pose holding his Greek New Testament by Pericles' bust, or rapaciously echoes "our Greek" atop Parthenon's looted frieze, it is eventually the student of Greek who unwittingly becomes shortchanged.

Since the day of Erasmus generations of key scholars such as Blass, Moulton, Robertson, Gignac, and Allen have appropriated the territory of Biblical and Classical Greek as "their Greek" while generously allotting the remaining centuries to "modern" Greek. But like Aesop's sour grapes, the sounds of the Historical Greek Pronunciation (HGP) are too sour for *their* Greek, their territorial interests at times overshadowing candid scholarship.

This arbitrary stance among leading Erasmian scholars today shows that what they have so abjectly failed to understand and accept is that the move being made for the HGP is far greater than merely the question of pronunciation. Indeed, the reason for bringing Erasmian into the discussion in this work is not just to beat it down in order to declare the other contestant a winner; there is a weightier issue at hand: the Erasmian harm, discussed next.

32. Moulton, *Introduction to New Testament Greek*, 11.

# Chapter 7

# The Erasmian Harm and the Remedy

## 7.1 THE ERASMIAN DICHOTOMY OF GREEK

The Erasmian harm is more than just an uncharacteristic, un-Greek pronunciation: it is a barrier planted in the center of Greek learning. When in the 1500s the Erasmian ax of dichotomy was brought down into the heart of the Greek language and scholarship, an insurmountable barrier between the two parts was formed and founded on the concocted notion that the Byzantines pronounced Greek in a manner unrelated to the true pronunciation of Ancient Greek (4.1). Renaissance Erasmians now could readily claim that the true pronunciation of Greek was distorted by the Byzantines and more so by their displaced remnants in Europe. For the past five centuries this tacit conspiracy has enabled leading non-Greek Western intellectuals to convince successive generations of scholars that from the Christian era onward, Greek is irrelevant to the earlier Greek in that it became corrupt by the Roman, Slavic, Frankish, Venetian, and Turkish influences, in effect producing a bizarre "modern" Greek idiom that is unrelated to Κοινή, let alone Classical Greek.

The truth is that early on, especially from AD 330 (1.7), the Greek language remained homogeneous within the Byzantine Empire, unaffected by the forces that gave rise to many of Europe's dialects; and Neohellenic is virtually "purified" of the Turkish influence. Besides, a grammatical comparison, the true test in the scientific study of language, can show that Neohellenic preserves not only the phonology but also the essentials of morphology and to a considerable extent the syntax of Attic Greek, three distinctive criteria of its being a direct descendant and representative of Attic. In fact, except for a number of simplified grammatical and morphological components, mainstream Neohellenic shares with Attic and Κοινή essentially the same parts of grammar, the same singular alphabet, the same orthography, a high percentage of the same vocabulary, and the same phonemic sounds.

The Erasmian divider has prevented scholars from conceding the significance of the later Greek, depriving scholarship not only of a fuller linguistic tool for the interpretation of the Greek language and literature but also of being enlightened by the later history of the language. What is at stake, as a result, is the meaning of the Greek texts, which needs to receive light exegetically not just from the earlier (Hellenistic and pre-Hellenistic) but also from the later (Byzantine and Late Neohellenic) history of the language.

Following is a brief description of the need for the Κοινή of the NT to receive light also from the later Greek.[1]

## 7.2 LIGHT FROM THE LATER GREEK

### 7.2.1 Neohellenic

Neohellenic is of chief significance in the interpretation of the earlier Greek language and literature and therefore of the Κοινή of the NT. Many terms in Neohellenic found also in the NT can affirm how they are applied in the NT text. Hasselbrook notes:

> [A] number of terms strongly associated with Christianity occur for the first time in the New Testament and continue in Modern Greek usage with the same meanings. . . . Furthermore, the nature of this connection is such that the New Testament contains many features that have more affinity with Modern than Classical Greek. Therefore, a unity exists between the New Testament and Modern Greek that should not be ignored or left unexplored.[2]

Hasselbrook also notes a one-sided emphasis in today's NT lexicons in that they depend largely on the meaning of words found in literary classical works, ignoring in other words the Demotic (vernacular) component of the language from which Κοινή primarily developed. He sees in them a deficiency resulting from "not analyzing the streams of tradition relative to word usage and meaning that are preserved in the later stages of the Greek language, in particular, from medieval to modern times."[3] Hasselbrook submits that in order to balance NT lexicons it would be necessary to use a full diachronic approach to the Greek language that takes into account the dimorphic—literary and vernacular—meaning of words, not only prior to or concurrent with, but also following NT times.[4] In one of his chapters, Hasselbrook compares certain NT words as defined in reputable Ancient Greek lexicons with the meaning of those same words as articulated in reputable Neohellenic lexicons. He then notes the resultant insights gained from their Neohellenic definitions. Hasselbrook's study

1. "Earlier" refers to Hellenistic and pre-Hellenistic (chiefly Classical) Greek, and "later" to the period consisting of Byzantine Greek (AD 300–1453) and Late Neohellenic (1453 to the present).

2. Hasselbrook, *Lexicography*, 48–49.

3. Hasselbrook, *Lexicography*, 206.

4. Hasselbrook, *Lexicography*, 115.

demonstrates that Neohellenic can illuminate NT usage and lead to new and deeper exegetical insights.

A novel exegetical example of this is given by Caragounis, who analyzes the meaning of the words κλῆμα and ἄμπελος. In an article titled "Is Jesus the Vine or the Vineyard?"[5] Caragounis takes the reader on a fully documented diachronic journey from Aesop (7th–6th c. BC) through classical, Hellenistic, Byzantine, and modern times to show how these words were used at different stages in their evolutionary spectrum, especially in NT times. By the end of the journey the reader realizes that what has been traditionally understood in John 15:1–7 as κλήματα *branches* (disciples) and ἄμπελος *vine* (Jesus) is to be understood instead as κλήματα *vines* (disciples) and ἄμπελος *vineyard* (Jesus). This "new" (and correct) interpretation of κλῆμα and ἄμπελος is based not on the "modern" usage of these words, but on their NT usage preserved in Neohellenic. While this "revised" meaning of κλήματα and ἄμπελος does not change the fundamental import of Jesus' metaphor, it does nevertheless paint a very different picture that reveals profound new truths.

As is the case with κλῆμα and ἄμπελος, NT words may show retention of their classical meaning, an added semantic dimension, or some distinct new nuance, with a significant number of such words and their meaning being preserved in Neohellenic. Looking at NT lexica through the full diachronic lens (from pre-/classical times to the present) brings into view a vast and virtually unexplored field for NT Greek lexicography.[6]

Neohellenic helps not only in the area of lexicography but also in the solution of text-critical issues—corrupt readings, permutations, substitutions, parablepsis, haplography, metathesis, dittography, conflation, etc. Many such readings are of an acoustic nature, that is, related to pronunciation. Space may be devoted here but to a couple of examples to show that a scholar who has an eye *and* ear attuned to the HGP is more fully equipped for textual criticism. Thus, one who sees, for instance, τοῖς misspelled in a MS as τῆς, τις as τεις, ἵνα as εινα, λέγετε as λεγεται, or γινώσκετε as γεινώσκεται, he detects scribal errors of an acoustic dimension because he *hears* τοῖς, τῆς, τεις, τις all as [tis], εινα as [ina], λεγεται as [lejete], and γεινώσκεται as [jinoskete], that is, the way a semiliterate scribe heard (but misspelled) these words in the scriptorium before he recorded them (2.3, fn.).

Conversely, an Erasmian adherent's ear is not attuned to these types of error. An Erasmian sees τοῖς [tis] as *toys*, but when τοῖς is misspelled τῆς, τις, or τεις (each pronounced [tis]), he sees τῆς as *tays*, τις as *'tis* or *ties*, and τεις as *tays* or *tees*. He also sees ἵνα [ina] as *high-/he-nah*, but when ἵνα is

**"The Erasmian system may lead to unforeseen negative consequences, particularly in the field of textual criticism."**

5. Caragounis, *Development of Greek*, 247–61.

6. There is virtually no lexicographical work that includes the period beyond Byzantine times. As Patrick James remarks, "Sophocles 1860 and . . . 1870 remain the only works to encompass postclassical Greek . . . superseded only in part by Trapp 1994–2005" (James, "Greek Lexicography," 13).

misspelled εἴνα [ina], he sees it as *hay-nah* or *high-nah*. He also sees λέγετε [lejete] as *leg-ə-teh*, but when λέγετε is misspelled λέγεται [lejete], he sees it as *leg-ə-tie*. And he sees γινώσκετε [jinoskete] as *guy-/gi-gnaws-kəteh*, but when γινώσκετε is misspelled γεινώσκεται, he sees it as *gay-/guy-/gi-gnaws-kə-tie*, and so on. Simply put, an Erasmian does not detect the acoustic cause of these misspellings.

Recurring orthographical errors of an acoustic nature involve other sounds besides ι-/ε-sounds and are found in MSS of all text types (Byzantine, Western, Caesarean, or Alexandrian), i.e., from the latest MSS to the oldest, added evidence that NT authors used the HGP. Misspellings are thus voluminous, and reliance on the Erasmian (visual) approach to text-critical issues can be a major drawback. As Campbell notes, "Use of the Erasmian system may lead to unforeseen negative consequences, particularly in the field of textual criticism."[7] In resolving therefore text-critical issues of an acoustic nature, would it not be logical for one to make sure that his pronunciation matches the scribe's?

### 7.2.2 Byzantine and Medieval Greek

No less significant is the light from the earliest Byzantine to medieval times. For well over a thousand years Byzantine scholars and the numberless clergy kept ancient works alive, and therewith linking Classical Greek, Κοινή, and Neohellenic (1.8). These scholars contributed enormously to Christian teaching, philosophy, and Greek learning, not to mention the arts and sciences. Their works are those of theologians, philosophers, historiographers, mathematicians, architects, doctors, scientists, astronomers, encyclopedists, artisans, poets, and others, all reflecting the varied genres to which they devoted their literary talents. Scholarly Byzantine works are Atticistic in style (imitative of classical authors). Because they discuss or allude to classical works frequently, they contain quotes, proverbial sayings, and expressions of ancient writers, scores of which are popularly used as idioms or adages in Neohellenic today.

A discussion of any Byzantine authors and their works would be beyond the scope of this work.[8] Suffice it to say that in AD 325, only within a few years of the end of the persecution of Christians in AD 311, the Byzantines formulated the Nicene Creed, the doctrine of faith adhered to virtually by all Catholic, Orthodox, and Protestant Christians. Most of their literary works were produced during the medieval period (9th–13th c.) and are based on Aristotelian logic or Platonic ideas often in combination with theological thought. Thus, at the start of the first Byzantine Renaissance in the 860s—after Byzantium came out of its Dark Age (650–750) and the Age

7. Campbell, *Advances*, 206.

8. Worthy of mention as an example is Ioannis Chrysostomos (John Chrysostom, "the golden mouthed"), Archbishop of Constantinople (347–407), who produced vast numbers of exegetical homilies and other theological studies. So did his contemporaries Vasilios, Grigorios, Athanasios, and other church fathers.

of Iconoclasm (750–850)—Byzantine historians again took up the pen and "preserved everything we have of Ancient Greek literature, for the oldest surviving manuscripts were copied in these years."[9] Of the fifty-five thousand Ancient Greek texts in existence today some forty thousand were salvaged and transmitted by the Byzantines; and virtually all of the Greek MSS (about 95 percent) are Byzantine.[10]

European Renaissance scholars, who until the fall of Constantinople in 1453 had seen only fragments of Ancient Greek manuscripts, were bedazzled by the full texts of antiquity Byzantine scholars brought with them and which they could read, translate, teach, and emulate with their pen in Thucydidean style. Those were also the scholars who furnished the Byzantine text that became the basis of Desiderius Erasmus' 1516 edition of the Greek NT during the Reformation, including the King James Version in 1611.

These facts are strong indicators of the intense interest both lay and clergy in Byzantium nurtured toward learning, especially in Attic grammar and literature, as well as in the LXX and NT MSS. Had the Byzantines not pursued the copying and preservation of manuscripts, the heritage of the ancient, early Christian, and Medieval Greek worlds would have most assuredly perished.

Doubtless, the works of Byzantine theologians and writers can strengthen the unity between the New Testament and Neohellenic by providing lexicographers and other scholars with invaluable insights in the diachronic investigation of biblical terms and usage, and thereby impact textual criticism, exegesis, and textual transmission.

## 7.3 THE ERASMIAN HARM

To say therefore that the light from the later Greek is irrelevant to the earlier Greek is tantamount to saying that Greek died around the time of the destruction of the NT autographs and no later than the end of the persecution of the first Christians. The Hellenic tongue, however, is anything but dead. And we know that the Erasmian cut-off point between the earlier and the later Greek was politically orchestrated by Renaissance scholars under the fabrication that the latter's pronunciation was corrupt. After five hundred years this dichotomy is still subject to the same pretext, still based on the association of the later Greek with Byzantine and modern-era Orthodoxy. Consequently, the message seminarians receive early on from such treatment of the Greek language is that post-NT Greek sounds different (that is, unlike Erasmian!) and is therefore unrelated to the earlier Greek—as though the value of the later Greek could be determined by pronunciation alone.

**The Erasmian pretext poses as a deterrent to the light from the later Greek.**

With the Greek language thus dismembered and its sounds altered, it becomes quite difficult, if not impossible, for those confined to the Erasmian side of the divider

9. Wells, *Sailing from Byzantium*, 41.

10. Brownworth (see p. 7, fn. 11).

to conceptualize the possible extent to which the resources of the later Greek can be harnessed to holistically and diachronically shed light on the Greek text. And that encapsulates the horrendous damage the Erasmian ax, abetted by the stance of leading modern Erasmuses, has succeeded in inflicting on the Hellenic tongue and learning.

## 7.4 THE ERASMIAN FORCE

As already mentioned, in the majority of institutions of higher learning, especially in America, Erasmian is paradoxically used both for Biblical and Classical Greek. This situation, coupled with the above description of the damaging effects Erasmian has inflicted upon the Greek language and learning, of necessity leads one to ponder over this pronunciation system's ubiquity after five whole centuries. As McLean observes,

> It is indeed surprising that the pronunciation system invented by a Dutchman living 500 years ago in Northern Europe, with no real contact with Greek culture, should still be in use in the modern university of the twenty-first century.[11]

So, what sustains Erasmian? What is the force behind this worldwide un-Greek pronunciation system? For the answer, one would need to take into account the propagators of Erasmian, of which there are three general groups.

The first group comprises today's influential Erasmian scholars who have not understood or for various reasons are not willing to accept the relation of the later Greek to the earlier Greek, let alone the nature and purpose of the HGP. The second group, also the largest, is made up of acolytes, namely, today's instructors and other users of Erasmian who imitate the pronunciation variety of their teacher.

Then there is a third group: past authors, particularly since the last part of the nineteenth century, such as Friedrich Blass (1843–1907), whose stance on the pronunciation of Greek became the modern pylons of the Erasmian stronghold and upon whose works subsequent generations of leading scholars have depended; and more recently, W. Sidney Allen (1918–2004), whose celebrated *Vox Graeca: The Pronunciation of Classical Greek* is viewed by many as today's "bible of 'restored' pronunciation."[12]

It is nevertheless the first group of scholars who, by their action or inaction, can make a difference today in how Greek will be viewed and treated on our campuses tomorrow.

Thanks to a growing global awareness and resultant renewed interest among NT scholars and students today regarding the pronunciation of NT Greek, most leading Erasmians would concede that NT Greek did not sound like Erasmian. At the same time, some die-hards hold that even though Erasmian "doesn't make it right," the "standard" Erasmian pronunciation in the majority of institutions today is reason

11. McLean, *New Testament Greek*, 4.

12. Dillon, *Classical World*, 323.

enough to keep using it. This *argumentum ad numerum* reasoning is unconvincing given the fact not only that Erasmian is not right, but also that there is no consensus among Erasmians as to whose pronunciation variety is standard in the first place.

In the same vein of thought is the concern that students who pronounce NT Greek the Modern Greek way encounter difficulties when mingling with students who use Erasmian. But while this may be a concern, it is a concern neither of students who use Erasmian nor of students who are cognizant of the evidence that Greek is read and pronounced today pretty much the way it was read and pronounced by the first Greek-speaking Christians; rather, it is a concern of the old die-hard Erasmians whose stay-the-course reasoning militates against the presence of the HGP.

One would not be amiss in inferring from the above sketch of the Erasmian state of affairs that the force that sustains Erasmian as the default pronunciation in the majority of institutions today is characterized not by what is required of Erasmian scholars but rather by what is not. The Erasmian force, in other words, may be seen as a scholastic comfort zone wherein professionals operate without having to measure up to any "correct" Erasmian pronunciation; a walled-in attitudinal environment that shelters not the English-speaking students—who would supposedly face difficulties in learning to read and pronounce Greek the Neohellenic way (5.2; 5.7)—but the scholars themselves. This academic milieu in turn presents itself as a gainful enterprise for Erasmian-based materials to flow into centers of Greek learning.[13] Simply put, the Erasmian force is a complacent, accountability-free capitalizing attitudinal system that feeds on itself.

## 7.5 AN ILL-FOUNDED FEAR

Scholars who speak of Erasmian, reconstructed, or other pronunciations of Greek have not perceived the depth of the aforementioned problem, that what is at stake here is the meaning of the Greek texts, which receives light exegetically from the later history of the language, as discussed above. Their fear has been that if they concede the importance of the later Greek they are going to find themselves standing outside the circle of native Greek speakers and those who sound more like Greeks. This is an ill-founded fear, however. It is the fear that pronunciation will be used to gauge one's Greek credentials. Doubtless, pronunciation can be an outward sign of familiarity with a language, but in no way does it indicate that a non-Greek scholar cannot contribute to the advancement of Greek studies without first becoming fluent in Neohellenic. On the contrary, many great works have been accomplished by scholars who have (or had) limited proficiency in Neohellenic—some, in fact, none.

13. It is strongly emphasized here that this observation pertains exclusively to the Erasmian pronunciation propagated through pronunciation keys, transliteration, treatises on the phonology of Greek, and instructional practices, not to the otherwise scholarly content found in many works produced by Erasmian adherents.

It must be underscored at the same time that there are some natural differences when it comes to the question of a *feeling* for the language. The Greek scholar, like any other national in regard to his own language, has an intuitive sense for the language that a non-native lacks. That is the natural difference between the speech of native speakers and that of second-language adult learners, a truth no second-language adult learner, especially one not thoroughly immersed in the language over lengthy periods of time, particularly wishes to hear. But that is true of any language. It is the stark reality of language acquisition and learning, and burying the head in the sand does not change that reality. Of course, this lays greater onus on non-Greek scholars in terms of the need to study more of the Greek language and to try to get to grips with its diachronic concerns.

## 7.6 APPLYING THE HGP: A STEP FORWARD

Neohellenic is the direct descendant of Attic Greek, its sounds having come down to us as they naturally evolved from antiquity to the present, unseparated from their post-Eucleidean alphabet and orthography. Applying therefore the HGP sounds and orthography to the Greek language diachronically is a scientific demand. Thus, introducing the HGP to institutions of higher learning is the remedial force that can (a) gradually remove the barrier created by the Erasmian pronunciation when it split the Greek language into ancient and modern as if the two parts were unrelated, (b) lead to a holistic approach to the Greek language, history, and literature, (c) help in the effective evaluation of variants in the process of textual transmission, and (d) allow the light from the later Greek to illuminate the NT text and enrich exegesis and interpretation.

Brilliant scholars spend decades applying Erasmian or pursuing some other type of "reconstructed" Greek pronunciation—enough time for immersion in any language. Of course immersion in Neohellenic in Greece for any reasonable amount of time may be inconvenient and in many cases nearly impossible for the majority of scholars and students. But the good news is that becoming familiar with the HGP requires literally a fraction of the time that it takes to reach a level of proficiency in the language. With today's technology, this step forward can be accomplished at home. That is one way to begin internalizing Greek words, for close familiarity with a language begins with the *sine qua non* method of basic words and phrases heard and rehearsed using natural sounds.[14]

14. If you sojourn in Greece to improve your Neohellenic language skills, it is recommended that you seek opportunities to be immersed in activities within a formal learning environment. In this way you may find yourself in situations in which you can share a few words in Greek before groups, the preparation for which activity would accelerate your progress enormously. Restricting your sojourn to visiting places, touring the islands, shopping, and engaging in other such fun activities may enhance your appreciation of Greece and the Greek culture but offer you an inadequate—and probably skewed—view of the Greek speech.

## 7.7 LIVING SOUNDS VS. ERASMIAN

The essence of the advantages of using the natural and living sounds of Neohellenic for NT Greek rather than Erasmian is captured in the words of Cohen and Sellers:

> One of these [advantages] is that the student is learning the sounds of a living language. A knowledge of the modern pronunciation will make it possible for the student to converse with native speakers, whether in his own country or abroad, . . . [which] makes much more possible an approach (however slight at first) toward the acquisition of language intuition. . . . The constant learning and speaking of a real pronunciation system will undoubtedly facilitate a better intuition for semantic range and grammatical nuance. . . . In the light of the advantages of the modern pronunciation and the easy access to modern Greek materials as well as native speakers of Modern Greek, there seems to be no compelling reason to retain the Erasmian pronunciation system.[15]

But the student can also be assured that in addition to the advantages of "learning the sounds of a living language" and "the acquisition of language intuition," applying the Neohellenic pronunciation takes one a giant historical step closer to New Testament times as well as to Alexander's day: for if the HGP is preserved in Neohellenic, then the words in a Κοινή text orthophonically pronounced the Neohellenic way would have sounded normal to the first Greek-speaking Christians, to Paul and his contemporary Athenians, to the disciples of Jesus, and yes, to Jesus himself. In fact, the same would have sounded as well no less intelligible and clear to the Septuagint scholars, a number of whom were doubtless contemporaries of Alexander and his private tutor, Aristotle (2.22; 3.4; 3.5).

And if, as so lucidly expressed by Cohen and Sellers, there seems to be no compelling reason to retain the Erasmian pronunciation in the study of Biblical Greek, then there should likewise be no compelling reason to retain the same for the study of Classical Greek.

## 7.8 CLOSING REMARKS

Today a worldwide precedent is being set, as an increasing number of scholars and students adopt the Neohellenic pronunciation—at times alongside Erasmian. This unprecedented phenomenon is largely owed to the rapid growth of online offerings of NT Greek by various entities and individuals that use or incorporate the Neohellenic pronunciation. It could very well be that this trend, globally fanned by the unbridled employment of social media, will precipitate an ever-increasing awareness of the advantages of the HGP and eventually cause the Erasmian preponderance to be overturned.

15. Cohen, *Theological Journal*, 200–201.

# Chapter 8

# Pronunciation Tips

## 8.1 TONE VS. STRESS

Tone refers to the pitch of sounds (high, mid, low) during speech. In a tone language like Chinese, the quality of the rising and falling of voice carries meaning. Stress, on the other hand, refers to the relative loudness of voice produced by the simultaneous pressure the speaker exerts on his lungs during the flow of air passing through the mouth (cf. 2.19.2).

## 8.2 STRESS IN ENGLISH

English is a stress language. The stressing of a syllable over unstressed syllables is one of the fundamental characteristics of spoken English, and the one that most distinguishes English from other languages. English uses *primary*, *secondary*, and *zero* stress. Unstressed vowels tend to become centralized in the mouth and take the quality of the *schwa* vowel [ə] as the *a* in *above*. The word *fá-mi-ly* [fæməlı], for instance, receives primary stress on the first syllable (*fá-*), causing the vowel in the unstressed syllable *-mi-* (the syllable immediately following) to become a schwa vowel [mə].

## 8.3 ENGLISH PHONETIC ENVIRONMENT VS. GREEK GRAMMAR

English vowel length is determined by phonetic environment. The *ea* in *bead*, for instance, is longer than the *ea* in *beat*. The reason is that for voiced *d* in *bead* the vocal cords must remain in vibration, thus it takes longer to articulate it than its voiceless counterpart *t* in *beat*. By contrast, vowel distinction in Greek is determined not phonetically but grammatically: ἄλλος *other*, ἄλλως *otherwise;* πόλις *city*, πόλεις *cities*;

πιστῆς *faithful* (gen. sg. f.) πιστοῖς *faithful* (dat. pl. m.). One not familiar with grammar rules, whether today, in NT times, or in Aristotle's day, is/was likely to write ο for ω, ει or η for ι, η for οι, ε for αι, etc., the misspelling causing no difference in pronunciation.

## 8.4 ENGLISH STRESS AND GREEK PITCH-ACCENT

If, for practical purposes, languages were rated on a stress scale of 1 to 5, English would be no. 5, while Greek would be about no. 1.5, that is, comparatively low on stress. Greek has a pitch-accent, a tonal accent system that borders on stress but relies on the raised (or lowered) pitch of the accented syllable of a word.

The following points sum up the major differences between Greek pitch-accent and English stress. Comparisons are made orthophonically—i.e., in isolation (1.12; 1.13)—hence free of idiosyncratic characteristics.

| | **Greek** | **English** |
|---|---|---|
| 1. | All syllables are accented and pronounced distinctly. | Unstressed syllables are pronounced less distinctly than stressed syllables. |
| 2. | All syllables are isochronous (equal in length or quantity). | Syllables are intrinsically long or short depending on phonetic environment:<br>bead~beat, have~half, pig~pick[1] |
| 3. | Regardless of the number of syllables, a word is accented on *only one* syllable:<br>ἀν-τι-δι-α-τι-θε-μέ-νους | One primary ´ and multiple secondary stresses are possible:<br>tràn-sub-stàn-ti-á-tion |
| 4. | The accented syllable must be one of the last three syllables:<br>κα-τε-κλη-ρο-νό-μη-σε, πε-ρι-το-μή | Primary stress is not restricted to the the last three syllables:<br>cá-te-gò-ry, hó-no-rà-ry, pó-me-grà-nate |
| 5. | The pitch of an accented syllable rises above (or falls below) the other syllables and may be slightly louder and longer than the unaccented syllables. | The stressed syllable rises above the unstressed syllables in pitch and is markedly louder and longer than the unstressed syllables. |

## 8.5 ACCENTUATION

Pitch-accent in Greek plays a most significant role in that it determines meaning. Accenting the wrong syllable can give the word a different meaning or render it incomprehensible. For instance, πότε *when*, ποτέ *ever, never*; ζήτω *long live!*, ζητῶ *I seek*. (There is no acoustic difference between the acute accent ´ and the circumflex ˜ .)

The accented syllable of a word pronounced orthophonically is raised to a higher pitch and is imperceptibly or slightly more stressed and longer than other syllables.

1. Phonetically transcribed as [bi:d] / [bit], [hæ:v] / [hæf], [pʰɪ:g] / [pʰɪk], where " : " indicates length. Notice that the vowels [i], [æ], [ɪ] become intrinsically (environmentally) lengthened when followed by a voiced consonant (here [d, v, g] respectively), but not lengthened when followed by a voiceless consonant (here [t, f, k] respectively).

This is somewhat similar to the distinction in English between *object* [ɑbdʒɪkt] (noun) and *object* [əbdʒekt] (verb), except that the stressed vowel *o* in *object* is [ɑ], but when unstressed the same becomes a schwa [ə]; and unstressed *e* is [ɪ], but when stressed it becomes [e].

In a Greek word all syllables are isochronous, accented, and distinct, with one—and only one—syllable being raised to a higher pitch, while the vowels of all other syllables retain their phonetic properties.

Listed below are Greek homographs (words spelled alike) accented differently. The only difference between the words in each pair is phonemic, not phonetic; that is, accentuation causes a change in meaning but not in the way a word is otherwise pronounced. Some of the words listed are not found in the Greek NT text.

**Significance of Greek Accentuation**

| | | | |
|---|---|---|---|
| ἄγων | *leading* | ἀγών | *contest* |
| ἄκρις | *extremity* | ἀκρίς | *locust* |
| ἄλλα | *other* (pl neut) | ἀλλά | *but* |
| ἄρα | *then, therefore* | ἀρά | *curse* |
| βάλω (βάλλω) | *I throw, place* (aor act subj) | βαλῶ | *I throw, place* (fut act ind)[2] |
| Δία (acc) | *Zeus* | διά | *by, through* |
| δόκος | *opinion* | δοκός | *beam* |
| εἶπε | *(he) said* | εἰπέ | *Say!* |
| ἕκτος | *sixth* | ἐκτός | *except* |
| θέα | *view* | θεά | *goddess* |
| λῆνος | *wool* | ληνός | *winepress* |
| μόνη | *alone* | μονή | *convent* |
| νόμος | *law* | νομός | *district* |
| Ξάνθος | *a proper name* | ξανθός | *golden, yellow, blond* |
| Ξένων | *a proper name* | ξενών | *guest's quarters* |
| ὄρος | *mountain* | ὀρός | *serum, whey* |
| πατροκτόνος | *patricidal* | πατρόκτονος | *slain by a father* |
| πότε | *when?* | ποτέ | *ever, never* |
| πρωτογόνος | *bringing forth first* | πρωτόγονος | *first-born* |
| Σταῦρος | *a proper name* | σταυρός | *cross* |
| τόμος | *volume, tome* | τομός | *cutting* |
| ὕβρις | *insolence* | ὑβρίς | *a night bird* |
| ὦμος | *shoulder* | ὠμός | *raw* |

Accenting the right syllable of a word is extremely significant in Greek phonology. This is also an area in which Erasmian is particularly deficient, especially when it comes to multisyllabic words. The word ἀποκάλυψις *revelation*, for instance, typically pronounced by Erasmians [əpòkəlúpsɪs], is accented twice, with a secondary stress placed beyond the antepenult; the vowel in -κά- (the syllable that ought to be stressed), being unaccented, turns into a schwa [ə] as does also the initial vowel α [ə]; and υ, unduly stressed and pronounced [u], contributes to rendering the pronunciation of the word incomprehensible.

2. This type of distinction can be seen in the personal endings and cases of many verbs and substantives.

## 8.6 NONDIPHTHONGIZATION

Unlike English, Greek has no diphthongs. Two adjacent vowels in Greek may resemble an English diphthong but each belongs in a different syllable. For example, ἐλέησον [eleison] *have mercy* to the English ear may sound as *e-lay-son* (three syllables), but the word actually consists of four syllables: ἐ-λέ-η-σον, -η- being a syllable by itself.

An English diphthong is defined as *a complex speech sound or glide that begins with one vowel and gradually changes to another vowel within the same syllable*—as [eᴵ] in *they* or [aᴵ] in *fine* (but not [e-ɪ] or [a-ɪ]). By contrast, in Greek each vowel in a word is, or belongs in, one syllable. Examples:

| | | | | |
|---|---|---|---|---|
| δι-α-νό-η-μα | **[o-i]** | not | [ɔᴵ] | *thought* |
| ἐ-λέ-η-σον | **[e-i]** | not | [eᴵ] | *(have) mercy* |
| ἀ-θῴ-ου | **[o-u]** | not | [oᵁ] | *innocent* (gen.) |
| Ῥω-μα-ϊ-στί | **[a-i]** | not | [aᴵ] | *in Roman* |
| Με-νε-λά-ου | **[a-u]** | not | [aᵁ] | *Menelaos* (gen.) |

## 8.7 NONASPIRATION OF [P, T, K]

English p, t, k are noticeably aspirated when followed by a vowel sound, particularly in initial position. In words such as *pair, take, kit* the initial plosive consonant is pronounced with a stream of air accompanying it during articulation. By contrast, Greek π, τ, κ (= p, t, k) are always unaspirated: [p, t, k], not [$p^h$, $t^h$, $k^h$].

## 8.8 THE SOUNDS B, D, G

The sounds b, d, g have always been a part of Greek phonology but there are no individual alphabet letters for these (2.12; 2.13). Instead, Greek uses the combinatory variants μπ, ντ, γγ/γκ medially thus: μπ = *mb* as in ti*mb*er, ντ = *nd* as in hi*nd*er γγ/γκ = *ng* as in E*ng*lish, where voiceless π, τ, γ/κ after a nasal sound become voiced b, d, g.

| | | | | | |
|---|---|---|---|---|---|
| Examples: | μπ | mb | ἔμπορος | (emboros) | *merchant* |
| | | | λάμπω | (lambo) | *I shine* |
| | ντ | nd | ἐντός | (endos) | *within* |
| | | | πάντοτε | (pandote) | *always* |
| | γγ, γκ | ng | ὄγγος | (ongos) | *weight* |
| | | | ἀγκάλη | (angali) | *embrace* |

The same phonetic effects occur at word juncture depending on conversational speed, speech habits, occasion, etc. In informal speech *mb, nd, ng* may sound as mere *b, d, g* respectively. These and combinatory variants μπ, ντ, γγ/γκ are nonphonemic.

## 8.9 PALATALIZATION OF VELARS Κ, Γ, Χ

In pronouncing the made-up words *koo-kee, koo-kee,* you may notice a slight change between the *k* in *koo* and the *k* in *kee*. The change is due to the shift in tongue position from the back vowel *oo* [u] in *koo* to the front vowel *ee* [i] in *kee*. At *koo*, lips are rounded and the tongue is humped high up in the back of the mouth. As you proceed from *koo* to *kee*, lips spread and the tongue moves slightly forward against the hard palate. The change in tongue position from *koo*, in which the back of the tongue is against the velum, to *kee*, in which the front of the tongue moves against the palate, causes *velar k* to become *palatalized*. This type of palatalization is more noticeable in Greek. Palatalization applies to κ, γ, χ when they are followed by [i] or [e] sounds. The following illustration shows this:

| **Velar κ, γ, χ** | | | **Palatalized κ, γ, χ**[3] | |
|---|---|---|---|---|
| κου | κο | κα | κι | κε |
| coo | *caw* | *car* | *key* | *ken* |
| γου | γο | γα | γι | γε |
| *woo* | *amigo* | *amiga*[4] | *ye* | *yen* |
| χου | χο | χα[5] | χι | χε |
| *who* | *haw* | *ha* | *he* | *hen* |

Digraphs γκ, γγ become likewise palatalized before [i] or [e]: ἄγγελος [aŋɟelos] *angel*, ἄγκυρα [aŋɟira] *anchor*. The English counterpart of [ɟ] is *g* in *gear* or *gu* in *guess*.

In certain cases the presence of γ betrays palatalization. Thus, Hellenistic papyri reflect palatalization in the spelling of ἱγεροῦ [ijeru] for ἱεροῦ, ἱγερῷ [ijero] for ἱερῷ, and γερῖς [jeris] for ἱεροῖς.[6] Here unaccented palatalized initial syllable ι [i] becomes conditionally palatalized [j] by joining front vowel ε to form the syllable γε [je]. This acoustically-guided informal spelling practice is indicative of inadequate schooling

3. When velars κ, γ, χ [k, ɣ, x] are conditionally palatalized, that is, when they are found before a front vowel sound [i] or [e], they may be represented by the IPA symbols [c], [ʝ], [ç], respectively.

4. The English sound closest to γ is the *w* in *woo* and *y* in *yes*. Spanish *amigo friend* is closer to γο, and *am*iga to γα.

5. The English sound closest to the Greek χ is the *h* in *have* and h*e*.

6. Papyri.info, http://www.papyri.info/ddbdp/bgu;4;1197.

on the part of the writer, and not of any widespread phonological process involving the softening of plosive [g] and turning into the velar fricative γάμμα [ɣ].[7]

The same palatalization effect occurs today in a number of words beginning with unaccented ι/υ+vowel. In such cases the letter γ is affixed to unaccented initial front vowel [i], leading to alternative (formal/informal) spelling and pronunciation, e.g., (formal) ἰ-α-τρός [iatros] > (informal) για-τρός [jatros] *doctor*, υἱ-ός [ios] > γιός [jos] *son*, ὑ-α-λί [iali] (from ὕ-α-λος) > γυα-λί [jali] *glass*, ἑ-ορ-τή [eorti] > γιορτή [jorti] *celebration*, ἰ-ῶ-τα [iota] > γιώ-τα [jota] the letter ι. The word ὑ-γεί-α [ijia] *health* becomes informal γειά [ja], though the initial υ- is retained after a word ending in [n]/[s]: εἰς ὑγείαν > συγείαν [sijian] *to health*, στην υγειά σου [stin ija su] *to your health*.

Some words beginning with δια- drop δ, thereby effecting the same change: δι-α-τί > για-τί [jati] *why*, δι-ά > γιά [ja] *for*. Other words, e.g., διάλεκτος [ðialektos] *dialect*, διατάσσω [ðiataso] *I command*, as a rule retain their nonpalatilized formal usage.

## 8.10 PALATALIZATION OF I [i] AS [j]

Many Greek words end in the cluster "consonant + accented front vowel + vowel." Some of those words, e.g., παιδία *children*, ἀρνία *lambs/sheep*, and μία *one* (fem.) alternatively shift their accent, thereby blending two syllables into one: παι-δί-α > παι-διά, ἀρ-νί-α > ἀρ-νιά, μί-α > μιά. The shift results in the palatalization of the consonant before the accented front vowel, thus δι in παιδιά becomes [ðj] hence [peðjá], νι in ἀρνιά becomes [nj] > [ɲ] hence [arɲá] (cf. Span. ñ), and μί in μιά becomes [mj] hence [mjá]. Phonemically [ðj], [nj], [mj] before a vocalic sound are analyzed as /ði/, /ni/, and /mi/ respectively. In such cases [j] may be interpreted as a conditional allophone of /i /. This type of conditional palatalization is present in Κοινή: ἀρνία > ἀρνιά (John 21:15); μία > μιά (nom.), μιᾷ (dat.) *one* (Acts 20:7); and παιδία *children* > παιδιά *children/friends* (John 21:5).[8]

Some words are accented on the vowel following the palatalized consonant and are thus given only in their palatalized form: πρασιά [prasjá] *garden area* (Mark 6:40); ἀνθρακιάν [anθrakján] (=[anθracán]) *(burning) coal* (John 18:18); διάβολος [ðjávolos] *devil* 1 Tim. 3:11; λαλιά [laljá] (=[laʎá]) *speech* (Mt 26:73), where [ʎ], the conditionally palatalized allophone of λ /l/, is also analyzed phonemically as /li/.[9]

7. I recall being in the third grade in Greece when I wrote "Καινοῦργιος Χρόνος" [kenurjos hronos] *New Year*. After staring at my "phonetic" spelling for a while, I hesitantly decided that I had never seen a γ in Καινοῦριος before. My mother, with spelling skills of a fifth grader, confirmed my error.

8. In John 21:5 Jesus, unrecognized by the disciples who have been struggling to catch some fish, gets their attention by shouting above the noise of the sea, ΠΑΙΔΙΑ! "Friends!" In this case Jesus would have used παι-διά! [pe-ðjá] as a two-syllable word accented on its palatalized ultima—exactly the way this word is casually used among adults today. The same word rendered παι-δί-α [pe-ðí-a] would have meant "Children!"—not an appropriate appellation among adult friends.

9. This type of palatalization should not be confused with any pronunciation peculiarities in parts of Greece where λ and ν are invariably heard slightly to heavily palatalized before front vowels. The standard Greek pronunciation, for instance, of βασιλεία *kingdom* is [vasilia], and of κοινωνία

## 8.11 ALPHABETICAL CONSONANTS

Below is a description of each Greek alphabetical consonant and its English counterpart or equivalent sound.

| Letter | IPA | Comments | Formal definition |
|---|---|---|---|
| Π π | [p] | **p**lay (unaspirated p) | voiceless bilabial stop |
| Τ τ | [t] | A**t**las (unaspirated t) | voiceless apicoalveolar stop |
| Κ κ | [k] | **K**leenex (unaspirated k)<br>**k** in **k**ey, **k**en before **i** or **e** sounds | voiceless dorsovelar stop |
| Β β | [v] | very | voiced labiodental fricative |
| Φ φ | [f] | **f**erry | voiceless labiodental fricative |
| Δ δ | [ð] | **th**at | voiced apicodental fricative |
| Θ θ | [θ] | **th**in | voiceless apicodental fricative |
| Ζ ζ | [z] | **z**oo (a single consonant) | voiced apicoalveolar fricative |
| Σ σ, ς | [s] | **s**o | voiceless apicoalveolar fricative |
| Γ γ | [ɣ] | Span. amigo; **w** in **w**att<br>**y** in **y**ield, **y**es before **i** or **e** sounds | voiced dorsovelar fricative |
| Χ χ | [x] | Span. ojo; **h** in **h**ave, **h**ot<br>**h** in **h**e, **h**elp before **i** or **e** sounds | voiceless dorsovelar fricative |
| Μ μ | [m] | **m**e | voiced bilabial nasal continuant |

*communion* is [kinonia]—not [vasiʎía] or [kinoɲía].

*Trivia*

It is said that γάϊδαρος *donkey* is accented on the *fourth* syllable from the end, proof that Greek trisyllabotony (limiting the accent of all Greek words to the last three syllables) no longer reigns in Greek. Wrong. The two contiguous vocalic syllables αϊ [a-i], when followed by a consonant as in νεράϊδα *mermaid*, in slower speech may be pronounced [ne-rá-i-ða], but in rapid speech as one syllable, hence [ne-ráj-ða] or [ne-rá$^{j}$-ða]. Greek [aj]/[a$^{j}$] is not analyzed as the English diphthong [a$^{I}$] in that it consists of the vowel [a] and approximant palatal consonant (semivowel) [j], a conditionally palatalized allophone of /i/. (In examples such as γῆ [ji] *earth*, in which γ occurs before a front vowel, [j] is a conditional allophone of [ɣ] as well.) As for γάϊδαρος [ɣáj-ða-ros]/[ɣá$^{j}$-ða-ros] *donkey*, there is no alternative pronunciation; for no native Greek would pronounce its first syllable [ɣa-i] (i.e., γά-ϊ-δα-ρος), only [ɣaj]/[ɣá$^{j}$], invalidating the claim that this word does not follow the Greek accentuation pattern of trisyllabotony. Besides, γάϊδαρος is from Arabic *gadar* or *gaidar* (plus the Greek suffix -ος). Greek for *donkey* is ὄνος [onos] (Matt 21:5). Thus, γάϊδαρος is acoustically a three-syllable word accented on its antepenult [ɣaj]/[ɣa$^{j}$], hence in harmony with the Greek accentuation system and its unbroken trisyllabotony rule (2.14).

| Ν ν | [n] | **n**o | voiced apicoalveolar nasal continuant |
|---|---|---|---|
| Λ λ | [l] | **l**et | voiced apicoalveolar lateral continuant |
| Ρ ρ | [r] | "tapped **t**" in bu**tt**er, Span. **r** in pe**r**o; a trill (not a retroflex, continuant, or stop) | voiced apicoalveolar trill |
| Ψ ψ | [ps] | Pe**psi** | |
| Ξ ξ | [ks] | than**ks** | |

## 8.12 CONSONANT PHONEMES

| Place (right) and Manner (down) of articulation | **bilabial** two lips | **labio-dental** lower lip, upper teeth | **apico-dental** tongue tip, upper teeth | **apico-alveolar** tongue tip, upper tooth ridge | **apico-alveolar** tongue tip near upper tooth ridge | **dorsovelar** back of tongue, velum |
|---|---|---|---|---|---|---|
| PLOSIVE/STOP voiceless | π | | | τ | | κ |
| CONTINUANT Fricative voiced voiceless | | β φ | δ θ | | ζ σ,ς | γ χ |
| Nasal | μ | | | ν | | |
| Lateral | | | | λ | | |
| Trill | | | | ρ | | |

## 8.13 VOWELS, VOWEL DIGRAPHS, AND DIERESIS

There is a general tendency among speakers of English to diphthongize particularly the vowels ε, αι [e] as [eᶦ] and ο, ω [o] as [oᵘ]. All Greek vowel phonemes /i, e, a, o, u/ are "straight" vocalic sounds, therefore none of them should be diphthongized.

| **Greek vowels** | **English equivalent** |
|---|---|
| ι, η, υ, ει, οι, υι | **ski** |
| ε, αι | **e**nd |
| α | **a**rt |
| ο, ω | **o**r |
| ου | y**ou** |

| **Digraphs with -υ** | |
|---|---|
| αυ | br**av**o / pil**af** |
| ευ | r**ev** / r**ef** |
| ηυ | **eve** / l**eaf** |

Dieresis (Division)

When ι or υ does not form a digraph with the preceding vowel, it is marked with two dots ( ¨ ) placed over it as ϊ, ϋ. This is called *dieresis:* Ῥωμαϊκός, πραΰς, ἄϋλος (pron. [a-i]).

## 8.14 NASAL γ

The initial γ in γγ or γκ is called "nasal γ" and pronounced [ŋ] as in *sing,* while the second letter (γ or κ) is pronounced [g] as in *go* (cf. 8.8). Nasal γ in γχ is pronounced [ŋh] as in *going home.* The rare γξ is pronounced [ŋks] as in *thanks.*

1. ἐγχρίω [eŋhrio] *I anoint*
2. σάλπιγξ [salpiŋks] *trumpet*

## 8.15 VOICED Σ [z]

Σ has two lowercase forms, σ and ς. The letter σ is used at the beginning of words or between letters—never at the end of words—while ς is used exclusively at the end of words. Voiceless σ [s] becomes voiced [z] before voiced consonants β γ δ λ μ ν ρ.

1. ἐσμέν [ezmen] *we are*
2. ἄσβεστος [azvestos] *unquenchable* (cf. *asbestos*)

The same occurs at word juncture when ς is followed by a voiced consonant.

3. τοὺς λόγους [tuz loɣous] *the words* (acc.)
4. τῆς μητρός [tiz mitros] *of the mother*
5. πρὸς Γαλάτας [proz ɣalatas] *to the Galatians*

## 8.16 THE SOUNDS TZ [dz] AND TΣ [ts]

The voiced apicoalveolar affricate τζ [dz] in which voiceless τ [t] by assimilation becomes voiced [d] before voiced ζ [z], and its voiceless counterpart τσ/ς [ts] are used in Neohellenic for the sounds [dʒ] and [tʃ], respectively, in foreign names and loanwords.

1. τζ [dz] as in *adz* for [dʒ] as in Τζωρτζ *George,* τζιπ *Jeep,* τζαμί *mosque* (Ar. *jami*)
2. τσ/ς [ts] as in *its* for [tʃ] as in ματς *match,* τσιμέντο *cement* (Ital. *cemento*)

Elsewhere, τζ and τσ/ς are used in diminutives (κορίτσι *little girl* < Ancient Greek κόρη *maiden*), onomatopoetic words (τζίτζικας / -ρας *cicada* < Ancient Greek τέττιξ), or words of uncertain etymology or variable developments (Μήτσος / Τζίμης *Jim* < *Δημήτριος; τσακίζω *break, fold;* τσακώνω *catch.*

Voiceless [ts] occurs in pre-classical (Homeric) forms: μέλιτσα > μέλισσα *bee* (2.15.1). τζ-τσ ([dz]-[ts]) are sometimes interchangeable (τζίγγος, τσίγγος *zinc*). The τζ-τσ voiced-voiceless distinction is nonphonemic.

## 8.17 SAMPLE READING EXERCISE USING THE HGP

### "The Lord's Prayer" (Matt 6:9–13)

| | | | | | | | | | |
|---|---|---|---|---|---|---|---|---|---|
| 9 | **Πάτερ** | **ἡμῶν** | **ὁ** | **ἐν** | **τοῖς** | **οὐρανοῖς,** | **ἁγιασθήτω** | **τὸ** | **ὄνομά** | **σου,**[1] |
| | Páter | imón | o | en | tís* | ouranís, | ayiasthíto | to | ónomá | sou, |
| | Father | our | the | in | the | heavens | let be hallowed | the | name | your |

| | | | | | | | | | | |
|---|---|---|---|---|---|---|---|---|---|---|
| 10 | **ἐλθέτω** | **ἡ** | **βασιλεία** | **σου,** | **γενηθήτω** | **τὸ** | **θέλημά** | **σου,**[1] | **ὡς** | **ἐν** |
| | elthéto | i | vasilía | sou, | yenithíto | to | thélimá | sou, | ós | en |
| | let come | the | kingdom | your | let be done | the | will | your | as | in |

| | | | | |
|---|---|---|---|---|
| **οὐρανῷ** | **καὶ** | **ἐπὶ** | **τῆς** | **γῆς.** |
| ouranó | ké | epi | tiz | yís.** |
| heaven | and | upon | the | earth |

* ν + τ = nt or euphonic nd
** σ/ς before a voiced consonant becomes euphonic **z**.

| | | | | | | | | |
|---|---|---|---|---|---|---|---|---|
| 11 | **Τὸν** | **ἄρτον** | **ἡμῶν** | **τὸν** | **ἐπιούσιον** | **δὸς** | **ἡμῖν** | **σήμερον·** |
| | Ton | árton | imón | ton | epioúsion | ~~d~~ós | imín | símeron; |
| | The | bread | our | the | daily | give | us | today |

~~d~~ = as in the (not d)

| | | | | | | | | | | |
|---|---|---|---|---|---|---|---|---|---|---|
| 12 | **καὶ** | **ἄφες** | **ἡμῖν** | **τὰ** | **ὀφειλήματα** | **ἡμῶν,** | **ὡς** | **καὶ** | **ἡμεῖς** | **ἀφίεμεν** |
| | ke | áfes | imín | ta | ofilímata | imón, | ós | ke | imís | afíemen |
| | and | forgive | us | the | debts | our | as | also | we | forgive |

| | | |
|---|---|---|
| **τοῖς** | **ὀφειλέταις** | **ἡμῶν·** |
| tis | ofilétes | imón; |
| the | debtors | our |

euphonic **z**.

| | | | | | | | | | |
|---|---|---|---|---|---|---|---|---|---|
| 13 | **καὶ** | **μὴ** | **εἰσενέγκῃς** | **ἡμᾶς** | **εἰς** | **πειρασμόν,** | **ἀλλὰ** | **ῥῦσαι** | **ἡμᾶς** |
| | ke | mí | isenéngis | imás | is | pirazmón, | ala | ríse | imás |
| | and | do not | lead | us | into | temptation | but | deliver | us |

| | | | | | | | | | | | |
|---|---|---|---|---|---|---|---|---|---|---|---|
| **ἀπὸ** | **τοῦ** | **πονηροῦ.** | **ὅτι** | **σοῦ** | **ἐστιν** | **ἡ** | **βασιλεία** | **καὶ** | **ἡ** | **δύναμις** |
| apo | tou | ponirou. | oti | soú | estin | i | vasilía | ke | i | ~~d~~ínamis |
| from | the | evil (one) | for | yours | is | the | kingdom | and | the | power |

| | | | | | | |
|---|---|---|---|---|---|---|
| **καὶ** | **ἡ** | **δόξα** | **εἰς** | **τοὺς** | **αἰῶνας.** | **ἀμήν.** |
| ke | i | ~~d~~óksa | is | tous | eónas. | amín. |
| and | the | glory | unto | the | ages. | Amen. |

---

[1] Unaccented pronouns and forms of εἰμί *I am* "lose" their accent to the preceding word and are called **enclitics.** Here σου loses its accent this way: τὸ ὄνομα σοῦ > τὸ ὄνομά σου; τὸ θέλημα σοῦ > τὸ θέλημά σου. The lost accent turns into an acute accent ( ´ ).

# Chapter Summaries

BY WAY OF RECAPPING this study, the following chapter summaries are given, after which appropriate conclusions are drawn.

Chapter 1. This opening chapter gives a historical overview of the development of the Hellenic language into the dimorphic (artistic and vernacular) Attic dialect of Athens. Following Alexander, the Attic vernacular spreads throughout the Hellenized world and becomes the Κοινή "common" speech of Hellenistic and Roman times, and further evolves through Byzantine times into Neohellenic.

Chapter 2. Numerous Hellenistic papyri contain orthographical errors by inadequately schooled individuals who are led by their ear to euphonic spelling practices and to interchanging graphemes that stand for the same sound. The sounds behind such errors, as well as all disputable Κοινή sounds, are traced back to mid-fifth century BC when older Attic writing begins to clash with Athens' newly adopted Ionic alphabet, *the post-Eucleidean grammar*, officially in 403 BC. The ensuing confusion, accentuated by the dimorphic nature of Greek, leads to misspellings that take root and which will be repeated by the less literate throughout subsequent centuries. Yielding phonemically evidentiary values, these errors are examined diachronically, their unbroken record bearing testimony to the preservation of the historical Greek sounds in Neohellenic. Referenced are works by native and nonnative Greek scholars as well as Erasmian scholars in order to show their respective treatment of the evidence of these historical sounds, herein collectively referred to as the Historical Greek Pronunciation (HGP).

Chapter 3. The focal point in this chapter is the emergence of the HGP. Formed by or initiated within classical times, the historical sounds make their entrance into the Hellenistic era, loyal post-Eucleidean orthography by their side. Barely four decades past Aristotle's death, seventy-two Jewish emissaries steeped in a Κοινή molded by the HGP and the orthography of Aristotle's day commence the translation of Hebrew Scriptures. Paul's speech to the Athenians some three centuries later speaks of Κοινή's tenacious HGP, the mainstream Greek sound system that prevails through Hellenistic and Byzantine times over all other potential pronunciations of Greek.

Chapter 4. An investigation of the politically orchestrated origins and spread of Erasmian in the 1500s, followed by an examination of the basis of its application by various scholars today, shows that as a pronunciation system Erasmian is artificial and inconsistent, whereas the Greek pronunciation is natural, consistent, and euphonic.

Chapter 5. Refuted are two misconceptions: reading and pronouncing the ι-sound Greek letters and digraphs the Neohellenic way presents difficulties for English-speaking students; and Κοινή and Neohellenic words are dissimilar. A comparison of Greek and English phonemes and conventional alphabets demonstrates that the English way of spelling, reading, and pronouncing is much more complex for learners of English than the Greek way is for English-speaking students, thereby rendering the concern of difficulty in language learning pointless. The chapter moreover shows that a high percentage of the Κοινή vocabulary in the New Testament is used or understood well by speakers of Neohellenic.

Chapter 6. This chapter is a critique of the far-fetched extent to which Erasmian scholars go in applying English phonological concepts to Attic Greek and Κοινή alike. As a case in point, the chapter analyzes the description of the pronunciation of Classical Greek by two Erasmian scholars, one being Sidney Allen, author of *Vox Graeca*, and shows that the Erasmian pronunciation of Classical Greek, which Erasmians indiscriminately apply to Hellenistic Κοινή as well, is untenable.

Chapter 7. This chapter describes Erasmian as the barrier that for five centuries now has inhibited viewing the Greek language holistically and diachronically, therewith preventing the light of the later Greek from illuminating exegetically the Greek NT text. This barrier is sustained by leading Erasmian advocates and other acolytes operating in accountability-free scholastic environments with respect to the pronunciation of Greek. The chapter shows that Neohellenic can shed light on NT usage, exegesis, and textual transmission; and that the application of the HGP can serve as the remedial force that may eventually cancel out the Erasmian effects on Greek scholarship.

Chapter 8. Tips on key differences between Greek and English phonologies help point out the features most crucial in pronouncing Greek. The chapter also summarily describes the features of the Greek phonemic sounds.

Appendixes. Annotated Attic decrees from the fifth and fourth centuries BC lend visual support to the basic premise in this book regarding Greek sounds: that the repeated misspellings seen in Hellenistic, Byzantine, and modern-day writings are traced to Attic Greek; and that such errors, judged diachronically by the same alphabet and orthography, are the strongest proof of the historical Greek sounds and their preservation in Neohellenic.

# Conclusions

As pointed out earlier in this study, it is from around the mid-5th c. BC that we can more confidently rely on the *written* evidence to track the sounds of Attic Greek. The evidence, discussed in chapter 2, formed the basis for the Historical Greek Pronunciation (2.23), which was further expounded in chapter 3. In light of these discussions, and with the definition of orthophonic pronunciation in mind (1.13), the following key conclusions can be drawn:

1) The Historical Greek Pronunciation was formed by, with certain of its elements initiated within, the Classical Attic period prior to entering the Κοινή period.

   *Wherefore*, no pronunciation system comes closer to the orthophonic pronunciation of Classical Attic than that of Κοινή.

2) Neohellenic, the latest phase of Attic Greek, preserves the historical sounds of Κοινή.

   *Wherefore*, no pronunciation system comes closer to the orthophonic pronunciation of the Κοινή of New Testament times and the Christian era than that of Neohellenic.

3) The Historical Greek Pronunciation advances a holistic view of the Hellenic language and literature and a full diachronic approach to New Testament usage, exegesis, and textual transmission. Erasmian does not.

   *Wherefore*, Erasmian is disadvantageous to the study of the Greek language and literature.

# Closing Remarks

All languages change, why not Greek?

"All languages change, so Greek has changed also." Such wholesale comparisons of Greek to other languages are eloquently expressed by a scholar at the University of California, Los Angeles (UCLA) who, having watched one of my videos on the development of the pronunciation of Greek, wrote, "Very nice, indeed! Latin and English haven't changed over the centuries, and so Greek hasn't either. Right?"

Granted, all languages change. Like any living organism, languages develop, grow, change, and even die. As they evolve, they change not only phonologically—as remarks such as the above primarily imply—but also morphologically, lexically, syntactically, semantically, graphically, and orthographically. Not all languages change at the same pace, however, nor do they all change within allotted amounts of time and in all these areas or to the same degree. Some languages may change more radically in less time than other languages. Behind such changes are geopolitical, cultural, sociolinguistic, technological, ideological, and other forces. Amassed, these forces can bring about tectonic linguistic shifts and changes in a relatively short time. Take, for instance, the historical events that led to the formation of all Romance and Germanic languages, or to the Great English Vowel Shift in sixteenth-century England.

Greek is not exempt. It, too, has changed since primordial times. By the classical period, changes such as discussed early in this work (the fricativization of postpositive υ of αυ, ευ, ηυ or the iotacization of diphthongs) had already taken place or been initiated. But since classical times Greek has changed minimally compared to the way Latin or the Germanic languages have changed in one-third that number of years. For one thing, Neohellenic, the latest phase of the Attic dialect, still uses the same twenty-four-letter alphabet *and* spelling, a circumstance that renders the centuries-old unbroken record of interchangeable letters (misspellings) a prized diachronic evidence of its historical sounds. Additionally, in its continuous evolution through Κοινή, Byzantine, and medieval times, today the Hellenic tongue still preserves all its basic grammatical categories intact. As Brown remarks, "In the preservation of the inflectional endings of noun, pronoun, adjective, and verb, in its approximation to the Ancient Greek order of words in phrases, clauses, and sentences, . . . Modern Greek is closer to Ancient Greek than is any other Modern Language to an ancient predecessor of even a few centuries."[1] These factors, coupled with a continuous literary tradition that makes antiquity "present" to any literate Greek, have variously shielded Greek from drastic changes.

With respect to the pronunciation of Attic Greek in particular, we cannot know exactly the speech patterns or intonational peculiarities of an Athenian in classical Athens. However, the historical evidence at hand enables us to trace the mainstream historical phonemic sounds from Neohellenic to the Κοινή of Hellenistic times and from there to Alexander and Aristotle's day, the latter being barely two dozen years before the conventional beginning of the Hellenistic period.

Thus, just because Latin and the Germanic languages changed so drastically since Dante and Chaucer, it does not necessarily follow that Greek underwent a similar or commensurate amount of change since Archon Eucleides. One cannot project the type and rate of changes of other Indo-European languages onto Greek just because Greek is an Indo-European language. Across-the-board comparisons of the development of Greek to that of other languages, even by the well educated, are uninformed and follow an *argumentum ad populum* logic that lacks scholarly merit.

1. Brown, *Classical Weekly*, 84.

# The HGP Today

Today the Historical Greek Pronunciation (HGP) is moving forward in strides as an increasing number of scholars and students around the world advance its application even while favoring greater familiarity with Neohellenic. It is hoped that the HGP will eventually be viewed by the majority as a step in the right direction, a departure from the confines of the Erasmian dichotomy of Greek and the grip of its anachronistic tradition, and into a linguistically sound approach to Hellenic studies. This could only invigorate interest in the Greek language and literature, lead to deeper New Testament insights, cultivate close articulation and academic commerce with the Greek-speaking world, and engender greater appreciation for the millennia-old authentic sounds of the Hellenic tongue.

It is also hoped that some parts in this book will seize the interest of students and scholars who might take the HGP to new heights of linguistic competence, thereby vindicating the tongue whose four hundred years of silence during captivity, and for half that number of years since, created a vacuum in countless centers of Hellenic learning around the world only to be filled with discordant sounds in place of her genuine voice.

# APPENDIX 1

# Decrees of Classical Athens and Their Historical Sounds

Following the defeat of the Persian invaders, the Athenians entered their Periclean Golden Age (479–404 BC). Able now to resume refining grammar and writing, they became increasingly aware of the deficiencies of their writing system, which did not adequately represent their Attic sounds and grammatical forms.

The Athenians dealt with this concern in 403 BC when, under Archon Eucleides, they ratified the 24-letter Ionic alphabet, a writing system their kinsmen, the Ionians, had perfected. Now they could formally distinguish, for instance, Ε(ε) from Ε(η), ΕΙ(ει) from ΕΙ(ῃ) , Ο(ο) from Ο(ω) or Ο(ου), and ΟΙ(οι) from ΟΙ(ῳ ); and represent the digraphs ΧΣ (ΚΣ) and ΦΣ (ΠΣ) as the monographs Ξ and Ψ respectively.

A comparison of 5th and 4th c. BC Attic decrees can show the differences between the older Attic script and the newly adopted Ionic, also known as the *post-Eucleidean grammar* ἡ μετ᾽ Εὐκλείδην γραμματική. Some of the differences are in fact reflected in the opening resolution typically found in Attic decrees:

5th c. BC ΕΔΟΧϟΕΝΤΕΙΒΟLΕΙΚΑΙΤΟΙΔΕΜΟΙ
εδοχσεν τει βολει και τοι δεμοι *Resolved by the council and the people*

4th c. BC ΕΔΟΞΕΝΤΗΙΒΟΥΛΗΙΚΑΙΤΩΙΔΗΜΩΙ
εδοξεν τηι βουληι και τωι δημωι ἔδοξεν τῇ βουλῇ καὶ τῷ δήμῳ

This section examines samples of Attic decrees from the 5th and 4th c. BC as presented in a special publication by the Hellenic Ministry of Culture.[1] Because the samples are limited in number (thus also in phonological inquiry), the purpose of this probe is to merely provide a comparison of key differences between the older Attic

1. *Athenian Democracy Speaking through Its Inscriptions* (Athens 2009, M. Lagogianni-Georgakarakos and K. Buraselis, eds.), auspices of the Hellenic Ministry of Culture, Epigraphical Museum. (Note: The decrees are shown transcribed on pp. 134–143. *SEG* 25:149 on p. 143, inscribed at the end of the classical period, is not part of said publication but is included here for comparison.)

alphabet and the new, and to point out the definitive form and phonemic value of the new graphemes at the threshold of the Κοινή period. The text of each decree, transcribed here in uniform typeface, is made to resemble somewhat the present shape of the original inscription. The larger inscriptions are not transcribed in their entirety for lack of space. The annotations highlight key areas in the discussion that follows later.

## *IG* I[3] 34 (EM 13044, P. 61) DECREE OF KLEINIAS (448/7 BC)

| | | |
|---|---|---|
| Θ Ε Ο Ι | OI = OI = οι proper diphthong | Θ Ε Ο Ι |
| ΕΔΟΧΣΕΝΤ**ΕΙ**ΒΟL | TEI = THI = τῃ spurious diphthong | εδοχσεν τει βολ |
| ΜΟΙΟΙΝΕΙΣΕΠΡΥ | ↑ same spelling associated with same sound ↓ | μοι Οινεις επρυ |
| ΔΙΑΣΕΛΡΑΜΜΑΤΕ | | διας εγραμματε |
| ΕΠΕΣΤΑΤΕΚL**ΕΙ**Ν | EI = EI = ει proper diphthong | επεστατε Κλειν |
| ΟLΕΝΚΑΙΤΟΣΑΡΧ | | ολεν και τος αρχ |
| ΙΠΟLΕΣΙΚΑΙΤΟΣ | | ι πολεσι και τος |
| ΠΙΜΕLΕΣΘΑΙΗΟΠ | | πιμελεσθαι hoπ |
| ΛΕΤΑΙΗΟΦΟΡΟΣΚ | H(h) is missing (line 10): | γεται ho φορος κ |
| ΕΚΑΣΤΟΝΚΑΙΑΠΑ | ΕΚΑΣΤΟΝ for ΗΕΚΑΣΤΟΝ | εκαστον και απα |
| ΙΕΧΣΥΜΒΟLΑΔΕΠ | I = Z | ζε χσυμβολα δε π |
| ΡΟΣΤΑΣΠΟLΕΣΗΟ | L = Λ | ρος τας πολες ho |
| ΕΙΑΔΙΚΕΝΤΟΙΣΑ | | ει αδικεν τοις α |
| ΟΡΟΝΛΡΑΦΣΑΣΑΔ | Λ = Γ | ορον γραφσασα δ |
| ΛΡΑΜΜΑΤΕΙΟΝΤΟ | | γραμματειον το |
| ΝΑΜΕΝΕ**ΤΟΙ**ΣΥΜΒ | TOI = TΩI = τῷ spurious diphthong | ναμενε τοι συμβ |
| ΠΑΛΟΝΤΑΣΑΠΟΔΟ | (compare with line 1) | παγοντας αποδο |
| ΝΑΛΝΟΝΑΙΗΟΤΑΜ | | ναγνοναι hoταμ |
| ΥΤΑΝΕΣΜΕΤΑΔΙΟ | In pre-Eucleidean writing, pronunciation and grammatical distinctions between homographs are determined by the context. | υτανες μετα Διο |
| ΣΗΕLLΕΝΟΤΑΜΙΑ | | ς hελλενοταμια |
| ΕΟΝΤΑΣΑΠΟΔΟΣΑ | | εον τας αποδοσα |
| ΣΑΣΧΟΡΙΣΗΟΣΑΙ | | σας χορις hoσαι |
| ΝΟΣΑΝΔΡΑΣΤΕΤΤ | | νος ανδρας τεττ |
| ΙΛΡΑΦΣΟΜΕΝΟΣ | | ι γραφσομενος |
| ΤΕΣΟΝΤΑΣ**ΤΟΜ**ΜΕ | TON + M = TOMM | τεσοντας τομ με |
| ΟΜΕΝΔΥΟΠLΕΝΕ | (assimilation) | ο μεν δυο πλεν ε |
| ΡΙΕΡΟΣΤΑΧΕΙΑΣ | | ριερος ταχειας |
| ΙΕΠΙΘΡΑΙΚΕΣΕ | | ι επι Θραικες ε |
| ΒΟLΕΝΚΑΙ**ΕΣ**ΤΟ | ΕΣ = ΕΙΣ | βολεν και ες το |
| LΕΥΕΣΘΑΙΠΕΡΙΤ | ↑ different spelling, same sound ↓ | λευεσθαι περι τ |
| ΕΙΕΑΝΔΕΤΙΣΑΘ | | ει εαν δε τις Αθ |
| ΝΦΟΡΟΝΗΟΝ**ΔΕΙ** | ΔΕΙ = ΔΕΙ = δει | ν φορον hoν δει |
| ΟΝΤΟΙΣΑΠΑΛΟΣ | | ον τοις απαγοσ |
| ΡΑΦΕΣΘΑΙΠΡΟΣ | | ραφεσθαι προς |
| ΙΟΝΚΑΙΤΟΝΧΣ | | ιον και τον χσ |
| ΕΣΤΕΜΒΟLΕΝ | N + B = MB [ɱv] | ες τεμ βολεν |
| ΥΝΕΣΘΟΔΟΡ | τημ βουλην for την βουλην | υνεσθο δορ |
| ΚΑΤΑΛΝΟΙΗ | (assimilation) | καταγνοι h |
| ΦΕΡΕΤΟΕΣΤ | | φερετο ες τ |
| ΝΛΝ**Ο**ΜΑΣΠΟ | Λ = Γ γν**ο**μας for γν**ω**μας O = Ω | ν γνομας πο |
| ΟΜΠΑΘΕΝΕΑ | N + Π = ΜΠ [mb] | ομ παθεν ε α |
| ΝΤΕΣΒΟΟΣΕ | (assimilation) (Cf. p. 139.) | ν τες βοος ε |
| ΙΚΑΤΑΥΤΟ | | ι κατ' αυτο |

## *IG* I[3] 46 (EM 6577, p. 81) Decree for the Foundation of a Colony at Brea (445 BC)

| Inscription | Note | Transcription |
|---|---|---|
| ΑΛΕΤΟΕΑΝΔΕΕΣΑΛΕΙΕΝΕΧ | | αγετο εαν δε εσαγει ενεχ |
| ΦΕΝΑΣΕΗΟΛΡΑΦΣΑΜΕΝΟΣΠΟ | | φενας ε ho γραφσαμενος πο |
| ΑΥΤΟΙΣΠΑΡΑΣΧΟΝΤΩΝΗΟΙΑΠ | | αυτοις παρασχοντον hοι απ |
| ΙΕΡΕΣΑΙΗΥΠΕΡΤΕΣΑΠΟΙΚΙΑΣ | | ιερεσαι hυπερ τες αποικιας |
| ΙΣΔΟΚΕΙΛΕΟΝΟΜΟΣΔΕΗΕLΕΣΘ | | ις δοκειγεονομος δε hελεσθ |
| **ΕΝΑ**ΕΧΦΥLΕΣΗΟΥΤΟΙΔΕΝΕΜΑΝΤ | ΕΝΑ for ΗΕΝΑ | ενα εχ φυλες hουτοι δε νεμαντ |
| ΟΚLΕΙΔΕΝΔΕΚΑΤΑΣΤΕΣΑΙΤΕΝΑ | H(h) is missing | οκλειδεν δε καταστεσαι τεν α |
| ΚΡΑΤΟΡΑΚΑΘΟΤΙΑΝΔΥΝΕΤΑΙΑ | | κρατορα καθοτι αν δυνεται α |
| ΕΝΕΤΑΕΧΣΕΙΡΕΜΕΝΑΕΑΝΚΑΘΑ | | ενε τα εχσειρεμενα εαν καθα |
| LΑΜΕΤΕΜΕΝΙIΕΝΒΟΥΝΔΕΚΑΙ | I = Ζ (line 15) | λα με τεμενιζεν βουν δε και |
| ΛΕΝΕΣΠΑΝΑΘΕΝΑΙΑΤΑΜΕΛΑL | Unlike Ξ or Ψ, | γεν ες Παναθεναια τα μεγαλ |
| ΑΦΑLLΟΝΕΑΝΔΕΤΙΣΕΠΙΣΤΡΑ | I or Z never appears | α φαλλον εαν δε τις επιστρα |
| ΝΤΕΝΤΟΝΑΠΟΙΚΟΝΒΟΕΘΕΝΤΑ | as a two-letter sound. | ν τεντον αποικον βοεθεν τα |
| ΤΑΤΑΚΑΤΑΤΑΣ**Χ**ΣΥΛΛΡΑΦΑΣΗ[ΑΙ] | ← epenthetic X | τατα κατα τας χσυγγραφας h[αι] |
| ΤΟΛΡΑΜΜΑΤΕΥΟΝΤΟΣΕΛΕΝΟΝ | | το γραμματευοντος εγενον |
| ΟΝΤΟΝΕΠΙΘΡΑΚΕΣΛΡΑΦΣΑΙ | | ον τον επι Θρακες γραφσαι |
| ΕΙΚΑΙΚΑΤΑΘΕΝΑΙΕ**ΜΠ**ΟLΕΙΠΑ | Ν + Π = ΜΠ | ει και καταθεναι εμ πολει πα |
| ΕΝΣΤΕLΕΝΗΟΙΑΠΟΙΚΟΙΣΦΟΝΑ | εμ πολει = εν πολει | εν στελεν hοι αποικοι σφον α |
| ΑΝΔΕΤΙΣΕΠΙΦΣΕΦΙIΕΙΠΑΡΑΤΕ | ← ΦΣ = Ψ, I = Ζ | αν δε τις επιφσεφιζει παρα τε |
| ΤΟΡΑΛΟΡΕΥΕΙΕΠΡΟΣΚΑLΕΣΘΑ | | τορ αγορευει ε προσκαλεσθα |
| ΡΕΣΘΑΙΕLΥΕΝΤΙΤΟΝΗΕΦΣΕΦΙ | | ρεσθαι ε λυεν τι τον hεφσεφι |
| ΕΝΑΙΑΥΤ**Ο**ΝΚΑΙΠΑΙΔΑΣΤ**Ο**ΣΕΧ | | εναι αυτον και παιδας τος εχ |
| ΡΕΜΑΤΑΔΕΜΟΣΙΑΕΝΑΙΚΑΙΤΕΣ | | ρεματα δεμοσια εναι και τες |
| ΤΟΝΕΑΜΜΕΤΙΑΥΤΟΙΗΟΙΑΠΟΙΚ | | τον εαμ με τι αυτοι hοι αποικ |
| ΟΝΤΑΙ::ΗΟΣΟΙΔΑΝΛΡΑΦΣΟΝΤΑ | | ονται:: hοσοι δ' αν γραφσοντα |
| ΝΣΤΡΑΤΙΟΤΟΝΕΠ**ΕΙ**ΔΑΝΗΕΚΟΣ → | ΕΙ = ει | ν στρατιοτον επειδαν hεκοσ |
| ΚΟΝΤΑΕΜΕΡΟΝΕΜΒΡΕΑΙ**ΕΝΑΙ**Ε → | Ε = ει ειναι | κοντα εμερον εμ Βρεαι εναι ε |
| **Χ**ΣΑΛΕΝΔΕΤΕΝΑΠΟΙΚΙΑΤΡΙΑ | | χσαγεν δε τεν αποικιαν τρια |
| ΙΣΧΙΝΕΝΔΕΑΚΟL**ΟΥ**ΘΟΝΤΑΑΠΟ | Ο = ΟΥ | ισχινεν δε ακολουθοντα απο |
| ΜΑΤΑ | | ματα |

ΧΣ = Ξ

H(h) is missing:
ΕΜΕRΟΝ for ΗΕΜΕRΟΝ > ημερων

## *IG* I³ 49 (EM 6849, P. 49) THE SPRINGHOUSE DECREE (432/1 BC)

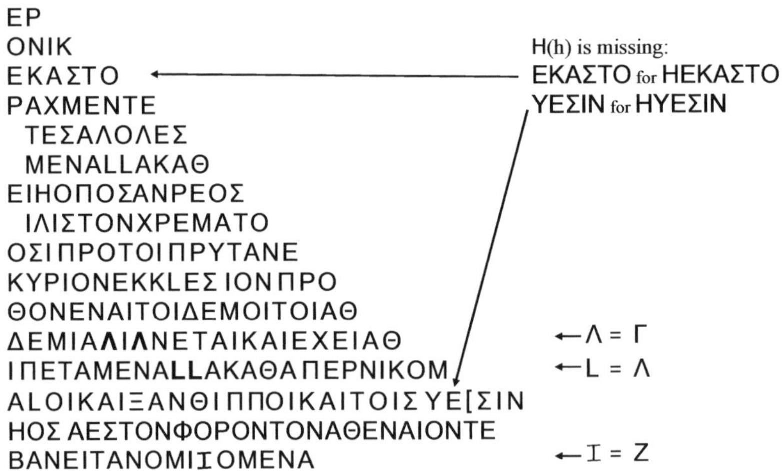


ερ
ονικ
εκαστο
ραχμεν τε
τες αγογες
μεν αλλα καθ
ει hοπος αν ρεοσ
ιγιστον χρεματο
οσι προτοι πρυτανε
κυριον εκκλεσιον προ
θον εναι τοι δεμοι τοι Αθ
δεμια γιγνεται και εχει Αθ
ιπε τα μεν αλλα καθαπερ νικομ
αλοι και ξανθιπποι και τοις υε[σιν
hοσα ες τον φορον τον Αθεναιον τε
βανει τα νομιζομενα

Attic H(h) as a symbol of aspiration had no acoustic value, so it was used inconsistently.

## *IG* I³ 35 (EM 8116 A, P. 51) DECREE FOR THE TEMPLE OF ATHENA NIKE, SIDE I (427/4 BC)

ΚΟΣΕΙΠΕ
ΕΙΗΙΕΡΕΑΝΗΕΑ
ΙΕΧΣΑΘΕΝΑΙΟΝΗΑΠΑ
ΘΑΙΚΑΙΗΙΕΡΟΝΘΥΡΟΣΑ
ΙΚΑΘΟΤΙΑΝΚΑLLΙΚΡΑΤΕΣΧΣΥΛΛΡΑΦΣ
ΕΙΑΠΟΜΙΣΘΟΣΑΙΔΕ**ΤΟΣΠΟLΕΤΑΣ**ΕΠΙΤ
ΕΣLΕΟΝΤΙΔΟΣΠΡΥΤΑΝΕΙΑΣΦΕΡΕΝΔΕΤ
ΕΝΗΙΕΡΕΑΝΠΕΝΤΕΚΟΝΤΑΔΡΑΧΜΑΣΚΑΙ
ΤΑΣΚΕLΗΚΑΙΤΑΔΕΡΜΑΤΑ**ΦΕΡΕΝ**ΤΟΝΔΕ
ΜΟΣΙΟΝΝΕΟΝΔΕΟΙΚΟΔΟΜΕΣΑΙΚΑΘΟΤΙ
ΑΝΚΑLLΙΚΡΑΤΕΣΧΣΥΛΛΡΑΦΣ**ΕΙ**ΚΑΙ**ΒΟ**
ΜΟΝLΙΘΙΝΟΝ
ΗΕΣΤΙΑΙΟΣΕΙΠΕΤΡΕΣΑΝΔΡΑΣΗΕLΕΣΘ
ΑΙΕΛΒΟLΕΣΤΟΥΤΟΣΔΕΜΕΤ[ΑΚΑ]LLΙΚΡΑ
ΣΧΣΥΛΛΡΑΦΣΑΝΤΑΣΕΠ
ΕΙΚΑΘΟΤΙΑΠΟΜ
ΕΙΤΟΣ

τος πολετας = τους πωλητας
Ο = ΟΥ / Ω, Ε = Η

φερεν = φερειν Ε = Ε / ΕΙ

Ο = Ω βομον = βωμόν

ΕΙ = ΗΙ (ηι = ῃ)

ΕΛ ΒΟLΕΣ ΤΟΥΤΟΣ Ο = ΟΥ / Ω
εγ βολες τουτος = εκ βουλης τουτους
εγ = εκ

κος ειπε
ει hιερεαν hε α
ι εχς Αθεναιον hαπα
θαι και το hιερον θυροσα
ι καθ' ο τι αν Καλλικρατες χσυγγραφσ
ει απομισθοσαι δε τος πολετας επι τ
ες Λεοντιδος πρυτανειας φερεν δε τ
εν hιερεαν πεντεκοντα δραχμας και
τα σκελε και τα δερματα φερεν τον δε
μοσιον νεον δε οικοδομεσαι καθ' ο τι
αν Καλλικρατες χσυγγραφσει και βο
μον λιθινον
hεστιαιος ειπε τρες ανδρας hελεσθ
αι εγ βολες τουτος δε μετ[ακα]λλικρα
σχσυγγραφοντας επ
ει καθ' ο τι απομ
ει το σ

SIDE I. Pre-Eucleidean Ε as ε, η, ει; ΕΙ as ει, ηι; and Ο as ο, ω, ου bespeak the need to graphically distinguish grammatical forms.

# *IG* I³ 36 (EM 8116 B, P. 51) DECREE FOR THE TEMPLE OF ATHENA NIKE, SIDE II (424/3 BC)

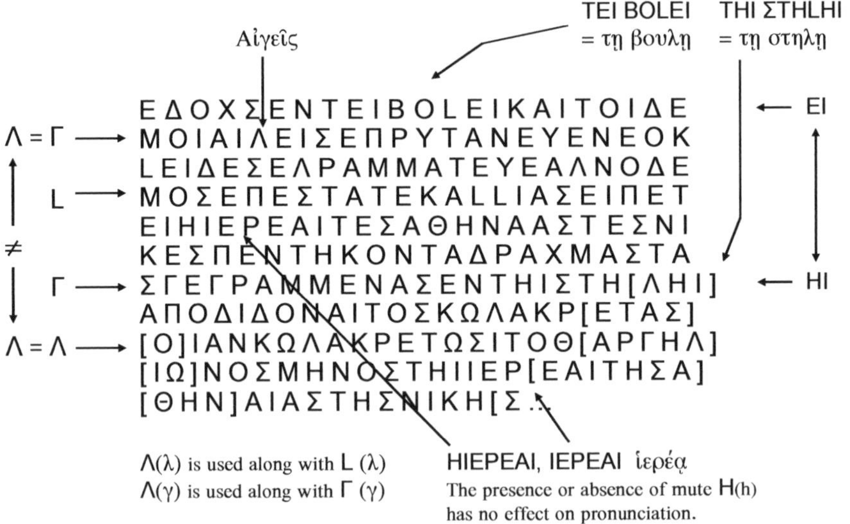

TEI BOLEI = τῃ βουλῃ
THI ΣTHLHI = τῃ στηλῃ
Αἰγεῖς
ΕΔΟΧΣΕΝΤΕΙΒΟLΕΙΚΑΙΤΟΙΔΕ
ΜΟΙΑΙΛΕΙΣΕΠΡΥΤΑΝΕΥΕΝΕΟΚ
LΕΙΔΕΣΕΛΡΑΜΜΑΤΕΥΕΑΛΝΟΔΕ
ΜΟΣΕΠΕΣΤΑΤΕΚΑLLΙΑΣΕΙΠΕΤ
ΕΙΗΙΕΡΕΑΙΤΕΣΑΘΗΝΑΑΣΤΕΣΝΙ
ΚΕΣΠΕΝΤΗΚΟΝΤΑΔΡΑΧΜΑΣΤΑ
ΣΓΕΓΡΑΜΜΕΝΑΣΕΝΤΗΙΣΤΗ[ΛΗΙ]
ΑΠΟΔΙΔΟΝΑΙΤΟΣΚΩΛΑΚΡ[ΕΤΑΣ]
[Ο]ΙΑΝΚΩΛΑΚΡΕΤΩΣΙΤΟΘ[ΑΡΓΗΛ]
[ΙΩ]ΝΟΣΜΗΝΟΣΤΗΙΙΕΡ[ΕΑΙΤΗΣΑ]
[ΘΗΝ]ΑΙΑΣΤΗΣΝΙΚΗ[Σ..
Λ = Γ
L
≠
Γ
Λ = Λ
EI
HI
Λ(λ) is used along with L (λ)
Λ(γ) is used along with Γ (γ)
HIEPEAI, IEPEAI ἱερέᾳ
The presence or absence of mute H(h) has no effect on pronunciation.


SIDE II. Old forms mixed with new:
Ionic letters, including Η and Ω, are peculiarly used right along with older Attic letters, a sign that Η and Ω forced their way into Attic writing years before the ratification of the Ionic alphabet.

εδοχσεν τει βολει και τοι δεμοι Αιγεις επρυτανευε Νεοκ-
λειδες εγραμματευε Αγνοδε-
μος επεστατε καλλιας ειπε τ-
ει hιερεαι τες Αθηνααις τες Νι-
κες πεντηκοντα δραχμας τα-
ς γεγραμμενας εν τηι στη[ληι]
αποδιδοναι τος κωλακρ[ετας]
[ο]ι αν κωλακρετωσι το Θ[αργηλ]-
[ιω]νος μηνος τηι ιερ[εαι της Α-
[θην]αιας της Νικη[ς...

## *IG* I[3] 93 (EM 6591B, P. 78) DECREES RELATING TO THE SICILIAN EXPEDITION (415 BC)

BOLEN ΚΑΘΟΤΙΑΡΙΣΤΑ
ΝΤΕΑΠΟΤΟΤΙΜΕΜΑΤΟΣΔΟΚΕ
ΤΕΤΕΜ ΠOLINANALONHOΣONA
ΣΗΕΧΣΕΚΟΝΤΑΝΑΥΣΕΑΜ ΠΡΟΣ
ΜΕΝΟΝΕΙΕΣΦΕΡΕΝΗΟΤΑΝΔΕ
LΕΣΙΑΝ ΠΟΙΕΣΑΝΤΟΝΔΕΚΑΗΕ
EPIALLΟΜΕΔΕΝΟΣΠΡΟΤΕΡΟΝ
ΕΕΚΚLΕΣΙΑΝ ΠΟΙΕΝΤΟΣΠΡΥΤ
ΑΙΤΟΙΣΣΤΡΑΤΕΛΟΙΣΤΟΝΝΕΟ
ΟΙΣ ΠΕΡΙΔΕΤΟΕΚ ΠLΟΤΟΝΝΕΟ
ΠΑΝΟΡΘΟΣΘΑΙΕΝΤΟΙΔΕΜΟΙΗ
ΚΚLΕΣΙΑΝ ΠΟΙΟΝΤΟΝΗΟΤΑΝΚΕ
ΟΝΚΑΙΤΕΣALLΕΣΗΥ ΠΕΡΕΣΙΑΣ
ΚΑΙΑΡΛΥΡΙΟΕΣΚALLΙΕΡΕΣΙΝ
ΗΕ...Α... ΣΙ...ILΙΟΝ

3 ΤΕΜ ΠΟΛΙΝ
τεμ πολιν = τὴν πόλιν

4 ΕΑΜ ΠΡΟΣ
εαμ προς = εαν προς
N+P → MP [mb]
(Cf. p. 134.)

In this decree, only a dozen years before the ratification of the Ionic alphabet, the older Attic script still holds sway.

1 Ο = ΟΥ βολεν = βουλην
1 Ο = Ο καθοτι = καθοτι
12 Ο = Ω ποιοντον = ποιουντων
6 ΟΙ = ΟΙ ποιεσαν = ποιησαν
11 ΟΙ = ΩΙ δεμοι = δημωι
5 Ε = Ε δε = δε
8 Ε = ΕΙ ποιεν = ποιειν
13 Ε = Η αλλες = αλλης
4 ΧΣ = Ξ ξ
8 L = Λ λ
14 Λ = Γ γ

βολεν καθοτι αριστα
ν τε απ  το τιμεματος δοκε
τε τεμ πολιν αναλον hοσον α
ς hεχσεκοντα ναυς εαμ προς
μενον ει εσφερεν hοταν δε
λεσιαν ποιεσαντον δεκα hε
ερι αλλο μεδενος προτερον
ε εκκλεσιαν ποιεν τος πρυτ
αι τοις στρατεγοις τον νεο
οις περι δε το εκπλο τον νεο
πανορθοσθαι εν τοι δεμο h
κκλεσιαν ποιοντον hοταν κε
ον και τες αλλες hυπερεσιας
και αργυριο ες καλλιερεσιν
hε...α...σι...ιλιον

# *IG* II[2] 145 (EM 6978, P. 105) HONORIFIC DECREES FOR EUKLES (402 BC) AND PHILOKLES (399 BC)

ΥΤΑΝΕΥΕΝ
ΕΥΣΕΓΡΑΜΜΑΤΕΥΕΝΣΙΜΙ
ΥΣΕΠΕΣΤΑΤ**Ε**ΕΥΡΙΠΠΙΔΗ
ΟΝΕΥΚΛΕΙΑΝΔΡΑΓΑΘΙ
ΕΠΕΙΔΗΑΝΗΡΑΓΑΘΟΣΕΓΕ
ΟΝΑΘΗΝΑΙΩΝΚΑΙΤΗΝΚΑΘ
ΑΙΩΝΚΑΙΤΗΝΕΛΕΥΘΕΡΙ
ΗΙΒΟΛΗΙΚΑΙΤΩΙΔΗΜΩ[Ι]
ΣΘΟΦΟΡΙΑΝΕΙΝΑΙΑΥΤΩ[Ι]

ΤΩΙΔΗΜΩΙ ΛΕΩΝΤΙΣΕΠΡΥ
ΑΙΟΣΕΓΡΑΜΜΑΤΕΥΕΝΕΥΦ
[Ε]ΠΕΣΤΑΤ**ΕΙ**ΜΕΛΑΝΩΠΟΣΕΙΠ
ΛΗΙΕΠΕΙΔΗΑΝΗΡΑΓΑΘΟΣ
ΙΛΟΚΛΕΟΥΣΠΕΡΙΤΟΝΔΗΜΟ[Ν]
ΗΓΚΑΘΟΔΟΝΤΟΥΔΗΜΟΕΨΗΦ
ΣΠΡΟΕΔΡΟΥΣΟΙΑΝΤΥΓΧΑΝ
ΕΙΣΤΗΝΠΡΩΤΗΝΕΚΚΛΗΣΙΑ
ΙΛΟΚΛΕΟΥΣΤΟΥΕΥΚΛΕΟΥΣ
ΣΚΑΙΚΟΣΜΙΟΣΔΟΚΕΙΕΙΝΑ[Ι]
ΠΡΥΤΑΝΕΣΙΤΟΙΣΑΕΙΠΡΥΤ
ΒΑΛΛΕΣΘΑΙΤΗΣΒΟΛΗΣΕ
ΤΗΙΒΟΛΗΙΕΙΝΑΙΤΗΓΚΗ
ΡΤΩΙ ΠΑΤΡΙΑΥΤΟΟ
ΜΟΝΤΟΝ ΑΘΗΝΑ[Ι]Ω[Ν]

ΕΠΕΣΤΑΤ**Ε** and ΕΠΕΣΤΑΤ**ΕΙ**
Ε = ΕΙ = [i] used interchangeably
(same word, same inscription, different spelling)

ΤΩΙ ΔΗΜΩΙ formerly ΤΟΙ ΔΕΜΟΙ

ΛΕΩΝΤΙΣ for ΛΕΟΝΤΙΣ
Ω = Ο = [o] used interchangeably; error due to same sound

post-Eucleidean Ψ introduced

ΤΟΥ ΔΗΜΟ for ΤΟΥ ΔΗΜΟΥ
Ο for ΟΥ persisted till 3rd c. BC

ΤΗΣ ΒΟΛΗΣ for ΤΗΣ ΒΟΥΛΗΣ
Ο for ΟΥ

υτανευεν
ευς εγραμματευεν Σιμι
υς επεστατε ευριππιδη
ον Ευκλει ανδραγαθι
επειδη ανηρ αγαθος εγε
ον Αθηναιών και τηγ καθ
αιων και την ελευθερι
ηι βοληι και τωι δημω[ι]
σθοφοριαν ειναι αυτω[ι]

τωι δημωι Λεωντις επρυ
αιος εγραμματευεν Ευφ
[ε]πεστατει Μελανωπος ειπ
ληι επειδη ανηρ αγαθος
ιλοκλεους περι τον δημο[ν]
ηγ καθοδον του δημο εψηφ
ς προεδρους οι αν τυγχαν
εις την πρωτην εκκλησια
ιλοκλεους του Ευκλεους
ς και κοσμιος δοκει ειναι[ι]
πρυτανεσι τοις αει πρυτ
βαλλεσθαι της βολης ε
τηι βοληι ειναι τηγ κη
ρ τωι πατρι αυτο ο
μον τον Αθηνα[ι]ω[ν]

This decree, written right after the ratification of the Ionic alphabet, shows a compromised transition from the old writing system to the new, as it reflects elements of both.

## *IG* I³ 61 (EM 6596, P. 63) DECREES CONCERNING THE METHONAIANS (430/29—424/3 BC)

H(h) is missing from underlined words, evidence of its erratic use.

ΜΕΘΟΝΑΙΟΝΕΚΠΙΕΡ[ΙΑΣ]
[Φ]ΑΙΝΙΠΠΟΣΦΡΥΝΙΧΟΕΓΡΑΜΜΑΤΕΥ[ΕΥΕ]
[ΕΔ]ΟΧΣΕΝΤΕΙΒΟΛΕΙΚΑΙΤΟΙΔΕΜΟΙΕΡΕΧΘΕΙΣΕΠΡ[ΥΤΑΝ]
[ΕΥΕ]ΣΚΟΠΟΣΕΓΡΕΜΜΑΤΕΥΕΤΙΜΕΝΕΔΕΣΕΠΕΣΤΑΤΕΔ[ΙΟΠ]
[ΕΙ]ΘΕΣΕΙΠΕΔΙ[Α]ΧΕΙΤΟΤΟΝΕΣΑΙΤΟΝΔΕΜΟΝΑΥΤΙΚ[ΑΠΡΟ]
[ΣΜ]ΕΘΟΝΑΙΟΣΕΙΤΕΦΟΡΟΝΔΟΚΕΙΤΑΤΤΕΝΤΟΝΔΕΜΟ[ΝΑΥΤ]
[ΙΚ]ΑΜΑΛΛΑΕΕΧ[Σ]ΕΡΚΕΝΑΥΤΟΙΣΤΕΛΕΝΗΟΣΟΝΤΕΙΘΕ[ΟΙΑΠ] ΗΟΣΟΝ
[ΟΤ]ΟΦΟΡΟΕΓΟΓΝΕΤΟΗΟΝΤΟΙΣΠΡΟΤΕΟΙΣΠΑΝ[ΑΘ]Ε[ΝΑΙΟ] ΗΟΝ
ΙΣΕΤΕΤΑΧΑΤΟΓΕΡΕΝΤΟΔΕΑΛΛΟΑΤΕΛΕΣΕΝΑ[ΙΤΟΝΣΕΟΦ]
[ΕΙ]ΛΕΜΑΤΟΝΗΑΓΕΓΡΑΦΑΤΕΤΟΙΔΕΜΟΣΙΟΙΤ[ΟΙΤΟΝΑΘΕ] ΗΑ
[ΝΑ]ΙΟΜΜΕΘΟΝΑΙΟΙΟΦΕΙΛΟΝΤΕΣΕΑΝΟΣΙΕΠΙΤ[ΑΔΕΙΟΙΑ]
ΙΘΕΝΑΙΟΙΣΟΣΠΕΡΤΕΝΥΝΚΑΙΕΤΙΑΜΕΙΝΟΣΕΠΙ[ΧΟΡΕΝΑΠ] ΟΣΠΕΡ
[ΟΥ]ΑΧΣΙΝΠΕΡΙΤΕΣΠΡΣΧΣΕΟΣΑΘΕΝΑΙΟΣΚΑΙΕΑΝ[ΚΟΙΝΟ]
[Ν]ΦΣΕΦΙΣΜΑΤΙΠΕΡΙΤΟΝΟΦΕΙΛΕΜΑΤΟΝΤΟΝΕΝΤΕ[ΙΣΙΣΑ]
[ΝΙ]ΣΙ ΓΙΓΝΕΤΑΙΜΕΔΕΝΠΡΟΣΗΕΚΕΤΟΜΕΘΟΝΑΙΟ[ΙΣ ΕΑΜΜ]
[ΕΧ]ΟΡΙΣΓΙΓΝΕΤΑΙΦΣΕΦΙΣΜΑΠΕΡΙΜΕΘΟΝΑΙΟΝΠ[ΡΕΣΒΕ]
[ΣΔ]ΕΤΡΕΣΠΕΜΦΣΑΙΗΥΠΕΡΠΕΝΤΕΚΟΝΤΑΕΤΕΓΕΓΟΝ[ΟΤΑΣ] ΗΥΠΕΡ
[ΗΟ]ΣΠΕΡΔΙΚΚΑ[Ν]ΕΙΠΕΝΔΕΠΕΡΔΙΚΚΑΙΗΟΤΙΔΟΚΕ[ΙΔΙΚΑ] ΗΟΤΙ
[ΙΟ]ΝΕΙΝΑΙΕΑΝΜΕΘΟΝΑΙΟΣΤΕΙΘΑΛΑΤΤΕΙΧΡΕΣΘΑ[ΙΜΕΔΕ]
[ΕΧΣ]ΕΝΑΙΗΟΡΙΣΑΣΘΑΙΚΑΙΕΑΝΕΙΣΕΜΠΟΡΕΥΕΣΘ[ΑΙΚΑΘ] ΗΟΡΙΣΑΣΘΑΙ
[ΑΠΕ]ΡΤΕΟΣΕ[Σ]ΤΕΝΧΟΡΑΝΚΑΙΜΕΤΕΕΔΙΚΕΝΜ[Ε]ΤΕ[Α]Δ[ΕΚΚΕΣ]
[ΘΑΙ]ΜΕΔΕΣΤΡΑ[Τ]ΙΑΝΔΙΑΤΕΣΧΙΡΑΣΤΕΣΜΕΘ[Ο]ΝΑΙΟΝ[ΔΙΑ]
[ΓΕΝΑ]ΚΝΤΟΜ[ΜΕ]ΘΟΝΑΙΟΝΚΑΙΕΑΜΜΕΝΟΜΟΛ[Ο]ΓΟΣΙΝ[ΗΕΚ] ΟΜΟΛΟΓΟΣΙΝ
[ΑΤΕΡ]ΟΙΧΣΥ[ΜΒΙ]ΒΑΣΑΝΤΟΝΗΟΙΠΡΕΣΒΕΣΕΑΝΔΕΜΕ[ΠΡΕΣ] ΗΟΙ
[ΕΙ]ΑΝΕΚΑΤ[ΕΡ]Ο[Ι]ΠΕΜΠΟΝΤΟΝΕΣΔΙΟΝΥΣΙΑΤΕΛΟΣ[ΕΧΟΝ] ΕΚΑΤΕΡΟΙ
. . . . . .
[ΣΙΣ] ΕΙΝ[ΑΙ ΕΧ]ΣΑ[ΓΟ]ΓΕΝ ΕΓ ΒΥΖΑΝΤΙΟ ΣΙΤΟ ΜΕΧ[ΡΙ . . . Α]
[ΚΙΣΧ]ΙΛΙΟΝΜΕΔΙΜΝΟΝΤΟΕΝΙΑΥΤΟΕΚΑΣΤΟΗΟΙ[ΔΕΕΛΛΕ] ΕΚΑΣΤΟ, ΗΟΙ
[ΣΠ]ΟΝΤΟΦΥΛΑΚΕΣΜΕΤΕΑΥΤΟΙΚΟΛΥΟΝΤΟΝΕΧΣΑΓΕΝΜ[ΕΤ]
[ΕΑΛ]ΛΟΝΕΟΝΤΟΝΚΟΛΥΕΝΕΕΥΘΥΝΕΣΘΟΝΜΥΡΙΑΙΣΙΔΡ[ΑΧ]
[ΜΕΙΣ]ΙΝΕΚΑΣΤΟΣΓΡΑΦΣΑΜΕΝΟΣΔΕΠΡΟΣΤΟΣΕΛΛΕΣΠ[ΟΝ] ΕΚΑΣΤΟΣ, ΕΛΛΗ-
[ΤΟ]ΦΥΛΑΚΑΣΕΧΣΑΓΕ[Ν]ΜΕΧΡΙΤΟΤΕΤΑΓΜΕΝΟΑΖΕΜΙΟΣ[ΔΕ] ΣΠΟΝΤΟΦΥΛΑΚΑΣ
[ΕΣ]ΤΟΚΑΙΕΝΕΑΥΣΕΕΧΣΑΓΟΣΑΗΟΤΙΔΑΝΚΟΙΝΟΝΦΣΗΦ[ΙΣΜ] ΗΟ
[ΑΠ]ΕΡΙ ΤΟΝ ΧΣΥΜΜΑΧΟ[Ν] ΦΣΦΙΖΟΝΤΑΙ ΑΘΗΝΑΙΟΙ ΠΕ[ΡΙΒ]
[ΟΕ]ΔΕΙΑΣΕΑ[Λ]ΛΟΤΙΠΡΟ[Σ]ΤΑΤΤΟΝ[Ν]ΤΕΣΤΕΣΙΠΟΛΕΣΙΕ[ΠΕΡ]
[ΙΣ]ΦΟΝ[Ε]ΠΕΡΙΤΟΝΠΟΛΕΟΝΗΟΤΟΑΝΟΝΜΑΣΤΙΡΕΠΙΤ[ΕΣΠ] ΗΟ
. . . . . .
[Ο]ΣΙ Ε[ΣΤΟ]ΝΔΕΜΟΝΗΟΙΠΡΕΣΒΕΣ[Η]ΟΙΠΑΡΑΠΕΡΔΙΚΚΟ[ΟΙΤ] [Η]ΟΙ
. . . . . .
[Ε]Ι Ε[ΔΡΑ]Σ ΕΟΣΑΝΔΙ[ΑΡΠ]ΑΧΘΕΙΑΛΛΟΔΕΠΡΟΧΡΕΜΑ[ΤΙΣΑΙ] ΕΔΡΑΣ, ΕΟΣ
[ΤΟ]Υ[ΤΟ]ΝΜΕΔΕΝΕΑΜΜΕΤΙΟΙΣΤΡΑΤΕ[Π]ΟΙΔΕΟΝΤΑ[Ι ΕΔΟΧ] ΟΙ
[ΣΕΝΤΕΙ]ΒΟΛΕΙΚΕΙΤΟΙΔΕΜΟΙΚΕΚΡΟΠΙΣΕΠΡΥ[ΤΑΝΕΥΕ . . .]
. . . . . .

N + M = MM εαμ μη τι = εαν μη τι

# *IG* I³ 102 (EM 6601, P. 102) HONORIFIC DECREE FOR THRASYBOULOS AND SEVEN OTHERS (410/9 BC)

This inscription is made up of six pieces. Below are sections of the majority of the readable parts. Spaces are not to scale.

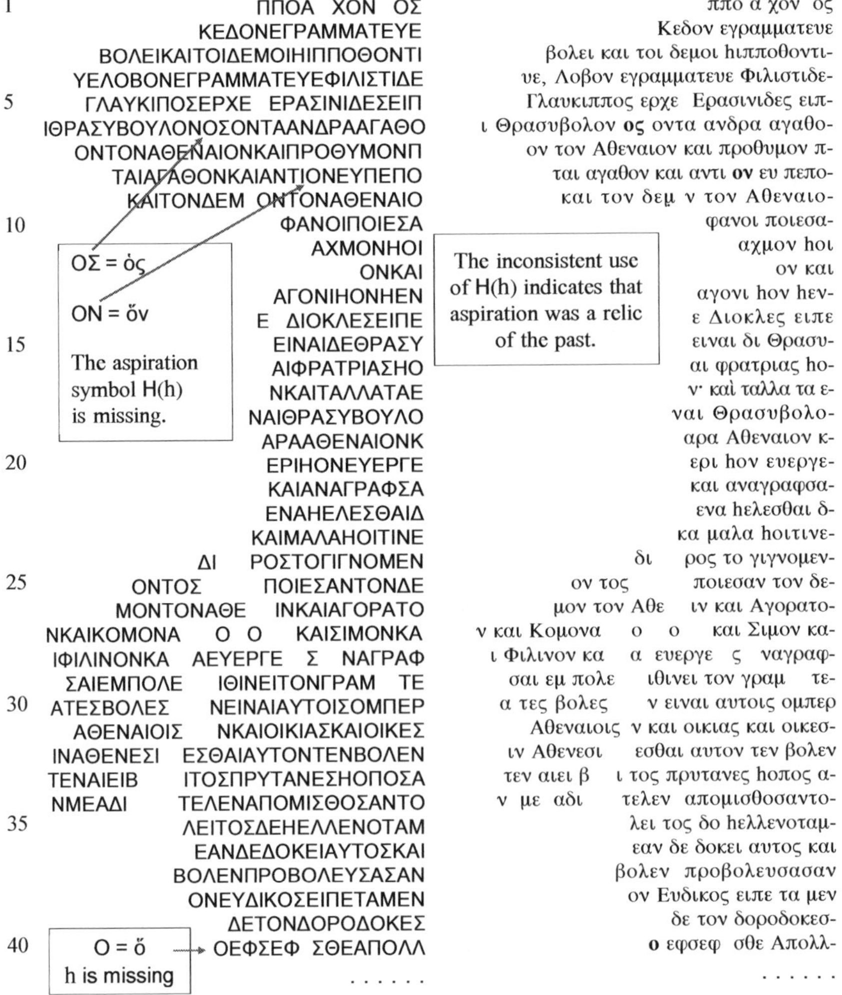

| | |
|---|---|
| ΠΠΟΑ ΧΟΝ ΟΣ | ππο α χον ος |
| ΚΕΔΟΝΕΓΡΑΜΜΑΤΕΥΕ | Κεδον εγραμματευε |
| ΒΟΛΕΙΚΑΙΤΟΙΔΕΜΟΙΗΙΠΠΟΘΟΝΤΙ | βολει και τοι δεμοι hιπποθοντι- |
| ΥΕΛΟΒΟΝΕΓΡΑΜΜΑΤΕΥΕΦΙΛΙΣΤΙΔΕ | υε, Λοβον εγραμματευε Φιλιστιδε- |
| ΓΛΑΥΚΙΠΟΣΕΡΧΕ ΕΡΑΣΙΝΙΔΕΣΕΙΠ | Γλαυκιππος ερχε Ερασινιδες ειπ- |
| ΙΘΡΑΣΥΒΟΥΛΟΝΟΣΟΝΤΑΑΝΔΡΑΑΓΑΘΟ | ι Θρασυβολον **ος** οντα ανδρα αγαθο- |
| ΟΝΤΟΝΑΘΕΝΑΙΟΝΚΑΙΠΡΟΘΥΜΟΝΠ | ον τον Αθεναιον και προθυμον π- |
| ΤΑΙΑΓΑΘΟΝΚΑΙΑΝΤΙΟΝΕΥΠΕΠΟ | ται αγαθον και αντι **ον** ευ πεπο- |
| ΚΑΙΤΟΝΔΕΜ ΟΝΤΟΝΑΘΕΝΑΙΟ | και τον δεμ ν τον Αθεναιο- |
| ΦΑΝΟΙΠΟΙΕΣΑ | φανοι ποιεσα- |
| ΑΧΜΟΝΗΟΙ | αχμον hοι |
| ΟΝΚΑΙ | ον και |
| ΑΓΟΝΙΗΟΝΗΕΝ | αγονι hον hεν- |
| Ε ΔΙΟΚΛΕΣΕΙΠΕ | ε Διοκλες ειπε |
| ΕΙΝΑΙΔΕΘΡΑΣΥ | ειναι δι Θρασυ- |
| ΑΙΦΡΑΤΡΙΑΣΗΟ | αι φρατριας hο- |
| ΝΚΑΙΤΑΛΛΑΤΑΕ | ν· καὶ ταλλα τα ε- |
| ΝΑΙΘΡΑΣΥΒΟΥΛΟ | ναι Θρασυβολο- |
| ΑΡΑΑΘΕΝΑΙΟΝΚ | αρα Αθεναιον κ- |
| ΕΡΙΗΟΝΕΥΕΡΓΕ | ερι hον ευεργε- |
| ΚΑΙΑΝΑΓΡΑΦΣΑ | και αναγραφσα- |
| ΕΝΑΗΕΛΕΣΘΑΙΔ | ενα hελεσθαι δ- |
| ΚΑΙΜΑΛΑΗΟΙΤΙΝΕ | κα μαλα hοιτινε- |
| ΔΙ ΡΟΣΤΟΓΙΓΝΟΜΕΝ | δι ρος το γιγνομεν- |
| ΟΝΤΟΣ ΠΟΙΕΣΑΝΤΟΝΔΕ | ον τος ποιεσαν τον δε- |
| ΜΟΝΤΟΝΑΘΕ ΙΝΚΑΙΑΓΟΡΑΤΟ | μον τον Αθε ιν και Αγορατο- |
| ΝΚΑΙΚΟΜΟΝΑ Ο Ο ΚΑΙΣΙΜΟΝΚΑ | ν και Κομονα ο ο και Σιμον κα- |
| ΙΦΙΛΙΝΟΝΚΑ ΑΕΥΕΡΓΕ Σ ΝΑΓΡΑΦ | ι Φιλινον κα α ευεργε ς ναγραφ- |
| ΣΑΙΕΜΠΟΛΕ ΙΘΙΝΕΙΤΟΝΓΡΑΜ ΤΕ | σαι εμ πολε ιθινει τον γραμ τε- |
| ΑΤΕΣΒΟΛΕΣ ΝΕΙΝΑΙΑΥΤΟΙΣΟΜΠΕΡ | α τες βολες ν ειναι αυτοις ομπερ |
| ΑΘΕΝΑΙΟΙΣ ΝΚΑΙΟΙΚΙΑΣΚΑΙΟΙΚΕΣ | Αθεναιοις ν και οικιας και οικεσ- |
| ΙΝΑΘΕΝΕΣΙ ΕΣΘΑΙΑΥΤΟΝΤΕΝΒΟΛΕΝ | ιν Αθενεσι εσθαι αυτον τεν βολεν |
| ΤΕΝΑΙΕΙΒ ΙΤΟΣΠΡΥΤΑΝΕΣΗΟΠΟΣΑ | τεν αιει β ι τος πρυτανες hοπος α- |
| ΝΜΕΑΔΙ ΤΕΛΕΝΑΠΟΜΙΣΘΟΣΑΝΤΟ | ν με αδι τελεν απομισθοσαντο- |
| ΛΕΙΤΟΣΔΕΗΕΛΛΕΝΟΤΑΜ | λει τος δο hελλενοταμ- |
| ΕΑΝΔΕΔΟΚΕΙΑΥΤΟΣΚΑΙ | εαν δε δοκει αυτος και |
| ΒΟΛΕΝΠΡΟΒΟΛΕΥΣΑΣΑΝ | βολεν προβολευσασαν |
| ΟΝΕΥΔΙΚΟΣΕΙΠΕΤΑΜΕΝ | ον Ευδικος ειπε τα μεν |
| ΔΕΤΟΝΔΟΡΟΔΟΚΕΣ | δε τον δοροδοκεσ- |
| ΟΕΦΣΕΦ ΣΘΕΑΠΟΛΛ | **ο** εφσεφ σθε Απολλ- |
| . . . . . . | . . . . . . |

ΟΣ = ὁς

ΟΝ = ὅν

The aspiration symbol H(h) is missing.

The inconsistent use of H(h) indicates that aspiration was a relic of the past.

Ο = ὅ
h is missing

## *SEG* 25:149—EM 12749 (303/2 BC)

**ΤΟΙΣΕΘΕΛΟΝΤΑΙΣΕΠ**
**ΜΕΓΑΣΑΦΙΚΟΜΕΝΟΣΕΙΣΤΗΝ**
**ΜΕΩΣΤΟΥΣΥΠΕΝΑΝΤΙΟΥΣΤΗΙΔ**
**ΧΩΡΑΝΤΗΝΑΘΗΝΑΙΩΝΚΑΙΤΩΝΑΛ**
**ΡΑΓΕΓΟΝΕΝΒΟΗΘΗΣΩΝΜΕΤΑΔΥΝ**
**ΓΕΝΟΜΕΝΟΣΠΟΛΛΑΣΜΕΝΗΔΗΠΟΛ**
**ΒΑΣΙΛΕΙΑΙΚΙΝΔΥΝΟΝΚΑΙΠΟΝ**
**ΤΟΥΤΙΜΩΝΚΑΙΠΕΡΙΠΛΕΙΣΤΟΥ**
**ΚΑΙΔΕΗΘΕΝΤΩΝΗΓΕΙΣΘΑΙΤΗ**
**ΚΑΤΑΠΕΛΟΠΟΝΝΗΣΟΝΠΡΑΞΕΩΝΠΟ**
**ΚΤΟΙΣΕΞΕΒΑΛΕΝΕΚΤΗΣΧΩΡΑΣΤΟ**
**ΘΑΙΤΟΙΣΕΘΕΛΟΝΤΑΙΣΕΠΙΛΕΚΤΟ**
**ΗΜΗΤΡΙΟΝΑΝΤΙΓΟΝΟΥΒΑΣΙΛΕΑΒ**
**ΦΙΠΠΟΥΕΝΑΓΟΡΑΙΠΑΡΑΤΗΝΔΗΜΟ**
**ΟΥΣΑΛΛΟΥΣΕΛΛΗΝΑΣΙΔΡΥΣΑΣΘΑΙ**
**ΘΙΣΤΑΜΕΝΟΥΣΕΙΣΤΑΣΘΥΣΙΑΣΤΑΣ**
**ΡΙΟΥΚΑΙΔΗΜΗΤΡΙΩΙΣΩΤΗΡΙΘΥΕΙ[Ν]**
**ΝΩΣΣΕΜΝΟΤΑΤΑΚΑΙΚΑΛΛΙΣΤΑΚΑ**
**ΤΩΝΕΠΙΛΕΚΤΩΝΤΩΙΒΑΣΙΛΕΙΔΕ**
**ΟΝΤΕΤΙΜΗΚΑΣΙΝΤΟΥΣΕΥΕΡΓΕΤ**
**ΜΑΙΣΤΙΜΩΣΙΝ.....**

τοις εθελονταις επ
μεγας αφικομενος εις την
μεως τους **υπεναντιους** τηι δ
χωραν την Αθηναιων και των αλ
ραγεγονεν βοηθησων μετα δυν
γενομενος πολλας μεν ηδη πολ
βασιλειαι κινδυνον και πον
του τιμων και περι πλειστου
και δεηθεντων **ηγεισθαι** τη
κατα Πελοποννησον πραξεων πο
κτοις εξεβαλεν εκ της χωρας το
θαι τοις εθελονταις επιλεκτο
ημητριον Αντιγονου βασιλεα β
φ ιππου εν αγοραι παρα την Δημο
ους αλλους **Ελληνας ιδρυσασθαι**
θισταμενους εις τας θυσιας τας
ριου και Δημητρι**ωι** Σωτηρι θυει[ν]
ν ως σεμνοτατα και καλλιστα κα
των επιλεκτων **τωι** βασιλει δε
ων τετιμηκασιν τους ευεργετ
μαις τιμωσιν.....

This Athenian decree is a sample of the definitive post-Eucleidean writing system at the threshold of the Κοινή period. Grammatical forms are distinct, and orthographical errors and phonopathy effects are absent. Notice the absence of aspiration in the four underlined words.

The decree is at a formal literary Attic level, yet from a Neohellenic standpoint the spelling is correct and the wording is well understood.

Note: From around the 12th c. AD, adscript Ι(ι) as in ηι, ωι, αι became subscript as in ῃ, ῳ, ᾳ.

# APPENDIX 2

# Changes in the Attic Alphabet and Their Significance

THE FOREGOING ANNOTATED ATTIC decrees lead to a number of observations regarding certain letters and the historical sounds they represent.

## CONSONANTS

Upon the ratification of the Ionic alphabet in 403 BC, the form of a number of Attic consonants becomes markedly different. The table below shows perhaps the most notable of those changes.

| **5th c. BC** | | **4th c. BC** | **5th c. BC** | **4th c. BC** |
|---|---|---|---|---|
| Λ | became | Γ | ΧϟΥΛΛΡΑΦϟΕΙ | ΣΥΓΓΡΑΨΗΙ [χ]συγγράψῃ |
| Ⱶ, L | became | Λ | ALLA | ΑΛΛΑ ἀλλά |
| Ι | became | Ζ | NOMIΙOMENA | NOMIZOMENA νομιζόμενα |
| Χ≶, Κ≶ | became | Ξ, Ξ | ΕΔΟΧ≶ΕΝ | ΕΔΟΞΕΝ ἔδοξεν |
| Φ≶, Π≶ | became | Ψ | Φ≶ΕΦΟ≶ | ΨΗΦΟΣ ψῆφος |
| ϟ | became | Σ | | |

## VOWELS

A more radical alphabetic change was effectuated by the adoption of H and Ω. The Athenians began using these two symbols from about the mid-5th c. BC first as compensatory marks in verse, and later in the century as regular letters in composition. This means that H and Ω may also be seen in 5th c. pre-Eucleidean inscriptions. The left column in the table below shows the letters in the 5th c. BC that stood for the same sounds that the letters in the second column represented in post-Eucleidean 4th c. BC.

| 5th c. BC | | 4th c. BC | | 5th c. BC Example | Possible grammatical form and meaning |
|---|---|---|---|---|---|
| E | stood for | E, EI, H, HI | as in | ΒΟΛΕ<br>ΦΕΡΕ | βολή, βούλει, βουλή<br>φέρε, φέρει, φέρῃ |
| EI<br>O | stood for<br>stood for | EI, HI<br>O, Ω, ΟΥ | as in<br>as in | ΒΟΛΕΙ<br>ΔΟΛΟΣ<br>ΔΟΛΟΙ | βούλει, βουλῇ<br>δόλος, δόλους, δοῦλος, δούλους<br>δόλοι, δόλῳ, δούλῳ, δοῦλοι |
| OI | stood for | OI, ΩΙ | as in | ΑΝΘΡΟΠΟΙ | ἄνθρωποι, ἀνθρώπῳ |

## E, EI AND O, OI

Pre-Eucleidean E and O, along with EI and OI, placed tremendous constraints on 5th c. Attic versifiers, grammarians, playwrights, orators, tragedians, sculptors, teachers, pupils, and ordinary citizens. The samples shown on the left column below, all gleaned from the foregoing set of decrees, show that E and O were multifunctional and therefore did not readily and adequately communicate fine grammatical distinctions.

| pre-Eucleidean | | | | | post-Eucleidean | |
|---|---|---|---|---|---|---|
| ΕΚΑΣΤΟΣ | E | = | E | ε | ΕΚΑΣΤΟΣ | ἕκαστος |
| KALLIKPATEΣ | E | = | H | η | ΚΑΛΛΙΚΡΑΤΗΣ | Καλλικράτης |
| ΠΟΙΕΝ | E | = | EI | ει | ΠΟΙΕΙΝ | ποιεῖν |
| NEOKLEIΔΕΣ | EI | = | EI | ει | ΝΕΟΚΛΕΙΔΗΣ | Νεοκλείδης |
| TEI BOLEI | EI | = | HI | ῃ | ΤΗΙ ΒΟΥΛΗΙ | τῇ βουλῇ |
| ΠΡΟΤΕΡΟΝ | O | = | O | ο | ΠΡΟΤΕΡΟΝ | πρότερον |
| BOLEN | O | = | ΟΥ | ου | ΒΟΥΛΗΝ | βουλήν |
| ΑΘΕΝΑΙΟΝ | O | = | Ω | ω | ΑΘΗΝΑΙΩΝ | Ἀθηναίων |
| ΑΘΕΝΑΙΟΙ | OI | = | OI | οι | ΑΘΗΝΑΙΟΙ | Ἀθηναῖοι |
| ΤΟΙ ΔΗΜΟΙ | OI | = | ΩΙ | ῳ | ΤΩΙ ΔΗΜΩΙ | τῷ δήμῳ |

## E, O AND H, Ω, ΟΥ

Some inscriptions in the last quarter of the 5th c. BC show sporadic, though clearly "post-Eucleidean," use of Ω(ω) and ΟΥ(ου) alongside their older associates O(ο) and O(ου); and of H(η) and monophthongized EI(ει) alongside E(η) and spurious EI(ηι). This strongly suggests that O and Ω were acoustically interchangeable as were also EI(ει) and H(η). Moreover, the use of H, Ω, ΟΥ indicates that 5th c. Athenians were becoming increasingly dependent on the Ionic script. These points find support from the following samples of a 5th c. Attic decree whose two sides, incribed a few years apart, depict the struggle for dominance between the older and the anticipated (post-Eucleidean) Attic script.[1]

1. See pp. 137–38.

p. 137, *Side I* (427/4 BC)

| | | | | | | |
|---|---|---|---|---|---|---|
| O | for | Ω | ΠOLETAΣ | for | ΠΩΛΗΤΑΣ | |
| | | | BOMON | for | BΩMON | |
| O | for | OY | TOYTOΣ | for | TOYTOYΣ | first vowel OY, second O |

p. 138, *Side II* (424/3 BC)

| | | | | | | |
|---|---|---|---|---|---|---|
| EI | for | HI | TEI BOLEI | for | THI BOYΛHI | spurious EI ει (= HI ῃ) |
| EI | for | EI | EIΠE | for | EIΠE | resembling genuine EI ει |
| HI | for | HI | THI ΣTHLHI | for | THI ΣTHΛHI | spurious HI shedding |
| | | | THI IEPEAI | for | THI IEPEAI | its older form EI |
| E | for | H | ΔEMOI | for | ΔHMΩI | |
| H | for | H | MHNOΣ | for | MHNOΣ | a mix of pre- and post- |
| | | | THΣ NIKHΣ | for | THΣ NIKHΣ | Eucleidean forms |
| OI | for | ΩI | ΔEMOI | for | ΔHMΩI | |
| Ω | for | Ω | KΩΛAKPETΩΣI | for | KΩΛAKPETΩΣI | |

## E(E) AND H(H)

Pre-Eucleidean E stood both for /e/ and /i/. After the adoption of Ionic H, the retention of the *first* E as ε /e / in ΠEPIKLEΣ, ΘEMIΣTOKLEΣ, EKKLEΣIA, ELLENON, ΣKELE, along with the change of the *second* E into H, i.e., ΠEPIKΛHΣ, ΘEMIΣTOKΛHΣ, EKKΛHΣIA, EΛΛHNΩN, ΣKEΛH, clearly shows that the *second* E represented a vowel other than the *first* E, yet one which, according to Plato, could be confused with ει or ι /i/ (2.2.2). Since the Attic vocalic system consisted of the five phonemes /i, e, a, o, u/, it follows that H(η) could have stood for no phoneme other than /i /.

Clearly, such changes speak not of phonological but strictly of graphemic adjustments.[2] To interpret changes of this nature in any other way would imply that upon the ratification of the Ionic alphabet, all contemporary Athenians, one being Plato—then in his mid-20s—would have had to make drastic overnight pronunciation changes in their mother tongue (2.17).

## H(η) AND H(h)

Some scholars hold that in the 5th c. BC Attic H was an aspirate (e.g., the *h* in *have*), whereas after 403 BC it was used as the vowel H(η). Still others, like Gignac, hold that H did not cease to be used as an aspirate until New Testament times (p. 48). Contrary

2. In English, for example, the letter *e* stands for a variety of sounds: *me* /i /, *effort* /e/, *crepe* /e$^{\mathrm{I}}$/, *sergeant* /a/, *dear* /ɪ /, *offer* /ə/. Replacing each sound of *e* with a different symbol would be an alphabetic adjustment, not a change in pronunciation.

to such claims, and as the foregoing Attic decrees show, by the 5th c. BC, H as an aspirate had long been a relic of antiquity (2.18).

For example, the inscription on p. 138 shows H both as *h* and as η nearly side by side. First, we see TEI HIEPEAI τει hιερεαι (τῃ hιερεᾳ), and a few lines below we see the same word as THI IEPEAI τηι ιερεαι (τῃ ιερεᾳ), that is, not only without the aspiration H(h), but also with H as η.[3]

The inscription shows H as η no fewer than seven times, including the article τηι (τῃ) before ιερεαι (ιερεᾳ) "priestess." This can only mean, on the one hand, that the presence of H(h) in 5th c. BC had no effect on pronunciation and, on the other, its presence did not confuse native Athenians capable of distinguishing *mute* H(h) from the *vowel* H(η).

That H as an aspiration symbol in Classical Attic had no acoustic value is further corroborated by the testimony of a number of pre-Eucleidean 5th c. BC Attic decrees. Listed below are samples of words which one would expect to see aspirated but whose aspiration mark H(h) is missing (i.e., not inscribed):

| Decree page and line # (L) | | Date | Words whose H(h) is missing | 4th c. post-Eucleidean spelling | |
|---|---|---|---|---|---|
| p. 134 | L10 | 448/7 BC | ΕΚΑΣΤΟΝ | ΕΚΑΣΤΟΝ | ἑκαστον |
| p. 135 | L11 | 445 BC | ΕΝΑ | ΕΝΑ | ἑνα |
| | L32 | | ΗΜΕΡΩΝ | ΗΜΕΡΩΝ | ἡμερων |
| p. 136 | L3 | 432/1 BC | ΕΚΑΣΤΟ | ΕΚΑΣΤΩ | ἑκαστῳ |
| | L14 | | ΤΟΙΣ ΥΕ[ΣΙΝ | ΤΟΙΣ ΥΙΕΣΙΝ | τοις υἱεσιν |
| p. 138 | L10 | 424/3 BC | ΙΕΡΕΑ | ΙΕΡΕΑ | ἱερεα |
| p. 141 | L12 | 424/3 BC | ΟΣΠΕΡ | ΩΣΠΕΡ | ὡσπερ |
| | L23 | | ΟΜΟΛΟΓΟΣΙΝ | ΟΜΟΛΟΓΩΣΙΝ | ὁμολογωσιν |
| | L25 | | ΕΚΑΤΕΡΟΙ | ΕΚΑΤΕΡΟΙ | ἑκατεροι |
| | L36 | | ΕΚΑΣΤΟ | ΕΚΑΣΤΩ | ἑκαστῳ |
| | L39 | | ΕΚΑΣΤΟΣ | ΕΚΑΣΤΟΣ | ἑκαστος |
| | L39 | | ΕΛΛΕΣΠΟΝΤΟ-ΦΥΛΑΚΑΣ | ΕΛΛΗΣΠΟΝΤΟ-ΦΥΛΑΚΑΣ | ἑλλησποντο-φυλακας |
| | L55 | | Ε[ΔΡΑ]Σ | Ε[ΔΡΑΣ] | ἑδρας |
| | L55 | | ΕΟΣ | ΕΩΣ | ἑως |
| | L56 | | ΟΙ ΣΤΡΑΤΕΓΟΙ | ΟΙ ΣΤΡΑΤΗΓΟΙ | οἱ στρατηγοι |
| p. 142 | L6, L8 | 410/9 BC | ΟΣ, ΟΝ | ΟΣ, ΟΝ | ὁς, ὁν, ὁ |
| | L40 | | Ο | Ο | |

## PHONOPATHY

A speaker's socio-academic background, speech idiosyncrasies, physical condition, mood, occasion, and articulatory speed are all forces that have a bearing on his or her pronunciation. During speech such forces are constantly at work, though more so at word juncture, where sounds more noticeably clash, emerge, separate, fade, or blend,

3. See p. 138, line 5, τει *h*ιερεαι; line 10, τηι ιερεαι.

often for reasons of euphony. Speech peculiarities of this nature may be collectively referred to as *phonopathy*.

Phonopathy may be reflected in spelling. In New Testament manuscripts there is no paucity of cases in which scribes followed their ear in spelling euphonically, for instance, "nasal γ" for ν before γ (τὸγ γραμματέα), λ for ν before λ (τὸλ λόγον), or μ for ν before φ (τὸμ φόρον) (cf. 2.12).

There is virtually no variation of phonopathy seen at word juncture in NT MSS that is not seen as well in Attic decrees, the only difference being that NT writings make use of the letters Ψ(ψ) and Ξ(ξ), neither of which is seen in older Attic decrees. Listed below are examples of phonopathy seen in the above decrees.

| Letters at word juncture (. . . ) | | Resultant spelling | Example | Regular spelling | |
|---|---|---|---|---|---|
| Κ. . . | Β | ΓΒ | ΕΓ ΒΟΛΗΣ[4] | ΕΚ ΒΟΥΛΗΣ | εκ βουλης |
| Ν. . . | Μ | ΜΜ | ΕΑΜ ΜΕ ΤΙ[5] | ΕΑΝ ΜΗ ΤΙ | εαν μη τι |
| Ν. . . | Β | ΜΒ | ΤΕΝ ΒΟΛΕΝ[6] | ΤΗΝ ΒΟΥΛΗΝ | την βουλην |
| Ν. . . | Π | ΜΠ | ΤΕΜ ΠΟΛΙΝ[7] | ΤΗΝ ΠΟΛΙΝ | την πολιν |
| Σ. . . | Σ | ΣΧΣ | ΤΑΣ ΧΣΥΓΓΡΑΦΑΣ[8] | ΤΑΣ ΣΥΓΓΡΑΦΑΣ | τας συγγραφας |
| intervocalic: | | | | | |
| ΜΠΣ | | ΜΦΣ | ΠΕΜΦΣΑΙ[9] | ΠΕΜΨΑΙ | πεμψαι |

An inscriptionist's acoustically-driven chisel is subject to phonopathy. Though he may know, for instance, that ΕΓ is not a word (not ΕΚ), by relying on his ear he writes ΕΓ before ΒΟΥΛΗΣ. This is due to the fact that in his pronunciation voiceless stop Κ becomes a voiced continuant as it meets voiced continuant Β [v]. Hence, Κ becomes its voiced continuant associate Γ.

Nasal Ν, on the other hand, is assimilated by nasal Μ, hence Ν + Μ = ΜΜ. And voiced Ν transfers its voiceness onto voiceless Π, causing it to become voiced, hence ΜΠ = [mb]—a common phonopathy feature in Neohellenic (2.13.1).

## SUMMARY AND CONCLUSIONS

1. The ratification of the Ionic alphabet included the replacement of a number of consonant letters with letters that were different in form yet representative of the same sounds as those represented by their replaced counterparts.

4. See p.137, line 16.
5. See p. 134, line 25; p. 141, line 56.
6. See p. 134, line 36.
7. See p. 134, line 41; p. 135, line 22; p. 139, line 3.
8. Epenthetic Χ before Σ. See p. 135, line 19.
9. See p. 141, line 17.

2. The adoption of H and Ω helped overcome the limitations on grammatical distinctions posed by E and O.
3. E continued to be used as [e], and H assumed the role represented by E [i].
4. O continued to be used as [o], and the role of O as [u] was assumed by OY.
5. HI replaced spurious EI(ῃ), while proper diphthong (digraph) EI(ει) remained.
6. ΩI replaced spurious OI(ῳ), while proper diphthong (digraph) OI(οι) remained.
7. The difference between O and Ω was grammatical, not phonological.
8. Familiarity with the phonopathy of Attic sounds can help detect a number of pronunciation-spelling peculiarities, virtually all of which are found as well in NT MSS.
9. There is no evidence that Attic H(h) had any acoustic properties, as H(h) is often seen used erratically or is missing altogether.
10. Post-Eucleidean graphemes and their phonemic values entered the Κοινή period in their definitive Attic form.

# APPENDIX 3

# Greek Dimorphia

The literary masterpieces of the classical Greek period marked the crowning age of a glorious history, an age that raised literary excellence of Greek to the limit. A greater gap was thus created between the artistic and literary form of the language (the form used in works by professionals and the well educated) and the Demotic or vernacular (the form used by ordinary citizens). The illustration below shows the dimorphic nature of Greek and the relation between the levels of the language, a diachronic characteristic of Greek from classical times to the present. It also shows that Κοινή developed from Demotic Attic, though Κοινή was heavily influenced by the artistic levels of Classical Attic.

Note: The size of boxes and gray areas is arbitrary. Gray areas indicate the overlapping of literary levels, and broken arrows the low-to-high or informal-to-formal vernacular levels.

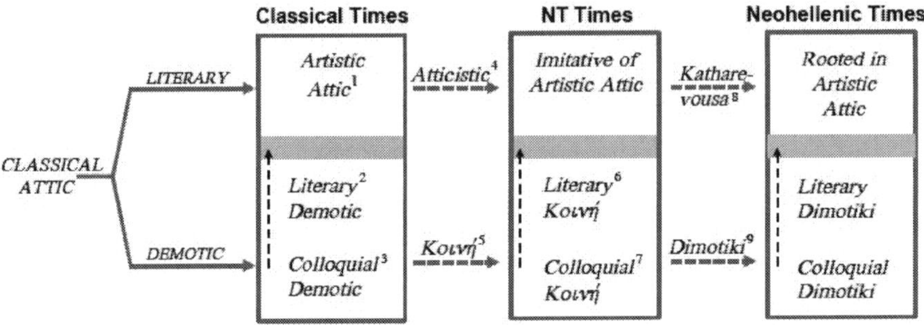


1. *Artistic Attic*. Literary Attic was the language of a highly artistic expression used by classical authors (philosophers, orators, tragedians, writers, versifiers, comedians) to create masterpieces of Attic literature. Unlike the well-educated, ordinary Athenians could not converse in artistic Attic, yet they could understand it.

2. *Literary Demotic Attic*. A medium between the ordinary vernacular and the highly artistic literary Attic, literary Demotic Attic was used by educated Athenians who could write and speak at this formal level. The language of the court, decrees, government records, professional documents, academia, etc. was at this level.

3. *Colloquial Demotic Attic.* The popular expression of ordinary Athenians was in informal, colloquial Attic. Many inscriptions were written at this level also.

4. *Atticistic.* The imitation of the artistic Attic expression, begun by the Atticists in the 1st c. BC, continued through Byzantine and modern times.

5. *Κοινή.* Κοινή is thought to have moved toward simplification respecting lexical, morphological, and syntactical forms, but one must use caution when comparing features of the Κοινή of the NT with those of artistic Attic, all the more so because no substantial literary works in Hellenistic Κοινή by non-Helleninized mainline Greek authors are available from NT times.

6. *Literary Κοινή.* A number of NT books are at this level: Hebrews, parts of Acts, most of Paul's writings, and much of Peter, James, and Jude, albeit there is no clear level demarcation from the other NT witings.

7. *Colloquial Κοινή.* Most of Mark, Revelation, and parts of the other gospels and NT books range between the colloquial and an intermediate literary level, albeit there is no clear level demarcation from the other NT witings. The vast majority of Hellenistic papyri found in Egypt are within this range.

8. *Katharevousa* "Purifying" is a conservative form of Neohellenic that emerged in the late 18th century as a compromise between Ancient Greek and Dimotiki.

9. *Dimotiki.* Rooted in Demotic Attic, Dimotiki is a component of Neohellenic dimorphia. In academic, political, religious, and other professional circles, Dimotiki and Katharevousa are notably mixed.

# APPENDIX 4

# Formal/Informal Pronunciation

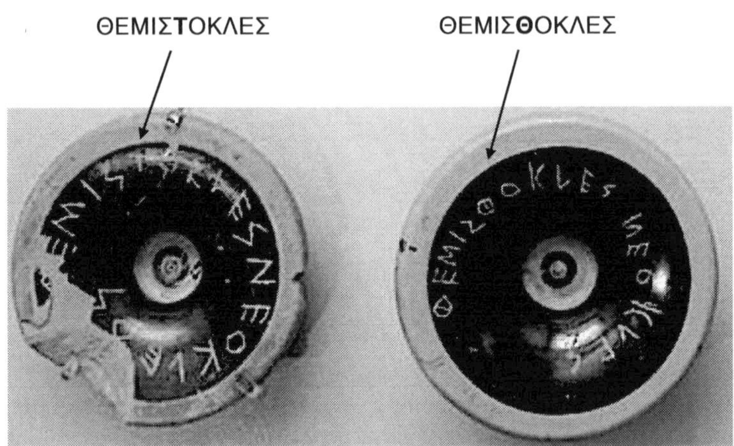


**Voting ostraka of classical Greece (482 BC)**

The name on the ostrakon on the left is spelled θεμιστοκλης (with Τ), while the same name on the ostrakon on the right is spelled θεμισθοκλης (with Θ). The difference in spelling (and sound) is indicative of the existence in classical Athens of a formal and informal use of speech sounds, a diachronic feature of Greek dimorphia.

# APPENDIX 5

# Chronological Table of the Changes in the Attic Alphabet[1]

| | | α | β | γ | δ | ε, ει, η | ζ | h | θ | ι | κ | λ | μ | ν | ο, ου, ω | π | ϙ | ρ | σ | τ | υ | φ | χ |
|---|---|---|---|---|---|---|---|---|---|---|---|---|---|---|---|---|---|---|---|---|---|---|---|
| I | 7th cent. B.C. | Ⱥ ᐅ | ... | ... | Δ (?) | ∃* | I | B | ... | ʕ* | ... | ⅂* | ... | Ч* | ○ | ꓶ* ꓶ* | ... | ꟼ* | ʕ* ʃ* | T† | V | ... | X |
| II | End of 7th and beginning of 6th century | A A A A | 8* | Λ | Δ | Ǝ ∃* ∃* ∃* Ǝ | ... | B | ⊗ ⊕ | I | K K* | ⅃* | M M M* M | ᴧ M Ч* Ч* | O | Γ Γ* | ϙ | P ꟼ* D | ʃ ʕ* ʃ* ʕ | T | V Y | Φ | X + |
| III | 1st quarter of 6th century | A A A A | B | Λ | Δ | Ǝ ∃* ∃* Ǝ Ǝ | ... | H | ⊕ | I | K K* | ⅃* | M M M* | M N(?) N Ч* Ч* N | O | Γ Γ(?) Γ* | ... | P D ᗡ* ꟼ* P | ʃ ʕ ʕ* | T | V Y | φ Φ | + X |
| IV | 2nd and 3rd quarters of 6th century | A A A | B | ... | Δ | F Ǝ Ǝ Ǝ | ... | H | ⊕ | I | K K | L | M M | M N N N | O | Γ | ... | R P Ϙ | ʃ ʃ | T | V | Φ | + X |
| V | 535—510 B.C. (approximately) | A A A | B | Λ | Δ | E E Ǝ E Ǝ | ... | H | ⊕ | I | K K | L | M M M (?) | N N | O | Γ | ... | P R | ʃ | T | V Y | Φ | + X |
| VI | About 508 B.C. | A A A A | ... | Λ | Δ | Ǝ E Ǝ F Ǝ E E | ... | H | ⊙ | I | K | L | M M | M N N N | O | Γ | ... | R P | ʃ | T | V Y | Φ | + |
| VII | 500—490 B.C. (approximately) | ... | ... | ... | ... | ... | ... | ... | ... | ... | ... | ... | (M) | (N) | ... | ... | ... | ... | ... | ... | ... | ... | ... |
| VIII | 490—480 B.C. (approximately) | (A) | ... | ... | ... | ... | ... | ... | ... | ... | ... | ... | (M M) | (N) | ... | ... | ... | ... | ... | ... | ... | ... | ... |
| IX | About 476 B.C. | A A A | B | Λ | Δ | Ǝ E Ǝ | ... | H | ⊙ | I | K K | L | M M | N N | O | Γ | ... | P R | ʃ | T | Y V Ƴ | Φ | X |
| X | About 460 B.C. | A A | B | Λ | Δ | E | ... | H | ⊙ | I | K | L | M | N N N | O | Γ | ... | R P P | ʃ Σ | T | Y V Ƴ | Φ Φ | X |
| XI | 460—447 B.C. (approximately) | A A A | B B | Λ | Δ | E | I | H | ⊙ | I | K | L | M | N N | O | Γ | ... | R P P | ʃ Σ | T | Y | Φ Φ | X |
| XII | About 446 B.C. | A | B | Λ | Δ | E | I | H | ⊙ | I | K K | L | M | N N | O | Γ | ... | P R R | Σ | T | Y Ƴ | Φ | X |
| XIII | 446—403 B.C. | "The 13th period is marked ... (1) by the gradual encroachment of Ionic forms ..., and (2) by the growing uncertainty in the use of the form for *spiritus asper*." | | | | | | | | | | "The asterisk denotes that the letter to which it is attached is written retrograde. The retrograde and βουστροφηδόν styles have disappeared with the 3rd period." | | | | | | | | | | | | | |

1. Adapted from *Greek Epigraphy*, Part I (E. S. Roberts, 106–7).

# Bibliography

Allen, W. Sidney. *Vox Graeca: The Pronunciation of Classical Greek*. 3rd ed. Cambridge: Cambridge University Press, 1987.

Angelopoulos, Nikolaos. "The Sound of Greek: A Critique of Greek Phonology." http://www.projethomere.com/ressources/PHONOLOGIE-Modern-Greek.pdf.

Angus, Samuel. "The Κοινή: The Language of the New Testament." *Princeton Theological Review*, January 1910.

Argyle, A. W. *An Introductory Grammar of New Testament Greek*. Ithaca: Cornell University Press, 1965.

Bagnall, Roger. *Reading Papyri, Writing Ancient History*. New York: Rutledge, 1995.

Bagnall, Roger, and Klaas Worp. *Chronological Systems of Byzantine Egypt*. 2nd ed. Leiden: Brill, 2004.

Balme, Maurice, and Gilbert Lawall. *Athenaze: An Introduction to Ancient Greek*. Book 1. Rev. ed. New York: Oxford University Press, 1990.

Beard, Mary, and John Henderson. *Classics: A Very Short Introduction*. Oxford: Oxford University Press, 2000.

Bekkeri, Immanuelis. *Anecdota Graeca*. Vol. 2. Berlin: Reimerum, 1816.

Black, David A. *Linguistics for Students of the New Testament Greek*. Grand Rapids: Baker, 1995.

Blackwelder, Boyce W. *Light from the Greek New Testament*. Anderson, IN: Warner, 1958.

Blass, Friedrich, and Albert Debrunner. *A Greek Grammar of the New Testament and Other Earlier Christian Literature*. Translated and revised by Robert W. Funk. Chicago: University of Chicago Press, 1961.

———. *Pronunciation of Ancient Greek*. Translated by W. J. Purton. Cambridge: Cambridge University Press, 1890.

Brown, Carroll N. "Modern Greek as an Aid to the Teacher of Ancient Greek." *Classical Weekly* 15 (1922) 82–85.

Brown, Gerald. *Bulletin of the American Society of Papyrologists* 6.1 (1969).

Brown, John Pairman. *Ancient Israel and Ancient Greece: Religion, Politics, and Culture*. Minneapolis: Fortress, 2001.

Browning, Robert. *Medieval and Modern Greek*. Cambridge: Cambridge University Press, 1995.

Brownworth, Lars. *Lost to the West: The Forgotten Byzantine Empire That Rescued Western Civilization*. New York: Crown, 2009.

Buth, Randall. "Η Κοινὴ Προφορά Koine Pronunciation." Biblical Language Center. 2008. https://www.biblicallanguagecenter.com/wp-content/uploads/2010/03/Greek_Pronunciation_2008.pdf.

Butler, Harold Edgeworth, trans. *The Institutio Oratoria of Quintilian*. London: Heinemann, 1922.

Bywater, Ingram. *The Erasmian Pronunciation of Greek and Its Precursors, Jerome Aleander, Aldus Manutius, Antonio of Lebrixa*. London: Oxford University Press, 1908.

Campbell, Constantine R. *Advances in the Study of Greek*. Grand Rapids: Zondervan, 2015.

Caragounis, Chrys C. *The Development of Greek and the New Testament: Morphology, Syntax, Phonology, and Textual Transmission*. Grand Rapids: Baker Academic, 2006.

———. *New Testament Language and Exegesis*. Tübingen: Mohr Siebeck, 2014.

Cartledge, Samuel A. *A Basic Grammar of the Greek New Testament*. Grand Rapids: Zondervan, 1959.

Clauss, James, and Martine Cuypers, eds. *A Companion to Hellenistic Literature*. Chichester, UK: Wiley-Blackwell, 2010.

Cohen, Gary G., and C. Norman Sellers. "The Case for Modern Pronunciation of Biblical Languages." *Grace Theological Journal* 5 (1984) 200–201. https://biblicalstudies.org.uk/pdf/gtj/05-2_197.pdf.

Conybeare, W. J., and J. S. Howson. *The Life and Epistles of St. Paul*. New ed. Grand Rapids: Eerdmans, 1964.

Davidson, Thomas. *Aristotle: Ancient Educational Ideas*. New York: Scribner, 1897.

———, trans. *The Grammar of Dionysios Thrax*. Reprinted from the *Journal of Speculative Philosophy*. St. Louis: Studley, 1874.

Decker, Rodney J. *Reading Koine Greek: An Introduction and Integrated Workbook*. Grand Rapids: Baker Academic, 2014.

Deissmann, Geoffrey A. *Light from the Ancient East: The New Testament Illustrated by Recently Discovered Texts of the Graeco-Roman World*. 4th ed. 1922. Reprint, Grand Rapids: Baker, 1965.

Dietrich, Karl. *Byzantinisches Archiv*. Leipzig: Druck und Verlag von B. G. Teubner, 1898.

Dillon, Matthew. "The Erasmian Pronunciation of Ancient Greek: A New Perspective." *Classical World* 94 (2001) 323–34.

Diringer, David. *The Alphabet: A Key to the History of Mankind*. London: Hutchinson, 1949.

Dobson, John. *Learn New Testament Greek*. 3rd ed. Carlisle, UK: Piquant, 2005.

Drumwright, Huber, Jr. *An Introduction to New Testament Greek*. Nashville: Broadman, 1980.

Durant, Will. *The Life of Greece*. New York: Simon and Schuster, 1939.

Fee, Gordon D., and Mark L. Strauss. *How to Choose a Translation for All Its Worth*. Grand Rapids: Zondervan, 2007.

Fowler, H. N., trans. *Plato*. Vol. 4. London: Harvard University Press, 1977.

Geldart, Edmund Martin. *The Modern Greek Language in Its Relation to the Ancient Greek*. Oxford: Clarendon, 1870.

Gignac, T. Francis, *A Grammar of the Greek Papyri of the Roman and Byzantine Periods*. Milan: Cisalpino-La goliardica, 1976.

Goethius, Eugene Van Ness. *The Language of the New Testament*. New York: Scribner, 1965.

Goodspeed, Edgar. *Chicago Literary Papyri*. Chicago: Chicago University Press, 1908.

Green, Samuel G. *A Brief Introduction to New Testament Greek*. London: Religious Tract Society, 1911.

Greenlee, Harold J. *A Concise Exegetical Grammar of New Testament Greek*. Grand Rapids: Eerdmans, 1963.

Grenfell, Bernard. *An Alexandrian Erotic Fragment and Other Greek Papyri, Chiefly Ptolemaic*. Oxford: Clanderon, 1896.

Grenfell, Bernard, et al., eds. *The Amherst Papyri*. Part 1. London: Frowde, 1900.

Grenfell, Bernard, et al., eds. *Fayum Towns and Their Papyri*. London: Kegan Paul, Trench, Trubner, 1900.

Grenfell, Bernard, et al., eds. *Greek Papyri Chiefly Ptolemaic*. Oxford: Clanderon, 1896.

Grenfell, Bernard, et al., eds. *The Oxyrinchus Papyri*. Parts 1–15. London, 1898–1922.

Grenfell, Bernard, et al., eds. *The Tebtunis Papyri*. London: Frowde, 1902.

Guthrie, W. *Quintilian's Institute of Eloquence*. Vol. 2. London: Printed for Dutton et al., 1805.

Hahn, Adelaine E. "Quintilian on Greek Letters Lacking in Latin and Latin Letters Lacking in Greek (12.10.27–29)." *Language* 17 (1941) 24–32.

Harkness, Albert. *The First Greek Book*. London: Appleton, 1866.

Harrop, Clayton K. *History of the New Testament in Plain Language*. Waco, TX: Word, 1984.

Hasselbrook, David. *Studies in New Testament Lexicography: Advancing toward a Full Diachronic Approach with the Greek Language*. Tübingen: Mohr Siebeck, 2011.

Hatzidakis, Georgios N. Ἀκαδημεικὰ Ἀναγνώσματα εἰς τὴν Ἑλληνικήν, Λατινικήν, καὶ Μικρὸν εἰς τὴν Ἰνδικὴν Γραμματικήν, Τόμος Α. Athens: Τύποι Σακελαρίου, 1902.

Hicks, E. L., and G. F. Hill. *A Manual of Greek Historical Inscriptions*. 2nd ed. Oxford: Clarendon, 1901.

Horrocks, Geoffrey. *Greek: A History of the Language and Its Speakers*. New York: Longman, 1997.

James, Patrick. "Greek Lexicography." Bibliography. 21 pp. https://www.academia.edu/7876131/Lexicography_Greek_2nd_ed._.

Jannaris, Antonios N. *An Historical Greek Grammar Chiefly of the Attic Dialect as Written and Spoken from Classical Antiquity down to the Present Time*. New York: MacMillan, 1897.

———. "Kratinos and Aristophanes on the Cry of the Sheep." *American Journal of Philology* 16 (1895) 46–51.

Jay, Eric G. *New Testament Greek: An Introductory Grammar*. London: SPCK, 1958.

Jenkins, Fred. *Bulletin of the American Society of Papyrologists* 29.1–2 (1992).

Jensen, Hans. *Sign, Symbol and Script*. New York: Putnam, 1969.

Jewett, B., trans. *The Dialogues of Plato*. Vol. 1. New York: Random House, 1937.

Johnson, J. de M., et al., eds. *Catalogue of the Greek Papyri*. Vol. 2. Manchester: Manchester University Press, 1915.

Joseph, Brian. "Irregular [u] in Greek." *Die Sprache* 25 (1979) 46–48. Available at https://www.asc.ohio-state.edu/joseph.1/publications/1979irregularu.pdf.

Katzner, Kenneth. *The Languages of the World*. New York: Routledge, 2002.

Kenyon, Frederic, ed. *Classical Texts from Papyri in the British Museum*. Oxford: Clarendon, 1891.

———. *The Palaeography of Greek Papyri*. Oxford: Clarendon, 1899.

Kenyon, John S., and Thomas A. Knott. *A Pronouncing Dictionary of American English*. Springfield, MA: Merriam, 1953.

Kubo, Sakae. *A Beginner's New Testament Greek Grammar*. Lanham, MD: University Press of America, 1979.

Ladefoged, Peter. *A Course in Phonetics*. Boston: Heinle, 2005.

Lagogianni-Georgakakos, M., and K. Buraselis, eds. *Athenian Democracy Speaking through Its Inscriptions*. Athens: Hellenic Ministry of Culture, 2009.

Lindsay, W. M. *The Latin Language: An Historical Account of Latin Sounds, Stems, and Flexions*. Oxford: Clarendon, 1894.

Machen, Gresham J. *New Testament Greek for Beginners*. 2nd ed. Chicago: Prentice Hall, 2003.

Marshall, A. *New Testament Greek Primer*. London: Bagster, 1962.

McLean, Bradley H. *An Introduction to Greek Epigraphy of the Hellenistic and Roman Periods from Alexander the Great down to the Reign of Constantine (323 B.C.–A.D. 337)*. Ann Arbor: University of Michigan Press, 2002.

———. *New Testament Greek: An Introduction*. New York: Cambridge University Press, 2011.

Miller, D. Gary. *Ancient Scripts and Phonological Knowledge*. Philadelphia: Benjamins, 1994.

Morris, William, ed. *The American Heritage Dictionary of the English Language*. Boston: Houghton Mifflin, 1978.

Moule, C. F. D. *An Idiom Book of New Testament Greek*. Cambridge: Cambridge University Press, 1953.

Moulton, James Hope. *A Grammar of New Testament Greek*. 3rd ed. Edinburgh: T. & T. Clark, 1919.

———. *A Grammar of New Testament Greek*. Vol. 1, *Prolegomena*. 3rd ed. Edinburgh: T. & T. Clark, 1908.

———. *An Introduction to the Study of New Testament Greek*. 5th ed. Revised by Henry G. Meecham. New York: McMillan, 1955.

Mounce, William D. *Basics of Biblical Greek Grammar*. 2nd ed. Grand Rapids: Zondervan, 2003.

———. *Basics of Biblical Greek Grammar Workbook*. 2nd ed. Grand Rapids: Zondervan, 2003.

Mynors, R. A. B., and D. F. S. Thomson, trans. *The Correspondence of Erasmus, Letters 594 to 841*. Toronto: University of Toronto Press, 1979.

Nestle, Eberhard, et al. *Novum Testamentum Greace*. 25th ed. New York: American Bible Society, 1963.

Nicole, Jules. *Les Papyrus de Gèneve*. Gèneve: Georg, Libraires de L'Institut, 1896.

Patsall, J. *Quintilian's Institutes of the Orator*. London: Printed for Law and Willis, 1774.

Porter, Stanley E., et al. *Fundamentals of New Testament Greek*. Grand Rapids: Eerdmans, 2010.

Potwin, Lemuel Stoughton. *Here and There in the Greek New Testament*. Chicago: Revell (original from the University of Michigan), 1898.

Reinach, Theodore, et al. *Papyrus Grecs at Demotique*. Paris: Leroux, 1905.

Rienecker, Fritz. *A Linguistic Key to the New Testament*. Vol. 1. Grand Rapids: Zondervan, 1977.

Rife, John. *A Beginning Greek Book*. Amelia, OH: Reiff, 1974.

Roberts, E. S., and E. A. Gardner, eds. *An Introduction to Greek Epigraphy*. Part 1, *The Archaic Inscriptions and the Greek Alphabet*. Cambridge: Cambridge University Press, 1887.

———. *An Introduction to Greek Epigraphy*. Part 2, *The Inscriptions of Attica*. Cambridge: Cambridge University Press, 1905.

Roberts, W. Rhys. *Dionysius of Halicarnassus on Literary Composition, Being the Greek Text of the De Compositione Verborum*. London: MacMillan, 1910.

Robertson, A. T. *A Grammar of the Greek New Testament in the Light of Historical Research*. Nashville: Broadman, 1934.

Roehl, Hermannus, ed. *Inscriptiones Graecae Antiqvissimae Praeter in Attica Repertas*. Berlin, 1882.

Royce, James. *Scribal Habits in Early Greek New Testament Papyri*. Leiden: Brill, 2008.

Russell, A. Donald, ed., trans. *Quintilian: The Orator's Education*. Vol. 1 Bks. 1–2. Loeb Classical Library. Cambridge: Harvard University Press, 2002.

Schwandt, John. "Guide to Greek Pronunciation Conventions." Institute of Biblical Greek. 2003. https://biblicalgreek.org/grammar/pronunciation/.

Scomp, Henry A. *A Manual of the Romaic, or Modern Greek, Pronunciation with Its Application to Ancient Greek*. Boston: Allyn and Bacon, 1892.

Stanwick, Paul E. *Portraits of the Ptolemies: Greek Kings as Egyptian Pharaohs*. Austin: University of Texas Press, 2002.

Stevens, Gerald L. *New Testament Greek*. 2nd ed. Lanham, MD: University Press of America, 1997.

Sturtevant, H. Edgar. *The Pronunciation of Greek and Latin: The Sounds and Accent*. Chicago: University of Chicago Press, 1920.

Summers, Ray, and Thomas Sawyer. *Essentials of New Testament Greek*. Rev. ed. Nashville: Broadman & Holman, 1955.

Tenney, Merrill C. *New Testament Survey*. Grand Rapids: Eerdmans, 1961.

Teodorsson, Sven-Tage. *The Phonology of Attic in the Hellenistic Period*. Gothenburg, Sweden: Acta Universrgensis, 1978.

Thompson, Edward M. *Handbook of Greek and Latin Palaeography*. London: Kegan Paul, Trench, Trubner, 1893.

Thompson, George T., and Laurel E. Hicks. *World History and Cultures*. Pensacola, FL: Beka, 1995.

Thornhill, Chadwick A. *Greek for Everyone: Introductory Greek for Bible Study and Application*. Grand Rapids: Baker, 2016.

Threatte, Leslie. *The Grammar of Attic Inscriptions*. Vol. 1, *Phonology*. New York: de Gruyter, 1980.

Timayenis, Telemachus T. *Modern Greek: Its Pronunciation and Relation to Ancient Greek*. Cambridge: Cambridge University Press, 1877.

Turner, E. G. *Greek Papyri: An Introduction*. Princeton: Princeton University Press, 1968.

Tzartzanos, Achilles. Γραμματικὴ τῆς Ἀρχαῖας Ἑλληνικῆς Γλώσσης [Grammar of the Ancient Greek tongue]. Athens, 1965.

Ventris, Michael, and John Chadwick. *Documents in Mycenaean Greek*. Cambridge: Cambridge University Press, 1973.

Vilborg, Ebbe. *A Tentative Grammar of Mycenaean Greek*. Gothenburg, Sweden: Almqvist & Wiksell, 1960.

Wallace, Daniel B. *Greek Grammar Beyond the Basics*. Grand Rapids: Zondervan, 1996.

Walters, Peter, and D. W. Gooding, eds. *The Text of the Septuagint: Its Corruptions and Their Emendations*. Cambridge: Cambridge University Press, 1973.

Watson, John Selby. *Quintilian's Institutes of Oratory*. Vol. 1. London: Bell, 1892.

Wells, Colin. *Sailing from Byzantium: How a Lost Empire Shaped the World*. New York: Bantam Dell, 2006.

Wuensch, Ricardus, ed. *Corpus Inscriptionum Atticarum*. Berlin, 1877.

# Index

Made in the USA
San Bernardino, CA
04 July 2020

74776824R00109